Soviet-American Security Relations in the 1990s

Soviet-American Security Relations in the 1990s

Edited by

Donald M. Snow
University of Alabama

Lexington Books
D.C. Heath and Company/Lexington, Massachusetts/Toronto

Library of Congress Cataloging-in-Publication Data

Soviet-American security relations in the 1990s.

    Includes index.
    1. Soviet union—Military relations—United States. 2. United States—Military relations—Soviet Union. 3. Nuclear arms control. 4. Nuclear crisis stability.
I. Snow, Donald M., 1943–   .
UA770.S653   1989   355'.033'0048   86-45291
ISBN 0-669-13152-0 (alk. paper)

Published simultaneously in Canada
Printed in the United States of America
International Standard Book Number: 0-669-13152-0
Library of Congress Catalog Card Number: 86-45291

The paper used in this publication meets the minimum requirements of American National Standard for Information Sciences—Permanence of Paper for Printed Library Materials, ANSI Z39.48-1984. ∞™

89 90 91 92 8 7 6 5 4 3 2 1

Contents

Preface

This book examines how Soviet-American relations have evolved over time and what they are likely to look like as we enter the last decade of the twentieth century. Because the dominant form that Soviet-American relations have taken and, to a large extent, continue to take is in the military realm, that aspect of the relationship forms the focus of this effort.

A central theme runs through this work, in some places explicitly and in others implicitly: stability and how, over the several decades in which the superpower relationship has been the dominant factor in international relations, a growing stability in the central relationship between the two has emerged. As argued variously by several of the authors (and most loudly by me), the central motor in this growing stability has been the nuclear relationship between the two. Both realize their mutual capacity for mutual incineration, and they understand that any direct confrontation between them could devolve into a nuclear war, the consequences of which could be mutually suicidal and thus unacceptable. Moreover, the realization of these possible consequences, and regardless of the actual probabilities in any given instance, has increasingly conditioned the way the two countries treat one another. The relationship, to borrow the title of my recent book, has been to create the "Necessary Peace: Nuclear Weapons and Superpower Relations."

The necessary peace has transformed the entire structure of Soviet-American relations and, by extension, world politics. In the early years after World War II, the focus was on the danger of war between East and West, and the emphasis was on a central war in Europe or a nuclear exchange, events to which a reasonably high level of probability was assigned. To deal with those problems, great priority was placed on building sufficient force to deter the Soviets from reaching the public policy decision of breaching deterrence.

The problem may have been solved too well. NATO and the Warsaw Pact, the Soviet Union and the United States face one another with the deadliest array of weapons in the history of peacetime. Their military abilities, capped by the awesome destructive capability of nuclear weapons, have made the world an incredibly potentially deadly place.

But there is an irony: in increasing deadliness to its current dizzying levels, the danger of war may have been decreased substantially. Not all observers would agree with that conclusion or take comfort from the dynamic underlying it. Nonetheless, it offers one plausible explanation of the relative calm and lack of violent interplay between the two superpowers.

It is the consequences of the stabilization of superpower military relations that is the principal concern here. The basic underlying assertion on which this book is organized is that the necessary peace has two consequences relevant to the future. First, the existence of enormous thermonuclear arsenals has virtually precluded the prospect that either side would begin a nuclear war as a conscious public policy choice. The problem of nuclear war thus becomes understanding the basis of thermonuclear-induced stability, seeing how that stability can be reinforced, and examining how changes in the thermonuclear balance affect that stability. Second, the nature of nonnuclear military relations has also been transformed. Central war in Europe has been averted for over forty years, and the continuing dynamic of that phenomenon needs examining. Also, since the superpowers cannot confront one another directly, their interaction increasingly occurs in the Third World, where their interests are not sufficient so that, if they come into direct conflict, the result is likely to be escalation to nuclear war.

In important ways, the great powers are forced to treat one another with caution and indirection. The United States and the Soviet Union can no longer afford to be heavyweight boxers standing toe to toe and slugging it out because their "haymakers" could destroy the world. Instead they have become like fencers, moving swiftly and deftly about one another's defenses, thrusting and parrying for advantage when possible but equally concerned that their swords remain tipped.

The organization of this book seeks to examine these dynamics. The first part looks at the phenomenon of stability in East-West relations. In the first chapter, I look specifically at how nuclear weapons have forced stability in the relationship. Paul R. Viotti then explains how patterns of behavior and specific agreements create stabilizing regimes between the powers, using arms control as a means to show both the prospects and limits on such arrangements. Robert C. Gray concludes the part by examining the concept of security in the context of strategic nuclear relations. Pointing out the importance of the idea of stability in American thinking, his chapter provides a bridge to the second part.

Part II looks explicitly at issues surrounding the strategic nuclear balance and how it might be transformed. The major issues that have emerged in the latter 1980s and promise to persist have dealt with the dual (and related) issues of nuclear defenses and arms control, and each of the chapters examines an aspect of those problems. Stephen J. Cimbala looks at the question of how one moves from a world in which there are no defenses against nuclear missiles to one where such defenses are prominent. Most observers agree that the transition will be most easily accomplished under a condition of arms control. A major hindrance to strategic arms control has been the charge that the Soviet Union has systematically violated arms control agreements, and Gary L. Guertner responds to the various arguments that are made about whether the Soviets do or do not honor their agreements. Finally, an adjunct to the question of missile defenses is the issue of how more conventionally delivered nuclear weapons by airplane and, recently, cruise missiles fits into a transformed nuclear world. David S. Sorenson exhaustively details the possible impact of a new generation of cruise missiles on the strategic balance.

The final part deals with the nonnuclear relationship. Much of Soviet-American military relations addresses the problem of a conventional war in Europe and the continuing problems it presents. This topic is viewed by Gale Mattox in her chapter on new challenges facing the alliance. At the same time, much of the debate in the 1980s has been over the proper role of maritime forces in various NATO contingencies, and John A. Williams looks at this aspect of the relationship. Finally, since Soviet-American relations have been pushed increasingly toward the periphery, the final two chapters address the nature of that changing relationship. Dennis M. Drew examines the problems that Soviet sponsorship of unconventional, low-intensity warfare movements pose for the United States military, while Daniel S. Papp takes the evolution of Soviet-American relations in the Third World as his principal task. Both agree that the Third World poses some unique problems for the United States and that Soviet-American relations will increasingly be affected by the Third World.

The chapters in this book were originally presented at the annual meeting of the Section on Military Studies (SOMS) of the International Studies Association in November 1986 in Cambridge, Massachusetts. The project was conceived nearly a year earlier while I was serving as secretary of the navy senior research fellow at the U.S. Naval War College, Newport, Rhode Island. I would like to take this opportunity to thank the SECNAV Research Fellows Program for providing me the time for organizing this project. Moreover, I would like to thank my editor at Lexington Books, Jaime Welch-Donahue, for her patience and encouragement of this project. Finally, I want to express personal thanks to all the authors, each of whom I consider a personal friend as well as valued colleague, for their contributions.

I
Stability and Soviet-American Relations

1

Stability in Soviet-American Relations: The Influence of Nuclear Weapons

Donald M. Snow

The nuclear age now spans more than four decades, and the period of mutual vulnerability of the superpowers to the ballistically delivered nuclear arsenals of the other has been the operational backdrop for superpower interactions for nearly three-quarters of that period. Particularly in times of tension and conflict with apparently escalatory potential, the nuclear shadow has apparently been cast as a sword of Damocles hanging perilously and tenuously over humanity. The cord from which the sword was suspended has often seemed fragile and frayed, but it has never snapped.

The centrality of the need to avoid nuclear war has been a central concern, at least in the United States, keyed by Brodie's famous 1946 admonition that in the nuclear age, the avoidance of war—deterrence—is the central role of military force.[1] The role that nuclear weapons play in superpower relations and in international affairs generally has been and continues to be highly controversial, sparking an ongoing, multilevel debate over strategies best capable of maintaining and reinforcing the deterrent condition. Central issues in this debate have been about what kinds of threats deflect the presumed aggressive intention of the Soviet opponent (declaratory strategy), what weapons and arsenal characteristics are necessary to enliven declaratory threats (development and deployment strategy), and what war plans will best convince the opponent to desist from nuclear attacks and, should deterrence fail, allow war termination on the most favorable (or least unfavorable) terms (employment or operational strategy).

The majority of the public, and especially scholarly, debate has focused on the area of declaratory strategy, leaving other levels of strategy to grow and mature outside the harsh rhetorical light that has often surrounded the debate over declaratory posture. The result, at least for employment strategy, has run along counterforce lines first suggested by Borden in 1946: "Victory in another conflict will not depend on destruction of civilians but on quick elimination of the opponent's forces and stockpiles in being."[2] Nacht traces this preference as part of policy "as early as August 1950 and certainly by 1952,"[3] and the documentary research done by Rosenberg shows the development of counterforce targeting from the end of World War II to 1960.[4] Ball, in his numerous works on the Single Integrated Operational Plan (SIOP) first developed by the Kennedy administration to coordinate planning, has emphasized this consistent orientation.[5] Only the reaction to President Jimmy Carter's Presidential Directive (PD)-59 brought employment policy under scrutiny.

Attention has focused instead on declaratory strategy, and hence the need for threats to the adversary in the absence of which it would or at least might start nuclear war. At this level of analysis, the major underlying assumption is the presumed hostile intention of the adversary, and the purpose of deterrence is to dissuade the opponent from activating that hostile intention.

The American declaratory strategy debate has vacillated between two answers to the question of what deters the Soviets: threats to wreak maximum death, destruction, and havoc in retaliation to a Soviet aggression (assured destruction) or threats to cancel out any projected Soviet gains through measured and proportional responses to any level of nuclear aggression (limited nuclear options or countervailance). The Soviets, meanwhile, maintain that "imperialism will unleash a world nuclear war against the Soviet Union unless prevented by the might of the Soviet Armed Forces"[6] and that it is only Western knowledge of certain defeat at the hands of those forces that prevents capitalist aggression.

What if these formulations are simply wrong or, more precisely, irrelevant? The Soviets have consistently derided both assured destruction and limited options, describing mutual assured destruction (MAD) as second-rate doctrine and expressing the belief that nuclear war was highly unlikely to remain limited.[7] If these views represent actual Soviet thinking on American strategy, is it possible to argue convincingly that the threats on which those strategies are based deter the Soviets? Similarly, Americans dismiss Soviet strategy as little more than a crudely stated excuse to continue procurement processes, a position deriving from the absence of U.S. aggressive intentions that require deterring.

What if both sides' derisions of the other are correct? If American threats do not deter the Soviets and Soviet threats do not alter American intentions, then who is deterring whom? Is it possible that the absence of nuclear war rests on a base both simpler and more subtle than the mutual threat system? Is it not possible that the central dynamic of nuclear deterrence is a shared superpower fear of the consequences of nuclear war? The unwillingness to accept the consequences of nuclear war may be the primary dynamic of the deterrence system. If that is the case, rather than the United States deterring the Soviet Union from crossing the nuclear threshold or vice-versa, the United States and the Soviet Union are deterring themselves. The principal dynamic of nuclear war avoidance may therefore be calculated and realistic self-restraint by the superpowers (hereafter referred to as realistic self-deterrence, RSD).

This possibility should not be shocking. With the growth of nuclear arsenals, it has become increasingly evident that "one of the few common goals the West and the Soviets share is the avoidance of nuclear war"[8] because "nuclear weapons create an uncommon interest between the two adversaries. Their fates are linked together—or the fate of each is in the hands of the other— in a way that was never true in the past."[9] This shared interest exists in a complex conflict-cooperation nexus. As the Harvard Nuclear Study Group puts it, "The shared objective is to keep the nuclear peace; neither superpower wants to fight a nuclear war. . . . Because of this combination of genuine rivalry and genuine common interest, both superpowers are cautious."[10] The nuclear embrace creates such a strong mutual interest in nuclear war avoidance that both seek to avoid and defuse situations that could lead to nuclear war. The result has been a gradual stabilization of relations and a situation where the likelihood of nuclear war is "extremely low."[11] This trend has continued through the gradual warming of Soviet-American relations during the Reagan presidency.

Leaders in both countries have publicly recognized realistic self-deterrence in fact if not in name. President Reagan, in a January 16, 1984, address, said, "We should always remember that we do have common interests. And the foremost among them is to avoid war and reduce the level of arms."[12] Using much the same language, Secretary of State George Shultz has stated that "we have a fundamental common interest in the avoidance of war. This common interest impels us to work toward a relationship between our nations that can lead to a safer world for all mankind."[13]

Soviet leaders have echoed the same sentiment. Official Soviet emphasis was particularly pronounced during the rule of Leonid Brezhnev. He argued the cataclysmic effects of nuclear war repeatedly in statements such as, "only he who has decided to commit suicide can start a nuclear war in the hope of emerging victorious from it,"[14] and ascribing to nuclear arsenals the ability to "destroy every living thing on earth several times."[15] This statement is repeated in the Soviets' response to *Soviet Military Power*[16] although without attribution: "Only a person who has decided to commit suicide can start a nuclear war in the hope of winning it."[17] Another group of Soviet commentators intones the official public position in Clausewitzian language: "As regards the socialist community countries they unconditionally reject all variants of a nuclear war as a means of attaining socialism's political aims. *Nuclear war is not a continuation of socialist policy. . . . Nuclear war cannot be permitted.*"[18] Before his banishment (and subsequent reinstatement to favor), no less a hard-line military figure than Marshall Ogarkov stated the official stance that the Soviets have no intention of initiating nuclear war: "Soviet military strategy views a future world war, *if the imperialists manage to unleash it*, as a decisive clash" (emphasis added).[19] The late Konstantin Chernenko stated the proposition most forcefully: "In a nuclear war, there can be no victors and no political aims can be achieved by means of it. Any attempt to use nuclear weapons would inevitably lead to a disaster."[20] Mikhail Gorbachev has repeatedly echoed the same theme.

One may initially be tempted to dismiss the statements by officials as propagandistic and politically motivated rather than as serious statements of policy. The notion that nuclear war avoidance is central to Soviet policy does not appear to comport, for instance, with the vaunted Soviet nuclear war-winning strategy.[21] On the other hand, these statements are consistent with overt policy so that realistic self-deterrence operates to create a stable nuclear relationship because the first foreign policy priority of both the United States and the Soviet Union is to avoid nuclear war with the other. This assertion flies in the face of conventional deterrence wisdom about the Soviet Union because it denies a Soviet intention to commit nuclear aggression that needs deterring. Yet there are at least three sorts of evidence that can be used to support the contention.

The first is substantial support within the expert community that analyzes Soviet policy. The consensus of that opinion is that "the Soviets assign the highest priority to the deterrence of nuclear war."[22] This assertion does not arise from any naive sense of Soviet benevolence but rather their assessment of the consequences of "that very devastating exchange which both they and the United States seek to avoid."[23] Moreover, adoption of nuclear war avoidance does not represent any particular moderation of Soviet goals, which remain constant: "The Kremlin leaders do not want war; they want the world. They believe it unlikely, however, that the West will let them have the world without a fight."[24] Moreover, abandoning nuclear war as a policy alternative argues neither that the Soviets "reject the notion of nuclear superiority, or at least the appearance of superiority . . . [as yielding] tangible political benefits"[25] nor that they "regard nuclear war as impossible."[26] Instead the policy represents a historical continuity: "For the Soviets, détente represented simply an updated variant of Leninist peaceful coexistence: an absence of direct military conflict between the major powers."[27] Avoiding the destruction of the Soviet Union in a nuclear war, in other words, is consistent with Soviet policy.

The pattern of Soviet-American relations, particularly in recent years, reflects the desire to avoid confrontations and nuclear war. As Schelling puts it, "We have what ought to be an important source of reassurance, a 'confidence-building' experience: 40 years of nuclear weapons without nuclear war."[28]

Viewing the entire postwar period in terms of superpower relations, one can discern two fairly distinct phases. The first spanned roughly the quarter-centruy after 1945 and was punctuated by fairly frequent confrontations with escalatory potential over problems and places such as Berlin, Cuba, and the Middle East. In the subsequent period, and especially since the Yom Kippur War of 1973, these confrontations have essentially ceased, despite ample opportunities for the superpowers to confront one another (for example, in Afghanistan or the Persian Gulf).[29] This period has also witnessed the Soviet achievement of nuclear equality with the United States and apparently reflects a reevaluation of that balance as well: "In the fifth phases (1971–1984), the Soviets recognized that assured destruction of Soviet society would result from fighting an all-out nuclear war."[30] This evolution occurred while Soviet-American relations generally deteriorated (under Carter, culminating with Afghanistan) to the point that exchanges between top leaders were suspended for four years (the first Reagan term).

The third and final source of support is Soviet profession. Recalling the rejoinder that leadership statements may include deception and manipulation among their purposes, the Soviets have consistently stated their position on nuclear war. "Soviet political and military commentators have repeatedly acknowledged the catastrophic consequences of general nuclear war and are certain to support its avoidance."[31] Consistency and honesty are not the same, of course, so that one can place varying amounts of weight on Soviet pronouncement. Nonetheless, the Soviets' consistency cannot be dismissed entirely.

If the intent to avoid nuclear war lies at the heart of U.S. and Soviet foreign policies, the question is why this is the case. This situation and the consequent stability that it has produced in U.S.-Soviet relations, after all, flies in the face of early (and even contemporary) warnings about the instability and delicacy of the balance of terror. As one observer puts it, "The superpower leaders and their allies in Europe have been more cautious than early theories of nuclear behavior predicted."[32]

The recent literature reflects substantial agreement about the absence of American or (particularly) Soviet intent to start nuclear war. Although these analyses are compatible and parallel to the realistic self-deterrence argument, they generally stop short of its conclusion. The basic dynamic cited is the recognition of "the objective reality of assured destruction in an all-out nuclear war," which has "led to important modifications in Soviet military and diplomatic strategy."[33] As a result of this realization, "the Soviets are likely to be self-deterred" because they realize fighting a nuclear war will bring "the destruction of both societies," meaning that "the chances of war between the United States and the U.S.S.R. are very slight."[34]

Different analysts label this phenomenon differently. McGeorge Bundy, for instance, has called it "existential deterrence."[35] Allison, Carnesale, and Nye refer to the crystal ball effect, by which they mean that "the unprecedented damage nuclear weapons can do has produced an unprecedented prudence."[36] Its effect is similar to Dyson's "live and let live policy."[37]

Analysts making this point quickly distinguish assured destruction (AD) as the likely outcome of nuclear war from AD as a conscious strategy. As Jervis puts it, "MAD as a fact is more important than MAD as a policy. The latter is in the realm of choice, the former is not."[38] Stating this a slightly different way, Knorr maintains, "Even though the superpowers do not follow deterrent strategies of Mutual Assured Destruction, mutual destruction is very likely to describe the consequences of substantial nuclear hostilities between them."[39]

This construction avoids embracing the genocidal consequences of advocating an assured destruction policy. Rather it argues that MAD "represents a condition, not an objective. . . . This condition exists today and is likely to persist for the foreseeable future. But MAD is not an objective of American policy. Its 'mutuality' is unattractive to most American policymakers (and presumably to Soviets as well)."[40] Although the assured destruction outcome is a likely result of nuclear exchange, that recognition should not be confused with policy advocacy. Rather, the danger is in equating the condition and the policy advocacy, which has the effect of creating a "mountain of confusion. . . . The mountain is the conclusion that this is the way we *should* design and plan the use of nuclear weapons."[41]

The conclusion must be that the motive force underlying Soviet and American determination to avoid nuclear war is a fear of its probable consequences. These consequences include the likelihood that any nuclear conflict, once initiated, would escalate to a general level with results as unacceptable as those associated with assured destruction, or worse, nuclear winter. This possibility is the result of the condition of mutual societal vulnerability to attack, against which there is no effective means of mitigating the disaster once it begins to unfold. The only way to avoid the disaster is to avoid letting the process begin—in other words, deterrence. Moreover, there is little near-term or medium prospect that this condition will or can be changed.

This formulation sounds a great deal like AD thought, but the distinction between AD as condition and as policy becomes critical. The basic contention here is that it is the assessment of AD as the likely—or at least a possible—outcome of any nuclear engagement, regardless of the deterrence strategies either side articulates in advance of that engagement, that forces both sides to adopt nuclear war avoidance as their first foreign policy priority. Neither the AD threat nor the countervailing strategy deters Soviet aggression against the United States any more than Soviet threats to prevail in nuclear war deter an American aggression. What deters nuclear war is the conclusion by the superpowers that the result of such a conflict would be devastating beyond any sensible conceivable purpose or gain. That assessment causes each superpower to deter itself from initiating nuclear war.

Other system dyamics reinforce the self-restraint nurtured by fear of nuclear war. Two stand out as illustrative examples: strategic uncertainty and the prospects for a nuclear winter. Each affects deterrence dynamics differently, but both reinforce the need to avoid nuclear war.

The nuclear winter hypothesis was first advanced in 1983.[42] The burden of the argument is that a nuclear war would ignite tremendous fires in urban areas, which would insert massive amounts of soot and other particulates into the upper atmosphere, girdling the globe and blocking out the sun's rays. The result would be an ecologically disastrous lowering of global temperatures to compound the other deleterious effects of nuclear war.

The nuclear winter phenomenon affects traditional declaratory positions perversely but reinforces self-restraint. At one level, it seems to reinforce AD by specifying the disaster. At the same time, it renders the AD threat incredible since carrying out the threat literally entails committing suicide. A strategy of limited nuclear options initially may seem more attractive, but there is always the danger one might inadvertently pass the threshold,[43] since nuclear winter "is only a possibility, and the triggering mechanism is complex and poorly understood." This likely will remain the case because "it is not possible to check the unique aspects of the effects against observation."[44] Nuclear winter reinforces self-deterrence; by making the consequences of nuclear war even worse, the incentive to remain self-deterred is made more compelling.

Strategic uncertainty also enters the calculus. The concept refers to "the role of uncertainty in military planning; the scale of risks and consequences in the use, or threat of use, of nuclear weapons; the unpredictability of warfare."[45] Uncertainty makes it more difficult to calculate gain from nuclear war because, for instance, "professional soldiers feel that the risks and uncertainties associated with first-strike are too great to be undertaken by a responsible government."[46] Uncertainty has been described as the basis of "the present state of nuclear deterrence,"[47] as an organizing device for future strategy,[48] and as the justification for the MX intercontinental ballistic missile[49] and the president's Strategic Defense Initiative (SDI).[50] The consistent rationale is that uncertainty complicates a potential aggressor's calculations about gains from nuclear weapons use to the point of paralyzing the ability to predict a "successful" outcome from nuclear weapons use. Such an effect is congruent with the self-deterrence dynamic of maintaining fear of the outcome of nuclear weapons usage.

The two concepts come together in uncertainty about when and how (or even if) nuclear winter might be triggered. The difficulty is that nothing truly analogous to nuclear winter occurs in nature, and uncertainty cannot be removed because "there can be no opportunity to experiment on earth."[51] The inability to gain exact knowledge leads Dyson to conclude, "The meteorological uncertainties of nuclear war will remain at least as great as the uncertainties of peacetime weather prediction."[52] As a practical policy consequence, "uncertainties will make it difficult for strategic planners to take into account the nuclear winter effect."[53] The absence of certainty, however, simply reinforces the inclination toward prudence that self-deterrence suggests.

Self-deterrence has strong implications for the nuclear debate and assessment about the stability of superpower relations. The debate over what kinds of threats best deter takes on a different and more academic quality. In addition, what actions contribute to a greater or lesser degree of stability in the ongoing condition are cast in a different light.

The discussion of system maintenance must occur within the context of the U.S.-Soviet geopolitical relationship. Although the military superpowers differ on political ideology and their views of a favorable world order (neither of which is inconsequential), the two are not historic enemies with long traditions of animosity. They clashed briefly during the Russian Civil War immediately after World War I, but otherwise relations have been cordial or at worst neutral. There are no deep cultural or historical animosities between the American and Russian peoples to fuel the righteous fires of nuclear genocide. Given the destructive capabilities the two possess, this situation is undoubtedly just as well; "it is perhaps fortunate that the U.S. and the Soviet Union are the ones to lay down precedents for dealing with the nuclear dilemma. It would be difficult to think of two great powers with less to fight about."[54]

The result of this observation is that one can remove atavistic passion from the list of incentives for starting a superpower nuclear war (a qualification one might not make so readily if, for instance, West Germany and the Soviet Union were the principal nuclear antagonists). Instead, the keys to maintaining nuclear war avoidance under the current regime of RSD appear to be more mechanical, dispassionate, and geopolitical.

Since fear of the consequences means nuclear war is unlikely to result from calculated intention, two categories of factors could lead to nuclear war. The first of these is nuclear war through inadvertence, where hostilities began without or even despite the intention or volition of either side. The second category would be if one or both sides lost their fear of the consequences of nuclear exchange, thus removing the continuing need to feel self-deterred.

War by inadvertence would most likely occur as the result of political causes, and so its remedies are political. Under current conditions, nuclear war is unlikely to occur unexpectedly as the result of either side's planning or executing something such as a surprise attack, because, as Lebow explains, "Most serious students of Soviet-American relations dismiss the notion that nuclear war could come in the form of a 'bolt out of the blue' sneak attack. . . . This is because such an attack would almost certainly be suicidal for the attackers as well as fatal for the victim."[55] Instead such an outbreak would likely be the result of events getting out of hand, a crisis degenerating because of either third party (perhaps Middle Eastern inspired) or direct superpower confrontation (such as a renewed Berlin crisis), or even possibly "because the Soviet Union attacked an ally of the United States."[56]

One deals with this problem by creating a political climate minimizing the prospects that a political crisis could inadvertently degenerate out of control, "a structure of political understanding and formalized restraint."[57] This structure has two purposes: crisis prevention to settle international differences before they can reach the level of confrontation and crisis and crisis management[58] through a "structure [of] greater crisis stability with the goal of preventing war in crisis situations."[59] Crisis prevention aims at keeping crises from occurring; crisis management tries to defuse crises that cannot be avoided altogether at the lowest and least dangerous levels of confrontation and escalatory potential.

The second category, perceptual changes, looks at weapons balance and is technological in character. Inhibitions against nuclear usage are imbedded in hard-headed assessments that arise from comparisons of arsenal characteristics. Such calculations have concluded that the outcome of initiating nuclear attack under any circumstances would be unacceptable for the initiator in the final outcome or at least that there is sufficiently great uncertainty about the outcome as to make the risk too great.

The problem here is to avoid either side's changing its perceptions. The key element is maintaining the perception either of the certainty of ultimate failure or the uncertainty of probable success because the "Soviet Union . . . ought to be deterred from attack given the massive penalties for even a slight failure."[60] Maintaining such perceptions requires avoiding a change in either the quantitative or qualitative weapons balance such that one or both sides could conclude it possessed such advantages that it could avoid the unacceptable consequences of nuclear exchange or that the consequences have been reduced sufficiently to contemplate gain. The effects of changes in the balance are important in reviewing proposals for large-scale nuclear force reductions, such as the Gorbachev three-step proposal for nuclear disarmament announced January 15, 1986, and largely reiterated at the Reykjavik summit of October 1986.

These ideas are hardly radical. Crisis avoidance and management are similar in concept to the AD requirement for crisis stability (although the latter, since it assumes hostility that needs deterring, is more weapons oriented), and perceptual change avoidance shares conceptual purpose with the AD goal of arms race stability, at least to the extent that such stability is associated with some symmetry and certainty of lethal effect.

The requirements also conform to how the system has evolved. The Harvard Study Group, for instance, describes the balance as essentially evolutionary: "Through trial and error the superpowers have developed some prudent practices for handling crises. Both sides continue to avoid direct clash of forces; each has avoided the use of nuclear weapons, and observes some restraint in the other side's sphere of dominant influence."[61] The result of this evolution is a nuclear stalemate with considerable resilience and stability. Nacht concludes, "It will take a truly revolutionary technological innovation or a massive exercise of human stupidity before this stalemate is seriously threatened."[62] Technological change, of course, is one factor that could change perceptions, and stupidity is a concern of crisis management, linking Nacht's conclusion to RSD.

RSD extends orthodox analysis in assessing what brings about stability and how to reinforce it. RSD divorces AD as policy from AD as fact, thus facilitating freer consideration of system maintenance in two senses. First, it removes the AD versus Limited Nuclear Options debate from the discussion, allowing a broader and less strictured debate. Second, accepting AD simply as a current description of the consequence of nuclear exchange allows discussion of alternative futures unfettered by doctrinal restrictions. Support or opposition to the various Gorbachev proposals, for instance, can be couched in broader terms than their effects on AD or LNOs. Instead RSD provides an alternative and broader way to think about the future of deterrence less encumbered by orthodox canons. Thus, the dynamic of self-deterrence has led to nuclear stability; how the elements leading to this situation can be improved warrants consideration.

Crisis Management

Somber calculations arrived at when there are no overt, dangerous sources of confrontation produce the self-deterring condition, but what circumstances might negate that judgment? One possible set of circumstances would be in the evolution of a crisis where superpower vital interests came into direct conflict. The evolution of such a crisis could render the avoidance of war less important than protecting the interest; in such circumstances, the crisis could alter perceptions of the unacceptability of nuclear weapons usage. More simply put, the danger is in a crisis getting out of hand.

Former secretary of defense James Schlesinger has looked at where this kind of problem might arise: "In the 'grey areas' the risks are low; incursions, subversions, and other pressures may occur without any major impact on the overall balance of power. . . . By contrast, a threat to Europe, Japan, or (for different reasons) the Arabian Gulf could start a process without limit."[63] This assessment, of course, reflects traditional American vital interests. Western Europe and Japan have been considered vital. Western Europe and Japan have been considered vital since the 1940s, and former President Carter conferred the same status on the oil-rich littoral areas of the Persian Gulf in that part of his 1980 State of the Union Address that became known as the Carter Doctrine.

If nuclear weapons have produced RSD and general restraint in U.S.-Soviet relations, then the crisis-escalatory prospects are not equally likely in the three regions. Both sides have long understood the escalatory potential in Europe and Japan, and East-West relations have been structured virtually to preclude interbloc actions not authorized by one superpower or the other. West Germany, for instance, is hardly likely to attack Czechoslovakia, or vice-versa, without superpower compliance.

The real danger lies in situations where the superpowers do not entirely control events. In those circumstances, crises can arise and expand before the superpowers, which often support but rarely control contending factions, are able to act decisively to defuse the crisis. The Persian Gulf is such an area, leading Schlesinger to conclude, "Only the Middle East region provides this potential for an uncontrolled clash between the Soviet Union and the United States."[64] Some observers would add the Korean peninsula to regions with this potential, and the resurgence of nuclear proliferation adds to the horror of the scenario. "Any use of nuclear weapons by small nations is likely to involve the superpowers and any use of nuclear weapons by the superpowers almost certainly would escalate to all-out exchange."[65]

The danger in a spiraling crisis is that the internal dynamics of the situation alter perceptions so greatly that judgments reached in a less hectic environment are reversed. Crises can occur rapidly, condensing decision time and both restricting and distorting information: perceptions about what is and is not sensible behavior change. As Allison, Carnesale, and Nye describe this process, "What starts out as rational is likely to become less so over time. And accidents that would not matter much in normal times or early in a crisis may create 'crazy' situations in which choice is so constrained that 'rational' decisions about the least bad alternatives lead to outcomes that would appear insane under normal circumstances."[66] Speaking directly to how perspective can be distorted, McNamara suggests, "What may look like a reckless gamble in more tranquil times might then be seen merely as a reasonable risk."[67] Crises create stress, leading to the most demanding requirement for the system: "Deterrence must work under terrible stress as well as in ordinary circumstances. . . . Deterrence is harder in a crisis."[68] Under a condition of psychological stress, there could be "a misreading of signals"[69] such that "fear might be forgotten, prudence set aside, and drastic action taken."[70] Given these problems, crisis management appears to have two basic imperatives: crisis avoidance where possible and crisis termination at the earliest and lowest level possible where avoidance proves impossible. The evidence suggests that superpower relations, implicitly if not always explicitly and often obscured in a fog of hostile, confrontational rhetoric, have been moving in the direction of both goals.

Crisis avoidance is the process of one or both parties staying out of situations that could lead to crises. The best evidence of this is the movement of interactions with confrontational potential away from such explosive places as Western Europe (for example, flash points such as Berlin) to the Third and Fourth Worlds, where interests are more peripheral and where either or both can withdraw before differences can become crises. Bracken agrees with this thrust, arguing that "it may be best to concentrate our energy on *preventing* confrontations, by diplomacy, wise foreign policy, and fostering of a cooperative relationship between the United States and the Soviet Union."[71] Although crisis prevention is clearly an important concern, George refers to it as "the orphan of strategic studies."[72]

The other problem is crisis termination at the lowest possible level, before a crisis can develop the intensity to trigger the dynamics by which crises get out of hand. Mechanisms such as the hot line and the recently instituted risk reduction centers are attempts to promote the communications that facilitate crisis termination. The vitality of the entire crisis management mission is underscored by Jervis: "We must pay more attention to convincing the Soviets that, even in an extreme crisis, war is not inevitable."[73] The key element is clear and noninflammatory communication, because "stability . . . requires that the Soviet Union not misread the intentions and capabilities of the West, particularly in times of crisis."[74]

Changed Perceptions

If the perception of unacceptable outcomes after a nuclear exchange activates the disinclination to initiate nuclear war, maintaining and nurturing this set of perceptions is one way to improve deterrence. The questions to be asked are: What about the current balance creates the perception? What could make that perception change to a belief that a nuclear war's consequences would be tolerable?

The key factor is the lethal balance, defined loosely as some form of equilibrium, and there is agreement on this factor on both sides of the iron curtain. A quasi-official Soviet pronouncement, for instance, intones, "Where there is a military strategic equilibrium, nuclear weapons will give neither side an advantage: their utilization only threatens to bring about a global catastrophe."[75] Secretary of State George Shultz agrees with this assessment: "The nuclear equilibrium has successfully deterred World War III."[76]

The size and lethal characteristics of the two arsenals create this equilibrium of deadly effects such that, for instance, "The most obvious requirement for American nuclear forces is that they provide the unquestioned ability to destroy the Soviet Union even if the Soviets stage a skillful first strike."[77] Traditionally, the high levels of mutually possessed force create the inhibition. Because of this size, "U.S. and Soviet strategic forces are not in delicate balance over a sharp fulcrum. Instead, they are counterpoised on a broad base of uncertainties that will permit a number of force alternatives on either side without cataclysmic results."[78] Peripheral changes in the equilibrium will not alter perceptions about gain. This helps reinforce stability: "An *attacker* will want high confidence of achieving decisive results before deciding on so dangerous a course as the use of nuclear weapons."[79] As long as arsenal sizes are large, calculations of gain from incremental change are stunted, a conclusion reinforced by the existence of strategic uncertainty and the suicidal potential of the nuclear winter.

Large, complex arsenals enter considerable operational uncertainties into any contemplations of initiating nuclear attack because such calculations can be answered positively only if one is reasonably certain the consequences will be tolerable. As John Weinstein puts this effect, "The vulnerabilities and uncertainties confronting Soviet leaders and military planners will continue to provide powerful incentives to avoid war with the West."[80] The philosopher Leon Wieseltier turns this factor around, arguing that it is the absence of certainty that one can succeed that deters: "In fact, deterrence does not require your enemy to believe that you will strike back; it requires only that he not believe you will not. Deterrence, in other words, does not require certainty. Doubt is quite enough."[81]

The large size of nuclear arsenals, the consequences of their use even after a victim has absorbed an initial attack, and operational uncertainties that frustrate plans to use nuclear weapons profitably have created the basis for stability. Were the balance of forces between the superpowers stagnant, one could consequently reduce the vigil with which that balance is eyed. The balance, however, is anything but stagnant, and its dynamism requires careful attention to ensure that the balance is not upset intolerably. Hoffman places this imperative specifically in the context of the SDI: "The point of departure ought to be reflection on the motives that might induce Soviet leaders and military planners to contemplate actually using nuclear weapons."[82] Guaranteeing that changes in the balance do not encourage altered perceptions about the utility of nuclear weapons employment is a major concern for maintaining the stability of the nuclear relationship.

Conclusion

The avoidance of nuclear war does not derive from the power of declaratory threats that the Soviet Union and the United States make against one another. Rather, any nuclear aggressive intentions either or both harbor against the other are dampened by their individual and collective unwillingness to endure their projected estimates of the effects of nuclear war. These somber calculations, which have the effect of inhibiting nuclear war, have been called realistic self-deterrence, and their effect is to produce considerable stability in superpower relations.

The existence of this stability is simultaneously an orthodox and radical notion. Its orthodoxy derives from a growing consensus among students of superpower relations that each shares the avoidance of nuclear war as their first foreign policy priority. Policymaker and analyst alike agree that nuclear war would be unacceptable to both, something akin (at least implicitly) to accepting assured destruction as factual consequence if not as policy preference.

The radicalism of RSD is to extend that consensus to conclude it is self-deterrence that powers nuclear war avoidance. If one accepts that notion, moreover, unsettling consequences flow. First, the debate over limited options (by whatever name) and assured destruction is tranformed, rendering much of it questionable relevance. Second, it creates an alternative agenda for deterrence maintenance, notably focusing on conflict management and perceptual maintenance as key concepts.

The self-deterrence hypothesis and its implementing criteria have implications in other aspects of the nuclear debate as well. How, for instance, does this notion meld with the growing concern over strategic uncertainty as part of nuclear strategy? Does it complement or undercut the conceptual attractiveness of missile defenses, especially the SDI? How does nuclear winter affect the ability or inability to calculate gain from nuclear weapons use?

The concerns raised by these observations extend to practical policy realities as well. One clear implication is that the nuclear world has become more stable; a world of superpower self-deterrence is not an intolerable place at all. That being the case, radical alterations to the system that might appear quite attractive on the surface need to be assessed in terms of their impact on the current system and the prospects that change will produce a more stable world. Gorbachev's entreaty for a nuclear-disarmed world by the end of this century suggests this need. Such a world would by definition have the nuclear yoke removed, but would that necessarily make it a better place? The Harvard Study Group is not so sure: "Ironically, while complete disarmament may be a worthy long-term goal, trying to achieve it before the requisite political conditions exist could actually increase the prospects of war. If the political pre-conditions of trust and consensus are missing, complete disarmament is inherently unstable."[83]

President Reagan's vision of a defense-dominant world is similar. Like disarmament, it would rid us of the nuclear terror that has activated the nuclear war avoidance system, but its effects could be similarly radical and conceivably leave us worse rather than better off. Moving away from the nuclear precipice is, in both cases, a lofty and praiseworthy objective but only if we are reasonably certain we are not trading that precipice for some new and unpredictable abyss.

Notes

1. Bernard Brodie (ed.), *The Absolute Weapon: Atomic Power and World Order* (New York: Harcourt, Brace, 1946).

2. William Liscum Borden, *There Will Be No Time: The Revolution in Strategy* (New York: Macmillan, 1946), p. 218.

3. Michael Nacht, *The Age of Vulnerability: Threats to the Nuclear Stalemate* (Washington, D.C.: Brookings Institution, 1985), p. 86.

4. See David Alan Rosenberg, " 'A Smoking Radiating Ruin at the End of Two Hours:' Documents on American Plans for Nuclear War with the Soviet Union," *International Security* 6, no. 3 (Winter 1981–1982): 3–38 and "The Origins of Overkill: Nuclear Weapons and American Strategy, 1945–1960," *International Security* 7, no. 4 (Spring 1983): 4–71.

5. See, for instance, Desmond Ball, "Targeting for Strategic Deterrence," Adelphi Papers No. 185 (London: International Institute for Strategic Studies, Summer 1985).

6. Harriet Fast Scott and William F. Scott, "Conclusions," in Harriet Fast Scott and William F. Scott (eds.), *The Soviet Art of War: Doctrine, Strategy, and Tactics* (Boulder, Colo.: Westview Press, 1982), p. 289.

7. For greater description, see Donald M. Snow, *Nuclear Strategy in a Dynamic World: American Policy in the 1980s* (Tuscaloosa, Ala.: University of Alabama Press, 1981), pp. 135–136, 141–142.

8. John G. Kelliher, "Discussion," in Richard F. Staar (ed.), *Arms Control: Myth Versus Reality* (Stanford, Calif.: Hoover Institution Press, 1984), p. 41.

9. Robert Jervis, *The Illogic of American Nuclear Strategy* (Ithaca, N.Y.: Cornell University Press, 1984), p. 30.

10. Harvard Nuclear Study Group (Albert Carnesale, Paul Doty, Stanley Hoffman, Joseph S. Nye, Jr., Scott A. Sagan), *Living with Nuclear Weapons* (Cambridge, Mass.: Harvard University Press, 1983), pp. 17–18.

11. Bernard Brodie, "On the Objectives of Arms Control," *International Security* 1, no. 1 (Summer 1976): 19. A sample of other recent writers making similar observations includes: Stephen M. Meyer, "Soviet Perspectives on the Paths to Nuclear War," in Graham T. Allison, Albert Carnesale, and Joseph S. Nye, Jr. (eds.), *Hawks, Doves and Owls: An Agenda for Avoiding Nuclear War* (New York: W.W. Norton, 1985), p. 167; Zbigniew Brzezinski, "Foreword," in Robbin E. Laird and Dale R. Herspring, *The Soviet Union and Strategic Arms* (Boulder, Colo.: Westview Press, 1984), p. xi; Charles Burton Marshall, "Dinner Address" in Staar (ed.), *Arms Control*, p. 183; and Thomas C. Schelling, "What Went Wrong with Arms Control," *Foreign Affairs* 64, no. 2 (Winter 1985/1986): 233.

12. Ronald Reagan, "The U.S.-Soviet Relationship," *Atlantic Community Quarterly* 22, no. 1 (Spring 1984): 5.

13. "U.S.-Soviet Relations in the Context of U.S. Foreign Policy," *Atlantic Community Quarterly* 21, no. 3 (Fall 1983): 202.

14. Dan L. Strode, "The Soviet Union and Modernization of the U.S. ICBM Force," in Barry R. Schneider, Colin S. Gray, and Keith B. Payne (eds.), *Missiles for the Nineties: ICBMs and Strategic Policy* (Boulder, Colo.: Westview Press, 1984), p. 146.

15. Laird and Herspring, *The Soviet Union and Strategic Arms*, p. 20.

16. *Soviet Military Power*, 4th ed. (Washington, D.C.: Government Printing Office, April 1985).

17. *Whence the Threat to Peace*, 2d ed. (Moscow: Military Publishing House, 1984), p. 13.

18. Gancho Ganev, Yevgeny Kazan, and Sarada Mitra, "The Nuclear Threat and Politics," *World Marxist Review* 27, no. 4 (April 1984): 46.

19. Nikolay V. Ogarkov, "Military," in Scott and Scott, *Soviet Art of War*, p. 246.

20. Quoted in *Whence the Threat to Peace*, p. 14.

21. The classic statement of this position remains Richard Pipes, "Why the Soviet Union Thinks It Can Fight and Win a Nuclear War," *Commentary* 64, no. 1 (July 1977): 21–34. Jervis rejoins this position, stating, "It is not clear that the Soviet doctrine has any relevance to deterrence at all. Instead, it may only be a discussion of what should be done if deterrence fails." See *Illogic of American Nuclear Strategy*, p. 108.

22. Edward L. Warner III, "The Defense Policy of the Soviet Union," in Reichart and Sturm, *American Defense Policy*, p. 53.

23. Robert Kennedy, "The Changing Strategic Balance and U.S. Defense Planning," in Robert Kennedy and John M. Weinstein (eds.), *The Defense of the West: Strategic and European Issues Reappraised* (Boulder, Colo.: Westview Press, 1984), p. 11.

24. Paul Nitze, "Strategy in the Decade of the 1980s," *Foreign Affairs* 59, no. 1 (Fall 1980): 90.

25. Kennedy, "Changing Strategic Balance," p. 12.

26. David Holloway, "The Strategic Defense Initiative and the Soviet Union," *Daedalus* 114, no. 3 (Summer 1985): 261.

27. James Schlesinger, "The Eagle and the Bear: Between an Unfree World and None," *Foreign Affairs* 63, no. 5 (Summer 1985): 949.

28. Schelling, "What Went Wrong," p. 219.

29. In their survey of postwar crises, Blechman and Kaplan report fifteen instances of crises with escalatory potential between 1948 and 1978, the most recent being the 1973 Yom Kippur crisis. See Barry M. Blechman and Stephen J. Kaplan, *Force without War; U.S. Armed Forces as a Political Instrument* (Washington, D.C.: Brookings Institution, 1978), pp. 98–100.

30. Laird and Herspring, *The Soviet Union and Strategic Arms*, p. 9.

31. Warner, "Defense Policy of the Soviet Union," p. 55.

32. Paul Bracken, "Accidental Nuclear War," in Allison, Carnesale, and Nye, *Hawks, Doves and Owls*, p. 28.

33. Laird and Herspring, *The Soviet Union and Strategic Arms*, p. 5.

34. Jervis, *Illogic* pp. 14, 34, 108.

35. McGeorge Bundy, "The Bishops and the Bomb," *New York Review of Books*, June 16, 1983, pp. 3–8.

36. Graham T. Allison, Albert Carnesale, and Joseph S. Nye, Jr., "Analytic Conclusions: Hawks, Doves, and Owls," in Allison, Carnesale, and Nye, *Hawks, Doves and Owls*, p. 216.

37. Freeman J. Dyson, *Weapons and Hope* (New York: Harper & Row, 1984), p. 294.

38. Robert Jervis, "MAD Is the Best Possible Deterrence," *Bulletin of the Atomic Scientists* 41, no. 3 (March 1985): 43.

39. Klaus Knorr, "Controlling Nuclear War," *International Security* 9, no. 4 (Spring 1985): 70.

40. Graham T. Allison, Albert Carnesale, and Joseph S. Nye, Jr., "An Agenda for Action," in Allison, Carnesale, and Nye, *Hawks, Doves and Owls*, p. 228. The same essential distinction is made by Freeman J. Dyson in *Weapons and Hope*, pp. 228–229.

41. Fred S. Hoffman, "The SDI in U.S. Nuclear Strategy," *International Security* 10, no. 1 (Summer 1985): 14.

42. For a thorough bibliography, see *World Armaments and Disarmament: SIPRI Yearbook 1985* (London: Taylor and Francis, 1985), pp. 127–129; for a good introduction to the subject, see Paul R. Ehrlich, Carl Sagan, Donald Kennedy, and Walter Orr Roberts, *The Cold and the Dark: The World after Nuclear War* (New York: W.W. Norton and Co., 1984).

43. For a fuller explanation of these effects, see Donald M. Snow, "Strategic Uncertainty and the Nuclear Winter: Implications for Policy," esp. pp. 64–67 in Paul R. Viotti (ed.), *Conflict and Arms Control: An Uncertain Agenda* (Boulder, Colo.: Westview Press, 1986).

44. Owen Greene, Ian Percival, and Irene Ridge, *Nuclear Winter: The Evidence and the Risks* (Cambridge, U.K.: Polity Press, 1985), pp. 85, 152.

45. Dmitri Simes, "Are the Soviets Interested in Arms Control?" *Washington Quarterly* 8, no. 2 (Spring 1985): 153.

46. Theodore A. Postal, "Strategic Confusion—with or without Nuclear Winter," *Bulletin of the Atomic Scientists* 41, no. 2 (February 1985): 14.

47. J.J. Gertler, "Some Policy Implications of Nuclear Witner," Rand Corporation Paper No. P-7045 (Santa Monica: RAND Corporation, January 1985), p. 15.

48. Donald M. Snow, *The Nuclear Future: Toward a Strategy of Uncertainty* (Tuscaloosa: University of Alabama Press, 1983), chap. 4. For a critical assessment, see Michael F. Altfield, "Uncertainty as a Deterrence Strategy: A Critical Assessment," *Comparative Strategy* 5, no. 1 (1985): 1–26.

49. Barry R. Schneider, "Soviet Uncertainties in Targeting Peacekeeper," in Schneider, Gray, and Payne, *Missiles for the Nineties,* pp. 109–134.

50. Paul H. Nitze, "SDI: Its Nature and Rationale," *Atlantic Community Quarterly* 23, no. 3 (Fall 1985): 265; Richard N. Perle, "The Strategic Defense Initiative: Addressing Some Misconceptions," *Journal of International Affairs* 39, no. 1 (Summer 1985): 25; Edward Teller, "Better a Shield than a Sword," *Defensive Science 2003+* 4, no. 5 (October–November 1985): 17.

51. Dan Horowitz and Robert J. Lieber, "Nuclear Winter and the Future of Deterrence," *Washington Quarterly* 8, no. 3 (Summer 1985): 59.

52. Dyson, *Weapons and Hope,* p. 21. Others sharing this view include Greene, Percival, and Ridge, *Nuclear Winter,* p. 154; and George F. Carrier, "Nuclear Winter: The State of the Science," *Issues in Science and Technology* (Winter 1985): 14–17.

53. Michael M. May, "Nuclear Winter: Strategic Significance," *Issues in Science and Technology* (Winter 1985): 18.

54. Michael M. May, "The U.S.-Soviet Approach to Nuclear Weapons," *International Security* 9, no. 4 (Spring 1985): 151.

55. Richard Ned Lebow, "Practical Ways to Avoid Superpower Crisis," *Bulletin of the Atomic Scientists* 41, no. 1 (January 1985): 22.

56. Leon Wieseltier, *Nuclear War, Nuclear Peace* (New York: Holt, Rinehart and Winston, 1983), p. 63.

57. John Steinbruner, "Arms Control: Crisis or Compromise," *Foreign Affairs* 63, no. 5 (Summer 1985): 1049.

58. Knorr uses the same categories to describe ways of lessening the likelihood of nuclear war. See "Controlling Nuclear War," p. 80.

59. Lebow, "Practical Ways to Avoid Superpower Crisis," p. 22.

60. Schneider, "Soviet Uncertainties," pp. 110–111.

61. *Living with Nuclear Weapons,* pp. 238–239.

62. Nacht, *Age of Vulnerability,* p. 201.

63. James R. Schlesinger, "The International Implications of Third-World Conflict: An American Perspective," Adelphi Papers No. 166 (London: International Institute for Strategic Studies, Summer 1981), p. 9.

64. Ibid., p. 10.

65. William T. Lee, "Soviet Perceptions of the Threat and Soviet Military Capabilities," in Graham D. Vernon (ed.), *Soviet Perceptions of War and Peace* (Washington, D.C.: National Defense University Press, 1981), p. 73.

66. "Analytical Conclusions," in Allison, Carnesale, and Nye, *Hawks, Doves and Owls,* p. 214.

67. Robert S. McNamara, "The Military Role of Nuclear Weapons: Perceptions and Misperceptions," *Foreign Affairs* 62, no. 1 (Fall 1983): 73.

68. Jervis, *Illogic*, p. 160.

69. Graham T. Allison, Albert Carnesale, and Joseph S. Nye, Jr., "Introduction to Allison, Carnesale, and Nye (eds.), *Hawks, Doves and Owls*, p. 19.

70. Harvard Nuclear Study Group, *Living with Nuclear Weapons*, p. 5.

71. Bracken, "Accidental Nuclear War," p. 49. He also argues crisis management as a major concern (p. 52).

72. Alexander R. George, "Toward a Soviet-American Crisis Prevention Regime," in Bernard Brodie, Michael D. Intriligator, and Roman Kolkowicz (eds.), *National Security and International Stability* (Cambridge, Mass.: Oelgeschlager, Gunn and Hain, 1983), p. 189.

73. Jervis, *Illogic*, p. 15.

74. Max M. Kampelman, "SDI and the Arms Control Process," *Atlantic Quarterly* 23, no. 3 (Fall 1985): 224.

75. Ganev et al., "Nuclear Threat and Politics," p. 42.

76. George Shultz, "A Forward Look at Foreign Policy," *Department of State Bulletin* 84, no. 2093 (December 1984): p. 7.

77. Jervis, *Illogic*, p. 168.

78. Kennedy, "Changing Strategic Balance," p. 22.

79. Hoffman, "SDI in U.S. Nuclear Strategy," p. 19.

80. John M. Weinstein, "All Features Grate and Stall: Soviet Strategic Vulnerabilities and the Future of Deterrence," in Kennedy and Weinstein, *Defense of the West*, pp. 42–43. Lieutenant General James A. Abrahamson recently made the same point in testimony to Congress. See Statement on the Strategic Defense Initiative, Statement to Committee on Armed Services, U.S. Senate, 99th Cong., 1st sess., February 21, 1985.

81. Wieseltier, *Nuclear War, Nuclear Peace*, p. 61.

82. Hoffman, "SDI in U.S. Strategy," p. 18.

83. *Living with Nuclear Weapons*, p. 190.

2
Soviet-American Conflict Rules: Constructing and Maintaining International Security Regimes

Paul R. Viotti

T his chapter deals with the construction and maintenance of international security regimes, particularly as they affect, and are affected by, superpower relations. First, management of conflicts that cannot easily be resolved is presented not just as a function of power considerations, but also as dependent on agreed rules or norms of behavior that can be constructed even between adversaries. After referring briefly to examples of managing unresolved conflicts in Berlin and Cyprus, attention is directed to management by Norway (a NATO ally of the United States) of its conflict relations with the Soviet Union. Finally, the chapter turns to the problems associated with constructing durable security regimes to govern strategic relations between the two superpowers.

Power, Rules, and the Routinization of Conflict Relations

Hugo Grotius, a sixteenth- and seventeenth-century jurist, was a practical scholar concerned with protecting the seafaring and other interests of his native Hollanders, and he looked to the rule of law among states. This Grotian insight of a rule-based order in international relations contrasts with the power- (or balance of power-) based order prominent in the works of Niccolò Machiavelli and Thomas Hobbes, whose writings spanned the same time period. Although power considerations were by no means absent in his thinking, Grotius focused more directly on the rules to which states subscribe. States ordinarily follow such rules because it is in their interest to do so. Indeed, these rules are the underpinning for much of what in international relations becomes routine. Without rules by which states voluntarily regulate their behavior, the discord

The views expressed in this chapter are those of the author and do not reflect the official policy or position of the U.S. Air Force, the Department of Defense, or any other branch of the U.S. government.

that inevitably inheres in their relations would likely lead to arms conflict with greater frequency than now occurs.

The late Hedley Bull noted the importance of power (or countervailing power) as a factor that constrains the behavior of states.[1] There are limits beyond which a state will not allow another one to go. If it is within its capability, it will block activities taken beyond these limits, if necessary through the use of force. There can be no doubt that statemen understand the threat posed by outside actors that would obstruct the pursuit of objectives beyond the limits of their tolerance. Peace in such a world depends on as clear an understanding of these limitations by statemen and a desire to avoid or, at least, manage conflicts that could lead to war. Both the United States and the Soviet Union exhibit the caution in dealing with one another that comes from realization of the danger posed if conflicts between them ever get out of hand.

In some instances in which conflicts cannot be resolved, the best one can achieve may be the routinization of conflict relations. Bull noted the prevalence of rules that along with power considerations provide some degree of order to international relations.[2] In Berlin, three Western allies (the United States, United Kingdom, and France) conduct business as usual, following elaborate procedures that have the appearance of ritual in their relations with the Soviet Union. The status quo is maintained by a series of agreements establishing rules of conduct, a regime that has its basis in the legal principle that all four states still remain allies with rights of occupation in the capital of a defeated German Reich. Dealing with one's adversary as if it were an ally is a unique way of managing conflict that without such arrangements could (and threatened many times in the past to) lead to war.[3]

Nor is Berlin the only place where disputes among parties tend to be reduced to routines. The case of Cyprus is particularly instructive in this regard. There is no agreed settlement of the dispute between Greek and Turkish Cypriots or between Greece and Turkey as to what should be done on the island. At the same time there has been an establishment of routines along the border dividing the two sectors and a certain acceptance of this situation, at least for the time being. A continuing U.N. peacekeeping presence lends legitimacy to efforts by the parties to establish rules and procedures by which conflict is managed.

Managing Norwegian-Soviet Conflict Relations

A most interesting case of a small state–large state regime for managing conflict relations involves an ally of the United States, Norway, and its relations with the Soviet Union. A member of the North Atlantic Treaty Organization (NATO) since 1949, Norway shares a border with the Soviet Union and administers the Arctic Ocean islands of Svalbard. The 130-mile territorial border was established in 1826 and is today very close to important Soviet naval facilities at Murmansk and other military installations on the Kola Peninsula.[4] An elaborate set of procedures along the frontier reduces uncertainty to routine ways of doing business, much like the rituals at the various checkpoints in Berlin and border crossings in Cyprus. Regularized communications channels among opposing parties exist in all three cases.

Both sides attempt to keep discussions between border officials technical—refining existing rules and coming to agreement on their application rather than politicizing them. New procedures were established after a 1985 incident in which "a Soviet soldier patrolling in the woods jokingly cocked his gun at his Norwegian counterpart." Officials agreed that "there would be no more lurking—only open patrolling." The patrols now exchange salutes whenever they meet.[5] As one Norwegian official has observed, the Soviets prefer to let their local border officials handle most issues.[6] This procedure also allows those at higher political levels to disclaim responsibility for particular arrangements they might not like, arguing that the arrangements in question had been made without proper authority.

Compared to seventeen Soviet border stations, Norway maintains only seven, with a total Norwegian contingent of about 150 border guards. Border commissions representing both parties meet once or twice monthly in headquarters on either side of the border (at Storskog near the town of Kirkenes on the Norwegian side and Boris Gleb on the Soviet). The meetings follow what amounts to a ritual that includes a welcoming by an honor guard, reviewing minutes from the last meeting, dealing with current issues, dining, and adjourning—usually over toasts. One border commissioner, a retired Norwegian Air Force general, comments that "we talk about music and ballet, and try to keep away from politics." He adds that "sometimes you get the feeling that you're taking part in a play by Chekhov." In this regard, the general notes that "halfway through the lunch, we decide that relations between Washington and Moscow have nothing to do with this border," and by the end of the meal "we decide that relations between Oslo and Moscow have nothing to do with it" either.[7]

Rules and procedures gain legitimacy with practice over time. Moreover, personal relationships often develop among individuals who meet and work together in the construction and maintenance of these regimes. Instances of this camaraderie are evident among air controllers of the four powers in the Berlin Air Safety Center. Similar cooperation in Norwegian-Soviet relations is the routine in joint air-sea rescue efforts in the Arctic Ocean, negotiations on fishing quotas, preservation of fish stocks, and other practical issues of common concern. Although both countries have yet to resolve their conflict over the border line that divides the continental shelf and defines their economic zones in the Barents Sea, each manages to live with the unsettled dispute.

Concerning the Arctic Islands of Svalbard (sometimes referred to as Spitsbergen, the name of the largest island), Norway gained formal sovereignty over them after World War I.[8] A forty-one-state multilateral treaty was signed in 1925, albeit without direct Soviet participation in the negotiations. The treaty limits Norway's sovereign rights by prescribing that the islands may not be used for warlike purposes, that all signatory powers have equal access to the islands to exploit natural resources found there, and that Norway may tax such economic activities only within rather strict limits.

The Soviet Union demanded changes in these arrangements during World War II, proposing a Norwegian-Soviet condominium on the islands. Norway was also to cede Bear Island (between Spitsbergen and the Norwegian mainland). The Norwegians successfully rejected these demands, and, for its part, the Soviet Union has dropped the issue. Indeed both parties benefit from coal mining, an exercise of their rights to permanent presence and the pursuit of economic activities. The Soviets administer their two mining towns based on precedents they have established in practice over time. Oslo did object in the 1970s to what it considered to be too assertive a Soviet role on the islands; low-keyed Norwegian persistence through diplomatic and political channels eventually led the Soviets to back off on at least some issues of contention.

Relations between Norway and the Soviet Union on Svalbard represent an excellent example of collaboration between potential adversaries in a strategically vital area. As such, the case is certainly worthy of further research.[9] Given the asymmetry in their military capabilities, the Norwegian position on Svalbard and along its border with the Soviet Union depends as much on agreed rules and procedures as on guarantees by its allies to take collective action in the event of aggression.

The Norwegians act on the presumption that national security depends ultimately on maintaining effective working relations with the Soviet Union. Thus, as Albert Wohlstetter has observed, the Norwegians stay about 500 miles "by road away from" the Soviet frontier "when exercising with allied military forces." They routinely "announce all maneuvers involving 10,000 or more troops" because they want "to reassure the Soviets of their nonaggressive intent," though the Helsinki Accords have required notifications only for allied exercises of 25,000 or more.[10] In short, maintenance of the regimes on the islands of Svalbard and along the territorial frontier goes well beyond considerations of military power. The two parties manage their conflict relations carefully, allowing both to preserve their interests.

Defining and Categorizing International Security Regimes

Formal and informal arrangements, explicit or tacitly understood rules, and institutions (when they exist) that construct and maintain these procedures and routines can be referred to as international regimes. The term *regime* is borrowed from the vocabulary of domestic politics by which we refer to a particular type of constitutional or governmental order—the set of rules or arrangements by which authoritative decisions are made and actions are taken within the jurisdiction of a given state that has the power and claims the right to make such policy binding on its citizens. *Regime* is used here, however, in an international context. Sovereign states agree formally or demonstrate by their actions that they will be bound voluntarily by certain rules governing a particular issue. The key word is *voluntarily*. Also, institutions may be created as part of a regime, but there need not be any formal organization for a regime to exist. Rules that have been agreed upon explicitly, or even just tacitly, are enough to constitute a regime. As such, international regimes are created in an attempt to regulate state behavior across a wide spectrum of diverse activities to include trade, the exchange of money, fishing, depletion of the upper atmospheric ozone layer, acid rain and other forms of pollution in the air and on the high seas, health, telecommunications, and postal exchange.

Most scholarly work on regimes has focused on nonmilitary or nonsecurity issues.[11] The focus in this chapter, however, is on international security regimes that regulate behavior between or among adversaries. Although many of the security regimes that now exist are multilateral arrangements that include coalitions of allies, the variant to be examined here is the set of regimes that define and constrain relations between the superpowers as adversaries.

Security regimes are by no means exclusively a post–World War II or otherwise twentieth-century phenomenon but were well-established modes of dealing with conflict in earlier centuries.[12] It is the case, however, that the advent of nuclear weapons and the threat of mass destruction associated with them have made the construction of security regimes to stabilize strategic relations compelling, particularly between the superpowers.

The most familiar category of security regimes is that which controls or regulates armaments quantitatively or qualitatively. For example, rules limit the numbers of particular weapon systems, the weapons that can be transferred to other states, and those that can be researched, developed, tested, or deployed. Conflict control is another, related category that includes attempts to routinize activities and set constraints related to conflict in particular geographic areas. The term also refers to efforts to establish communications with an eye toward avoiding misperception and improving trust and confidence among adversaries. The typology is shown in table 2–1.

The categories overlap to some extent. Although they are not mutually exclusive in all respects, it is useful analytically to differentiate rules and norms concerning military hardware or armaments per se from those dealing with the actual use of this hardware. The former—arms control—is defined here as dealing with research, development, test, or deployment of armaments. The latter is the domain of conflict control and includes both instrumental means

Table 2–1
International Security Regimes for Conflict and Arms Control

Arms Control: Armaments and Military Capabilities	Conflict Control: Spatial or Geographic Limits	Conflict Control: Instrumental Means
Strategic arms: SALT/START	Antarctica	Communications Hot line
Conventional force reductions: MBFR/CSCE	Atmosphere	Nuclear accidents SCC
	Space	Crisis centers
Nuclear nonproliferation		
Nuclear test bans	Nuclear-free zones: Latin America	Confidence-building measures: CSCE/MBFR
Chemical, biological, and radiological weapons	Seabed	National technical means of verification (NTM)
Conventional arms transfers	European security: CSCE/MBFR	
	Tacit spheres of influence	

Abbreviations: SALT = Strategic Arms Limitation Talks
START = Strategic Arms Reductions Talks
MBFR = Mutual and Balanced Force Reductions
SCC = Standing Consultative Commission
CSCE = Conference on Security and Cooperation in Europe

for preventing or limiting armed conflict and rules establishing agreed limits within geographic areas.

Constructing and Maintaining Security Regimes between Adversaries

Establishing security regimes—the routinization of conflict relations—is an extension of Weberian thought to the foreign policy and national security bureaucracies of adversaries.[13] Formal agreement or de facto consensus on rules to govern conflict relations forms the basis of security regimes between the superpowers. Weber saw efficiencies in the establishment of standard operating procedures, the routines of administration for performing recurrent functions. Graham Allison has observed that bureaucracies, consistent with their organizational ethos, tend to act or respond in predictable ways.[14] Management of conflict is effective to the extent that these patterns of behavior reflect regime rules put into practice by bureaucracies on both sides. By establishing such rules of behavior, foreign policy and national security bureaucracies learn how to cope with their environments. Repetition reinforces these modalities of behavior already learned. Uncertainty is reduced when both parties, particularly adversaries, act and respond predictably.

Explicitly stated rules, some with the binding force of international law, constrain activities on the high seas. Formal rules have evolved over the centuries by custom and have been codified in treaties relating to the law of the sea. Other rules governing relations on the high seas are less formally defined but understood tacitly nonetheless. Another example of tacitly understood rules that amount to a superpower regime is the interception by one superpower's fighters of the other's bombers or other aircraft approaching its national air space. Conducted with the precision of a dance, the shadow boxing between adversaries is orchestrated precisely to avoid armed conflict while at the same time defending matters of principle: the right of passage for military aircraft in international airspace on the one hand and the right of defense for territorial airspace on the other. Rules of engagement are specified by the military bureaucracies of both sides and become known to each through practice. This is not to say that such activity could not break into armed conflict if limits specified in the rules of engagement were exceeded by either party. But such instances are rare precisely because both sides have come to understand the limits each can approach but not exceed.

Regime rules are sometimes ambiguous by design. Some ambiguity on particular points may be deemed acceptable by negotiators on both sides as necessary to produce an agreement. Thus, in the SALT (Strategic Arms Limitation Talks) II agreement, the parties agreed to constrain changes to existing silo volume due to modernization and replacement of existing ICBM launchers as not to exceed 32 percent. Changes to existing ICBM systems in terms of length, diameter, launch weight, and throw weight were to be less than 5 percent. It was not clear, however, precisely how these margins were to be measured. Subsequent disagreement on measurement (coupled with accusations of violating the SALT II accords or, at the very least, pushing ambiguities to take advantage of these rules in the extreme) is hardly surprising.

Disputes in which one party understands the other to be in violation of one or more rules associated with a given regime may contribute to breakdown of the entire regime or, in any event, make the construction of other regimes more difficult. Far from building trust and confidence between the superpowers, such occurrences may well have the opposite effect. Thus, opposition by some in the United States to further reduction of the existing 150 kiloton threshold on nuclear testing or eliminating tests altogether in a comprehensive test ban stems from the view that the Soviets have already exceeded the 150 kiloton limit and consequently cannot be trusted to comply with an even more extensive set of regime rules.

The 1972 Anti-Ballistic Missile (ABM) Treaty is another example of ambiguity in terms.[15] Under Article V of the treaty, both parties agreed "not to develop, test, or deploy ABM systems or components which are sea-based, air-based, space-based, or mobile land-based." On the other hand, the meaning of Agreed Statement D is not altogether clear even to American officials, who have offered both broad and narrow interpretations. According to the statement, "In the event ABM systems based on other physical principles and including components capable of substituting for ABM interceptor missiles, ABM launchers, or ABM radars are created in the future, specific limitations on such systems and their components would be subject to discussion." A broad interpretation would allow for the research, development, and testing of such advanced technologies as lasers and particle beams so long as they were not actually deployed in space. A narrow interpretation, by contrast, reads the intent of the statement, consistent with the overall spirit of the treaty, as constraining the development of strategic defenses to include advanced technologies. From this perspective, Agreed Statement D provides grounds for further discussion as advanced technologies that run counter to the spirit of the treaty become clearer. The underlying issue, however, is not so much a question of legal semantics concerning terms in the treaty as it is fundamental disagreement on the appropriate balance between strategic offense and strategic defense. Proponents of the narrow interpretation oppose the shift in the strategic offense–strategic defense balance from the former to the latter. Proponents of the broad interpretation, by contrast, are more favorably disposed toward implementation of the SDI and the shift in the offense-defense balance it represents.

Another well-publicized area of dispute associated with the ABM Treaty is contained in provisions relating to radar deployments. In Article I, ABM radars are defined as those "constructed and deployed for an ABM role, or of a type tested in an ABM mode." Beyond the limited allowable ABM deployment, neither party, according to Article VI, is to give radars a capability "to counter strategic ballistic missiles or their elements in flight trajectory." Nor is either "to test them in an ABM mode" or "to deploy in the future radars for early warning of strategic ballistic missile attack except at locations along the periphery of its national territory and oriented outward." Thus, the deployment near Krasnoyarsk of a large, phased-array radar not located on the periphery of the Soviet Union and not oriented outward is seen by the United States as a violation of these provisions. Indeed, most American observers are in agreement that deployment of the Krasnoyarsk radar is, in fact, a violation of the ABM Treaty. For their part, the Soviets have denied that the radar in question has been tested in an ABM mode or is intended for strategic early warning. The point here is to underscore how easily any ambiguity in a provision can be used by a party to claim innocence. On the other hand, the cost of acting in what is perceived as bad faith can be quite high, making future agreements much more difficult to achieve.

Crises have been the source of regimes constructed in their aftermath in an attempt to avoid their recurrence. A classic case is the Cuban missile crisis of October 1962 that brought the superpowers to the brink of nuclear war. After several very intense days, the crisis was finally defused when the Soviet Union agreed to remove existing nuclear-capable offensive systems from Cuba and not to deploy offensive weapons or delivery systems there in the future. As part of the package, the Soviets extracted a reciprocal pledge from the United States not to use military force against Cuba—a reference to American support in 1961 for Cuban exiles in the Bay of Pigs invasion that had attempted unsuccessfully to overthrow the Castro regime. Although these reciprocal prohibitions were apparently clear to both parties and have been observed since that confrontation, other rules stemming from the crisis have been less clear and, as such, have been the cause of some dissension, among them calls to Cuba by Soviet nuclear submarines beginning in 1969, the arrival of MiG-23-D ground-attack aircraft in 1978, and the discovery of a Soviet combat brigade in 1979.[16] Nevertheless, the relative stability of the U.S.-Soviet regime over a quarter of a century is underscored by the continuing presence in Cuba of the U.S. Navy at Guantanamo and acquiescence by the Cubans (and the Soviets) to the assertion of American rights on the island.

Doctrinal Asymmetry and Problems in Regime Construction

Construction of stable, long-term security regimes can be facilitated if the negotiating parties are able to reach consensus on mutually desirable ends and on cause-effect relations leading to those ends. There is at present no agreement on the American side, much less between the United States and the Soviet Union, on how to establish and maintain security between the superpowers. It is a lack of such consensus that accounts, at least in part, for the great difficulties experienced by the United States and the Soviet Union in their joint attempt to construct strategic arms limitations or reductions regimes.

If there is no agreement in principle on what strategic forces are necessary to provide security to each party, how are negotiators to proceed? In the absence of an agreed, overarching security framework or strategic blueprint, negotiations amount to little more than tactical bargaining—for example, trading limits on one weapons system for limits on another. Unfortunately, however gratifying tactical successes may be to either or both parties, the durability of such agreements made in the absence of agreement on a larger security design may not be long-lasting.

There is no certainty that the United States and the Soviet Union have common security objectives. Is one party really pursuing arms control only as a means to constrain the technology of the other? To what extent are the parties driven by economic or budget considerations—that arms control can be a means for constraining defense expenditures? Apart from concern with the cost of arms competition, is the effort intended to reduce the likelihood of war through pursuit of arms control? Are both sides seeking to maintain peace through deterrence? Even if both are so motivated—and there is no clear consensus among observers on this point—do they share common doctrinal views on the ways and means leading to this outcome?

How deterrence is to be achieved—the doctrinal question—is enormously important. Doctrinal considerations are closely tied to decisions on the types and numbers of forces each side is to have. Perhaps because it may seem too difficult to achieve a meeting of the minds on security objectives and doctrinal prescriptions for accomplishing them, differences are often papered over by asserting that the parties do have common aims such as maintaining peace through "essential equivalence" in strategic forces (the term preferred by the American side) or "equality and equal security" (the term preferred by the Soviets)—language used in the late 1970s during negotiations on strategic arms limitations. Whatever may have been their diplomatic value, these terms were so general as to have had little substantive meaning. Indeed they obscured differences between the parties on security objectives and, if deterrence was the common aim, on the ways and means by which deterrence was to be maintained. Because strategic doctrine both affects and is affected by the numbers and types of military forces a party acquires and maintains, arms control negotiators cannot overlook or merely brush doctrinal differences aside. Even if the parties cannot agree on strategic doctrine concerning deterrence, their differences still need to be taken into account. Otherwise the strategic arms control regimes that are constructed cannot be expected to have much durability.

If deterrence is the aim, is it to be achieved through maintaining a credible, assured destruction capability for the military establishments of both parties? Is the driving criterion to be deterrence stability—assuring the survival of second-strike, retaliatory capabilities for both the United States and the Soviet Union? Prior to the Reagan administration, maintaining deterrence based on MAD and ensuring the stability of these deterrence relations had become the dominant American view, at least in terms of publicly stated or articulated doctrine. The MAD logic is that if each side retains the capacity and perceived willingness to wreak devastation on the other, then neither will be so foolish as to provoke such a war. Emphasis is placed on maintaining the invulnerability of an offensive strategic retaliatory force. Strategic defense, to the extent it is allowed, serves primarily to limit damage to one's offensive forces, national command and control authorities, and their communications networks.

Such an approach holds civilizations hostage in the hope that doing so will reduce the likelihood of war. The latter is a desirable end but one to be achieved by means strongly opposed by many. Reflecting this concern, American doctrinal statements shifted during the Reagan administration toward advocacy of strategic defense of populations—so-called area defense. Under MAD, by contrast, populations are left with few passive (civil defense or early warning) or active (interceptor aircraft or missile) defenses. Following this MAD logic (or illogic), the more vulnerable people are, the less likely they will need protection because, it is assumed, the mutual devastation of nuclear war and its likelihood are inversely related. The prospect of nuclear war is made so awful that neither side would consider undertaking it. All of this, of course, rests on the assumption that states (or decision makers acting for them) will act rationally, trying to avoid confrontations that could lead to nuclear war. Indeed, the superpowers have exhibited considerable caution in their relations with one another, particularly since the October 1962 Cuban missile crisis, which brought them to the brink of war.

American doctrinal premises under MAD had led to advocacy of limitations on ABM defenses and constraints on offensive systems that would preclude either side's achieving a credible first-strike posture—the ability to attack first, reducing the enemy's ability to retaliate to some minimally acceptable level. Consistent with this thinking, American strategic planners not only did not put much emphasis on, but also actively discouraged, civil or other defense preparations beyond the early warning necessary to alert retaliatory forces as part of a second-strike deterrent posture. The balance between strategic offense and strategic defense under MAD clearly favored the former over the latter.

Notwithstanding an articulated doctrine in the 1960s and 1970s that put emphasis on assured destruction and the stability of deterrence based on this condition, the push of American technology was in the direction of greater accuracy for delivery systems capable of carrying a larger number of nuclear reentry vehicles or warheads. Although the yield in kilotons or megatons of each of the multiple, independently targeted, reentry vehicles (MIRVs) was reduced compared to the larger yield of earlier, single-warhead land-based ICBMs or their submarine-launched counterparts (SLBMs), whatever was lost in magnitude of yield was more than compensated by numbers and accuracy of delivery. Increasing accuracy made it possible to engage in fairly precise targeting of the adversary's missile fields, bomber bases, and other military targets—so-called counterforce targeting.

High accuracy and a proliferation of warheads with effectiveness against hardened targets is not needed for holding populations at risk. Such capabilities are essential, however, if one plans to target an enemy's warmaking capabilities, limiting further damage such an adversary can wreak upon one's own society or military forces. Research suggests that over several decades, such targeting has been the consistent American approach to govern use of strategic forces—so-called operational doctrine.[17] If this is so, then nuclear force targeting by the two superpowers may not have been as divergent as was previously thought. In any event, targeting an adversary's strategic forces with a large number of accurately delivered warheads serves damage limitation more than it does assured destruction. Military requirements in terms of numbers of warheads and accuracy for the latter are far less demanding than the former. Of course, the danger in seeking damage limitation, as advocates of assured destruction have been quick to point out, is that an adversary may perceive that one is building a war-fighting or even first-strike capability, particularly if increasing offensive capabilities is coupled with development of strategic defenses.

From time to time since the early 1960s, American strategic discourse in the Kennedy-Johnson, Nixon-Ford, and Carter administrations has allowed for "city avoidance" with emphasis on counterforce targeting, damage limitation, and limited nuclear war-fighting options. This aspect of articulated doctrine has been consistent with target planning or operational doctrine. Seen in this context as a form of damage limitation, the Reagan administration's push for strategic defense is not as radical a departure from the status quo as it may first have appeared. It has been presented and understood, however, in terms of a longer-term vision of eventually displacing MAD and deterrence thinking with a condition of mutually assured survival in which effective strategic defenses are maintained by both sides.

Nevertheless, MAD has remained the overarching strategic condition between the superpowers. Although targeting military forces may reduce civilian or noncombatant casualties to some degree, still the massive casualties that would be produced due to collateral damage and other nuclear weapons effects make it hard to argue that counterforce targeting in fact represents any meaningful departure from assured destruction, holding populations at risk.

The dialectic between a deterrence based on assured destruction (with or without some damage-limitation targeting) on the one hand, and heavy emphasis on damage limitation or war fighting on the other, has divided American strategists over the years and has led to considerable uncertainty about U.S. strategy and policy. Is it to be a deterrence based on the punishment of assured destruction that would be wrought in a retaliatory strike, or is it to be a deterrence based on denial of any rational purpose to be served by taking on an adversary with credible war-fighting capabilities? Whatever their doctrinal views, however, both the United States and the Soviet Union have had to accept the reality or condition of assured destruction as a given, at least for the present.

There is considerable evidence that the Soviets did not share the earlier American commitment to an assured destruction doctrinal perspective. To be deterred by an American assured destruction threat does not mean that the Soviets have to subscribe to MAD as the doctrine to guide development of their own strategic forces. To the extent that the Soviet Union wishes to achieve a deterrent posture regarding the United States (and has not been building a credible first-strike posture, as a few have contended), it is to be a deterrent based on a credible war-fighting capability. With such military forces in being, what rational adversary would ever take them on in that mode? Si vis pacem, para bellum. Rather than deterrence based on the threat of punishment as under MAD, it is deterrence based on denial of any rational military purpose to be served by resort to force by any adversary. Acceptance of this view that Soviet and American strategic doctrines have diverged along these lines can account for at least some of the difficulties experienced by negotiators in the regime construction process.

The more recent American shift in articulated doctrine to a strategic defense that would protect populations does not signal doctrinal convergence with the

Soviet Union. The stated purpose of strategic defense is not for an improved war-fighting capability; it is to provide an area defense for population centers. Much more would be required to achieve the degree of nuclear war-fighting capability necessary to achieve deterrence based on denial. Indeed, the Soviet preference for maintaining such a war-fighting posture requires continuing commitment to development of both active and passive defenses, as well as to offensive capabilities capable of destroying or reducing an adversary's war-fighting capabilities. In short, strategic doctrines have important implications concerning the types and numbers of forces the superpowers will want to deploy. Some of these implications for force posture (and thus for arms control) are summarized in table 2–2.

A less ambitious notion of strategic defense as limited defense of one's offensive systems or command centers (damage limitation) would not be a departure from MAD. Some Americans see this as no particular problem since deterrence based on the threat of mutually assured destruction has successfully avoided general war for decades. Others see point defense of offensive weapons systems not as an end in itself but rather as part of a longer-term transition to a more comprehensive system of area defense designed to shield population centers.

Even if the United States and the Soviet Union aim to maintain peace through deterrence, there is still very little agreement or consensus on the means to that end or, consequently, on what would constitute a set of strategic arms control proposals acceptable to both sides. Not only is there a lack of consensus between the parties, but there also appears to be a lack of consensus within the civilian and military elites of each party on desired ends, much less on means to these ends.

Not all students of the strategic literature even agree that deterrence is central to Soviet strategic thinking as it has been in the United States in the post–World War II period. Some have argued that Soviet views are much more

Table 2–2
Strategic Doctrine: Implications for Force Posture

Force Posture	Doctrinal Objectives		
	Assured Destruction	*Assured Destruction plus Damage Limitation*	*Credible War-fighting Capability*
Strategic offense			
High accuracy	No	Yes	Yes
Quantity numbers	Enough to ensure retaliatory capability	More	Most
Strategic defense			
Active defenses	Only to defend offensive systems	More	Most
Passive defenses	Yes	Yes	Yes

traditional than the American—that is, much closer to the Clausewitzian text. From this perspective, seeking (or maintaining) a credible war-fighting capability (regardless of whether it is employed in a nuclear or nonnuclear mode) is considered justifiable in itself. Even if the Soviet Union does not want a war, if one were thrust on it, it would wish to respond so as to maximize its chances of "winning" such an encounter, or at least minimizing the damage it need sustain. From this point of view, Soviet strategists have not conceded that such wars are inherently unwinnable. Nor have they accepted the commonly held Western premise that applying Clausewitz to general war in the nuclear age is anachronistic.

Theater deployments of nuclear and conventional forces complicate the security equation. Western deployments since the 1950s of nuclear weapons in Europe as part of the American extended deterrent are in part a response to the conventional force numerical imbalance in Europe that favors the Soviet Union and its Warsaw Pact allies over the United States and NATO. Thus, if Western reliance on nuclear weapons for the defense of Europe is to be reduced, conventional forces on both sides would either have to be increased or reduced disproportionately to equivalent levels (however it is that equivalence may be defined) or to the level necessary to defend or resist effectively an offensive launched by the other side. Although reducing or eliminating intermediate-range nuclear forces on both sides is feasible, as the recently ratified Intermediate Nuclear Forces (INF) Treaty is testimony, total elimination of nuclear weapons in the absence of establishing conventional force equivalence or defense sufficiency would leave the West vulnerable to numerically superior Warsaw Pact conventional forces.

Thus, reductions in European-based or theater nuclear forces (TNF) would seem conceptually to be closely tied to reductions in conventional forces. On the other hand, negotiations in Vienna or Stockholm on the latter have occurred quite independently of negotiations in Geneva on the former. Talks on conventional forces within the Conference on Security and Cooperation in Europe (CSCE) framework are also kept distinct from nuclear weapons questions. Indeed the conceptual links among central strategic, theater nuclear, and conventional forces remain blurred. On the other hand, construction of a comprehensive arms reductions regime would necessarily be based on a design that took account of the relations between these three categories and their subelements.

Arms negotiations between the United States and the Soviet Union have thus proceeded in the absence of any commonly held blueprint or grand design stipulating desirable end points (much less specifying means to these ends) that would create the foundation for a more stable set of strategic relations. An underlying consensus between the two parties on the desirability of ends and on means to these ends would make possible the construction of a durable security regime.[18] Instead of a pattern in which issues being negotiated are substantively linked so as to achieve a coherent set of logically related agreements, negotiations more frequently involve tactical maneuvers designed to increase bargaining leverage or make concessions in one area in return for gains in another. Linkage is also made even to issues logically unrelated to the strategic questions at hand.

The SALT II negotiations were an extended and arduous process of trade-offs and compromises over diverse weapons systems within the strategic inventories of the superpowers as the two groped toward agreement. In the absence of a commonly accepted strategic doctrine to guide the negotiations, already established agreements (such as the 1974 Vladivostok Accords) became the important precedents on which subsequent agreements were forged; substantial departures from such decided matters (as were embodied in the comprehensive proposal offered early in the Carter administration) tended to lead to nowhere.

The problem has not gone away. Although the American strategic vision of the late 1980s differs from that of the late 1970s, the American and Soviet views still remain far apart. Both sides have made sweeping proposals that make President Carter's comprehensive proposal seem rather modest, but negotiations have moved at a glacial pace. Some rules, as were established in SALT II, have even been set aside.

In principle, the most durable of regimes would have an underlying strategic logic accepted by both sides. Lack of a clear understanding of each side's strategic views, not to mention the absence of consensus on the appropriate balance between strategic offense and strategic defense and how this might be realized, makes any comprehensive agreement difficult. Under such circumstances negotiators seeking an agreement are forced to deal tactically with the myriad of issues on the table, finding compromises among often unrelated elements and judging an overall agreement by the somewhat difficult-to-measure balance of gains and concessions.

The best regime outcome one can expect in such a situation tends to be far less stable or durable than one built on a substantive linkage of causally related security issues. Indeed, any regime that lacks this conceptual foundation can easily be upset by a new technological breakthrough, modification in doctrinal underpinnings, or unsettling events like the Soviet intervention in Afghanistan in 1979 that undermined support for SALT II.

Institutionalization and Regime Maintenance

Bilateral diplomatic channels proved less than adequate in the October 1962 Cuban missile crisis. As a result, the hot line was established in 1963. Since then, these crisis communications facilities have been upgraded. The superpowers agreed in 1987 to establish communication centers for routine notifications and the exchange of information required by various agreements.

The Geneva-based Standing Consultative Commission (SCC) was established in 1972 as a bilateral organization charged with overseeing implementation of the SALT agreements, reconciling differences, and laying the basis for expansion of the existing regime. More than just a common framework for the exchange of information, the level of institutionalization represented by the SCC would appear to conform more closely to what Ernst Haas refers to as a "joint facility" that attempts "to harmonize and standardize the behavior of the participants through the imposition of common routines."[19] The SCC has been charged to "consider possible changes in the strategic situation," to "agree upon procedures" for implementing treaty terms, and to "consider" possible amendments to the treaty and "proposals for further measures limiting strategic offensive arms." In short, the SCC has an important regime maintenance (and expansion) function,[20] although in recent years it has been not much more than a contentious forum for the exchange of charges on treaty violations.

To be sure, merely establishing facilities for communications between the United States and the Soviet Union does not ensure that good relations will result. Military liaison missions set up in Potsdam and Frankfurt as part of the post–World War II occupation of Germany were originally established for the recovery of war dead and to provide a communications link between heads of occupying forces. Although viewed by some as prototypical confidence-building measures (CBMs) between adversaries, in fact they have often been points of controversy between the two sides. Other instrumentalities that would serve as CBMs have emerged from the CSCE process and have also been discussed as part of the earlier Mutual and Balanced Force reductions (MBFR) negotiations in Vienna. Thus, notifications of exercises and sending of observers are among the CBMs that have been adopted. The work continues within the CSCE framework.

Superpower Regimes and International Security

This chapter has addressed some of the security regimes or sets of rules and institutions constructed by the superpowers and other states to govern their relations. Although other regimes have been mentioned, the focus has been on bilateral, U.S.-Soviet strategic regimes that affect the security of all states. Difficult as it is to construct, maintain, and expand regimes between two superpowers, the problem becomes even more complex when one addresses the larger number of actors and concerns associated with constructing and maintaining multilateral security regimes.

Beyond power and balance of power considerations, order in international relations stems from the rules and norms that states follow. Regimes functioning well effectively reduce the uncertainty that would otherwise obtain without them. Security comes in this sense from knowing that one's adversary will act with restraint in areas both parties have agreed to delimit.

The quality or overall climate of superpower relations has varied considerably since World War II. U.S.-Soviet relations in the Gorbachev period are better than they were earlier in the 1980s. Relations may not have returned to the high point reached during the period of détente in the 1970s, but there has been no return either to the poor climate that existed during the cold war. The overall climate of relations between the superpowers both affects and is affected by the functioning of the security regimes they and other states create. Just as a reasonably favorable climate in their relations is conducive to security regime construction, routine adherence to rules previously agreed upon also contributes positively to the climate of relations between the superpowers. Similarly, success in creating confidence- and security-building measures, formulating new rules, and expanding existing regimes makes a positive contribution to superpower relations. By contrast, violations and perceptions of violations undermine security regimes and make construction of new or expanded ones much more difficult. Indeed, the distrust and bad faith that result from real or apparent violations are hardly conducive to the construction and maintenance of international security regimes.

The importance of the cognitive underpinning of security regimes is frequently overlooked. Agreements that last are about much more than the surface issues being negotiated. Security regimes based on tactical bargains made in the absence of any consensus on the underlying strategic objectives and means to these ends may well be of short duration, tending to break down when the climate of relations is poor. Instances of noncompliance in such circumstances may contribute even further to deterioration in the quality of relations.

Intense discussions between adversaries on what constitutes security that go beyond delivering polemics or scoring propaganda points are indeed rare. A lack of consensus within the decision-making elites of either or both parties compounds the problem. Nevertheless, such discussions would appear to be essential if negotiations are to go beyond purely tactical considerations to the construction of durable and stable security regimes. In the unlikely event that the parties somehow achieve conceptual consensus on such fundamental security questions as the relation between war-fighting and deterrence capabilities on the one hand and security objectives on the other, the correspondence among strategic nuclear, theater nuclear, and conventional (or general purpose) forces, and other theoretical questions relevant to the security equation, there would still be more than enough on the agenda to challenge negotiators for years to come. Given asymmetries in the present force postures of the two superpowers, it will be no easy task to determine armaments limits (numbers and kinds of forces to be researched, developed, tested, or deployed) and associated conflict control regimes within this overall security framework.

Even if agreement on objectives and, in particular, strategic doctrine remains elusive (as seems more likely to be the case), then at least a better understanding of points of divergence would provide a stronger intellectual foundation for negotiations. Regimes can be constructed to accommodate divergent security blueprints when the differences have been more clearly identified. They may not be as stable or durable as security regimes constructed upon a common conceptual base, but in the nuclear age even fragile regimes would seem to be better than none at all.

Notes

1. See Bull's discussion of the Hobbesian tradition in Hedley Bull, *The Anarchical Society: A Study of Order in World Politics* (New York: Columbia University Press, 1977), pp. 24–25.

2. Ibid., pp. 26–27, and 67–74. These are excerpts from his discussion of the Grotian tradition.

3. I developed this theme in "Berlin and Conflict Management with the USSR," *Orbis* 28, no. 3 (Fall 1984), pp. 575–591.

4. See the discussion in Karen De Young, "All's Quiet on Norwegian-Soviet Frontier," *Washington Post*, August 4, 1987, p. A10.

5. Ibid.

6. A retired Norwegian general shared insights on Norwegian-Soviet relations in conversations with me.

7. DeYoung, "All's Quiet," p. A10.

8. I am indebted to my Norwegian colleague, Baard Knudsen, for his comments on the Norwegian-Soviet section of this chapter and in particular for the information he provided concerning Svalbard.

9. As Knudsen indicates, a comprehensive analysis of the Svalbard Treaty and Norwegian-Soviet relations on the islands is contained in Willy Ostreng, *Politics in High Latitudes: The Svalbard Archipelago* (London: C. Hurst and Co., 1977). The main center in Norway for research on political and international issues related to Svalbard is the Fridtjof Nansen Institute.

10. See Albert Wohlstetter, "Swords Without Shields," *National Interest*, no. 8 (Summer 1987): 33.

11. For a review of the literature on regimes and associated theory, see Stephan Haggard and Beth A. Simons, "Theories of International Regimes," *International Organization* 41, no. 3 (Summer 1987): 491–517.

12. See Bull, *Anarchical Society*, pp. 9–22, 27–52.

13. See Max Weber's classic "Parliament and Government in a Reconstructed Germany" in Guenther Roth and Claus Wittich (eds.), *Economy and Society* (Berkeley: University of California Press, 1978), 2: 1393–1395.

14. See his discussion of Model II in his classic "Conceptual Models and the Cuban Missile Crisis," *American Political Science Review* 63, no. 3 (September 1969): 689–718. Cf. his *Essence of Decision* (Boston: Little, Brown, 1971).

15. Reprints of the ABM Treaty and associated documents are found in various publications, including U.S. Arms Control and Disarmament Agency, *Arms Control and Disarmament Agreements* (Washington, D.C.: Government Printing Office, 1982), pp. 139–47. For a discussion of alternative interpretations of the ABM treaty,

see William J. Durch, "The Future of the ABM Treaty," Adelphi Paper No. 223 (London: International Institute for Strategic Studies, Summer 1987).

16. For an excellent summary, see Gloria Duffy, "Crisis Prevention in Cuba," in Alexander L. George (ed.), *Managing U.S.-Soviet Rivalry: Problems of Crisis Prevention*)Boulder, Colo.: Westview Press, 1983), pp. 285–318.

17. See Desmond Ball, "Targeting for Strategic Deterrence" Adelphi Paper No. 185 (London, International Institute for Strategic Studies, Summer 1983).

18. For a thorough discussion of cognitive aspects of regime construction, see Ernst B. Haas, "Issue Linkage and International Regimes," *World Politics* 32, no. 2 (April 1980): 357–405.

19. Ibid., pp. 398–399.

20. See the SALT II Treaty, Article XVII in Arms Control and Disarmament Agency, *Arms Control*, pp. 267–268.

3
The Idea of Stability in the Current Strategic Debate

Robert C. Gray

One of the most enduring aspects of deterrence theory has been the concept of stability. In a well-known essay on surprise attack published in 1959, Thomas C. Schelling observed that "it is not the 'balance' . . . that constitutes mutual deterrence; it is the *stability* of the balance. The balance is stable only when neither, in striking first, can destroy the other's ability to strike back."[1] The idea is still alive and well. In 1983, when President Reagan's Commission on Strategic Forces (the Scowcroft commission) sought to construct a broadly acceptable framework for arms control and strategic force modernization, the central organizing concept was that of stability, defined as "the condition which exists when no strategic power believes it can significantly improve its situation by attacking first in a crisis or when it does not feel compelled to launch its strategic weapons in order to avoid losing them."[2]

Because no one favors instability, almost everyone who writes or speaks about nuclear issues throws in at least a nodding reference to the virtues of stability. From early deterrence theorists and officials of the Kennedy administration to President Reagan, the Scowcroft commission, and legislators such as Senator Albert Gore (D–Tennessee) and Congressman Les Aspin (D–Wisconsin), stability has been a popular theme.

To be sure, there are divergent ideas as to what weapons and doctrines produce stability. Not all analysts, for example, view stability of the sort envisaged by the Scowcroft commission as desirable. From one perspective, Colin S. Gray has suggested that stability theory has led many in the United States to neglect damage limitation and operational aspects of nuclear planning. From quite another perspective, George W. Rathjens and Jack Ruina have expressed dismay that reductions in the numbers of nuclear weapons may be resisted by analysts who "argue, as they have too often, that particular kinds of reductions must be avoided so as to maintain 'strategic stability.' "[3]

I would like to thank Robert J. Bresler, Lynn E. Davis, and Stanley J. Michalak for reading a draft of this chapter.

Still there are few strategic ideas more popular than stability. Yet often there is insufficient attention to careful use of the term. The purpose of this chapter is to trace the origins and development of the idea of stability and to analyze the role it plays in the current debate over nuclear weapons and arms control.

Origins and Development of the Concept of Stability

The idea of deterrence is not unique to the period since Hiroshima. The concept of stable deterrence, however, is a postwar development. A prospective military structure based on a deterrent balance of forces is identifiable in the writings of some interwar air power theorists. But such a balance was viewed as unstable; war was considered an integral part of the system. Alexander George and Richard Smoke have suggested that the absence of the idea of "an indefinitely stable balance of deterrence" reflected the historical and technological conditions of the interwar period. Analysts of the time lived in a multipolar world in which wars could be fought without decimating entire societies. War between the great powers was an integral part of international political reality. As George and Smoke conclude: "The atomic bombs that ended World War II and the bipolar world that emerged out of it set the stage for the emergence of contemporary deterrence theory: the former made stable deterrence necessary, and the latter made it possible."[4]

The emphasis on stability was particularly evident in the major theoretical writings on deterrence that began to appear in the late 1950s.[5] Considerable attention was paid to analyzing the conditions under which one or the other side might be tempted to strike first. Bernard Brodie concluded that "stability is achieved when each nation believes that the strategic advantage of striking first is overshadowed by the tremendous cost of doing so."[6] As manned bombers were augmented by less vulnerable ICBMs and Polaris submarines and missiles, the mechanism for imposing the "tremendous cost" seemed to be at hand.

Enthusiasm for stability was not confined to deterrence theorists. The Kennedy administration elevated the concept to a position of overriding national policy. As Lawrence Freedman has written, Secretary of Defense Robert S. McNamara "put his efforts into reinforcing stability. The concept was recast as mutual assured destruction."[7] Neither side would be able to attack the other without suffering an unacceptably large retaliatory strike from the surviving portions of the other side's strategic forces.[8] While the Soviet Union built up its land- and sea-based ballistic missiles, the United States held constant the size of its ballistic missile force pending arms control negotiations to codify a condition of stable deterrence.

From the viewpoint of mutual assured destruction, the major threat to stability in the 1960s was the possible deployment of ABMs. If one side (or both) thought that incoming ballistic missile warheads could be intercepted in numbers sufficient to avoid "assured destruction," then incentives could exist for a preemptive attack. The ABM Treaty of 1972 was designed to deal with this prospect. The agreement to forgo significant ABM defenses seemed to signal Soviet and American agreement on the deterrent strategy on which stability was based.

Elements of Stability

Discussions of stability are typically divided into the separate dimensions of crisis stability and arms race stability. Following this practice, each of these elements will be discussed in turn.

Crisis Stability

Since the Cuban missile crisis in 1962, the phenomenon of crisis has been the subject of countless books and articles. Initially the focus was on crisis management. More recently attention has been paid to crisis prevention. Whatever the focus, however, the topic has attracted analysts because of the belief that an acute confrontation between the superpowers carries with it an increased probability of nuclear war.

The concept of crisis stability seems to be unproblematical at first glance. Albert Carnesale and his colleagues defined it in terms of "creating forces of a type which provide no incentive for either side to launch a first strike in a time of crisis."[9] The U.S. government has embraced a similar idea. Secretary of Defense Harold Brown, for example, listed crisis stability as one of the objectives of U.S. strategic policy. He defined it as "insuring that even in a prolonged and intense confrontation the Soviet Union would have no incentive to initiate an exchange, and also that we would feel ourselves under no pressure to do so."[10] Although the basic concept may seem simple, however, there are serious disputes over what policies, capabilities, and actions are required for crisis stability to be maintained.

Historically the most important prerequisite of crisis stability has been invulnerable strategic forces. As long as retaliatory forces could inflict a level of damage meeting the criteria of assured destruction, there would be little incentive to strike first in a crisis. As John Steinbruner has pointed out, from this viewpoint, the submarine leg of the triad is the source of greatest stability, strategic bombers are in a middle position, and silo-based ICBMs constitute the least stable component. ICBMs have been viewed as a source of instability not only because of their vulnerability to attack but also because of their superior ability (compared with SLBMs and bombers) to destroy hardened targets on the other side. As Steinbruner put it, "the combination of greater capability and greater vulnerability is clearly destabilizing under the established logic."[11]

Steinbruner argued in 1978 that the prevailing concept of stability had led analysts and policymakers to focus too much on force vulnerability and too little on command, control, and communications. He argued that from the perspective of command vulnerability, the stability potential of SLBMs and ICBMs was the reverse of what it was in terms of force vulnerability. Because of the difficulties in communicating with them, submarine-based forces constituted the least stable component in command terms. ICBMs, by contrast, were the most stable because of the security of communications. Bombers, as in the case of force vulnerability, occupied a middle position. (Closer examination reveals that SLBMs are deficient mainly in terms of prompt retaliation. As Ashton Carter recently put it, the Soviets would not be able to discount the possibility that submarines would eventually retaliate.)[12]

Steinbruner argued that communication systems and command structures "are vastly more vulnerable to attack than individual force elements."[13] This has a dual impact on crisis stability. If one side thought that it could cripple the command structure of the other side in a first strike, the dividend to the attacker would be larger than in the case of a first strike on ICBMs. Since each side knows this, there are incentives to use forces early—incentives to preempt—out of fear that an initial, decapitating attack on the command structure could preclude any response at all. Based on his analysis, Steinbruner called for a reformulation of the concept of stability that would place much more emphasis on command structure issues.

Although the injunction to pay more attention to command structure vulnerability remains valid, analysis of such vulnerability has progressed since 1978. Ashton Carter's work suggests that literal decapitation is unlikely. What analysis of command vulnerability does demonstrate, however, is that "some disorganization, delay, and failure to fire of surviving forces in a retaliatory response is likely under a wide range of assumptions." This could lead to some strategic forces never being launched, to some being used inefficiently, and to the use of others being delayed.[14]

Beginning with the Carter administration, there has been an upsurge of interest in improving C³I (command, control, communications, and intelligence), a fact reflected in both government programs and the writings of strategic analysts. The Reagan administration has put great emphasis on improving this portion of U.S. strategic assets, and the Scowcroft commission designated improvements in C³ as "our first defense priority." In a 1985 study, however, Bruce Blair argued that not enough was being done. Like Steinbruner seven years earlier, Blair concluded that too much attention had been devoted to force structure issues and not enough to maximizing the survivability of the command structure.[15]

Although virtually every observer agrees that survivability of C³I assets should be improved and most analysts want to decrease the vulnerability of strategic offensive forces, there is disagreement over whether these measures should be accompanied by increases in U.S. prompt hard-target kill capability. In one camp are those who view plans to attack political and military control targets and time-urgent military ones as destabilizing. Bruce Blair, for example, has proposed the idea of "no immediate second use," a revised version of assured destruction. He would rely more heavily than at present on submarine-based forces and greatly improved C³I. Defending the idea, he wrote that

> critics may argue that the doctrine of no immediate second use undermines crisis stability because the Soviet Union would perceive a defeatist attitude and an opportunity to prosecute an offensive campaign without the interference, disruption, and devastation that a prompt US counter-attack would produce. But such criticism misses the key point that *the certainty of retaliation is more important for deterrence than its timing.*[16]

A second view—that of the Scowcroft commission and the Reagan administration—holds that improved C³I by itself is insufficient. To maintain the integrity of NATO doctrine and to deter the Soviet Union from limited use of nuclear weapons, the United States must, according to the Scowcroft commission, "be able to put at risk those types of Soviet targets—including hardened ones such as military command bunkers and facilities, missile silos, nuclear weapons and other storage, and the rest—which the Soviet leaders have given every indication by their actions they value most, and which constitute their tools of control and power."[17] Although no one can know with certainty what best deters, the strategy recommended by the Scowcroft commission—which has been U.S. policy for a number of years—is a prudent response to Soviet developments since the early 1970s.

The force structure requirements of this strategy could include deployment of several hundred small, single-warhead ICBMs on hardened mobile launchers and the Trident II, D5 submarine-launched ballistic missile. These weapons would enable the United States to threaten targets thought to be of great importance to the Soviets without providing fixed missile targets for a Soviet first strike.

Improving Crisis Stability

Both cooperative and unilateral measures can be adopted to improve crisis stability. Of cooperative approaches, arms control agreements are the most familiar. These should be designed to improve the survivability of the nuclear weapons of the two sides. Harold Brown and Lynn Davis have cataloged a number of measures that could be incorporated into agreements. Weapons survivability can be improved by reducing the overall number of nuclear weapons and particularly of ballistic missile warheads; by permitting certain kinds of modernization (e.g., mobile missiles); by allowing the rebasing of ICBMs; by regulating the introduction of new missiles; and by phasing out, or preferentially reducing, certain kinds of older systems (e.g., MIRVed missiles).[18]

Reducing the vulnerability of each side's nuclear forces addresses the most enduring formulation of stability and constitutes one of the most pressing goals of arms control.

Other arms control measures could address C³I or command vulnerability, possibly by limiting antisatellite (ASAT) systems.[19] Banning tests of SLBMs launched in depressed trajectories would inhibit the ability to conduct an attack with reduced warning time.[20]

An arms control agreement is an example of a broader cooperative approach, confidence-building measures (CBMs). One proposal recently implemented—the establishment of jointly staffed U.S.-Soviet nuclear risk-reduction centers—illustrates this broader category. Among the functions relating to nuclear terrorism that these centers will perform are the following:

Joint planning for nuclear terrorism.

Exchanging information about nuclear safety devices and safeguards.

Exchanging information about relevant activities of subnational groups.

Notification of missing weapons or nuclear materials.

Cooperation in the event of a third-party detonation.

Cooperation in the event of nuclear threats by subnational groups.[21]

Beyond this, such centers will be able to address potential or developing superpower conflicts, although this would be a more challenging mission than dealing with third-party and terrorist actions.[22]

The measures discussed—from arms control to risk-reduction centers—presuppose a Soviet willingness to take certain actions in cooperation with the United States. Other efforts to improve crisis stability are less dependent on Soviet cooperation.

The unilateral actions that the United States can take can be divided into those related to force vulnerability and those pertaining to command vulnerability. Force vulnerability can be improved by moving away from high-value MIRVed ICBMs in silos toward mobile missiles. The December 1986 decision of the Reagan administration to move forward with full scale development of the small ICBM (Midgetman) in hard mobile launchers is a constructive development.[23] Command vulnerability can also be improved by unilateral measures. The goal is to make a decapitating attack even more difficult by, for example, hardening key assets and/or increasing their number.

In sum, crisis stability can be improved by a combination of cooperative and unilateral measures. Efforts should proceed on both fronts.

Arms Race Stability

Albert Carnesale and his colleagues have defined arms race stability as "controlling the weapons buildup [in the United States and Soviet Union] so that the military relationship is more predictable and resources can be used for purposes other than weaponry."[24] Although not all analysts who use the concept include the point about resource allocation, there is consensus on the first part of the Carnesale definition. Advocates of arms race stability frequently call upon the participants in an arms race to exercise caution in testing or deploying new weapons that could undermine an existing balance of forces. "Bounding the threat" enables each side to focus on maintaining survivable forces. Arms control is viewed by many as a productive way of increasing predictability in force structures and improving arms race stability.

The idea of arms race stability should reflect one's theory of arms races and their causes. Because there is debate over the causes of the U.S.-Soviet arms race (or, indeed, whether it can be said that there is such a race), there is some confusion over the prerequisites of arms race stability.

Secretary of Defense Robert McNamara set forth the classic action-reaction view in 1967:

> What is essential to understand here is that the Soviet Union and the United States mutually influence one another's strategic plans. [The] actions—or even realistically potential actions—on either side relating to the buildup of nuclear forces . . . necessarily trigger reactions on the other side. It is precisely this action-reaction phenomenon that fuels an arms race.[25]

This view of the arms race emphasizes military-technological competition rather than the larger fabric of U.S.-Soviet geopolitical or ideological struggle. The implication is that the nuclear arms race can be separated from the overall competition.

Officials of the Kennedy administration believed, moreover, that reducing the number of weapons and the risk of nuclear war could be accomplished by "nonnegotiated techniques and unilateral actions." As Assistant Secretary of Defense John T. McNaughton stated, "we must, in every decision we make, concern ourselves with the factors of stability and of the dynamic effect on the arms race."[26] Perhaps because of their view of the arms race as an action-reaction phenomenon, officials in the McNamara Pentagon welcomed unilateral initiatives that could interrupt the cycle of competition.

The action-reaction view of the arms race came under vigorous attack in the 1970s. It has not, however, completely disappeared and is readily identifiable in the ongoing SDI debate.[27] Today, however, most analysts reject such a unidimensional view in favor of multicausal explanations that, in addition to elements of action-reaction, also stress institutional-bureaucratic factors, strategic doctrine, ambiguities in intelligence analysis, and domestic politics.[28]

If the unidimensional action-reaction view is inadequate to account for the U.S.-Soviet arms competition, however, so is the view that Soviet behavior is not responsive to U.S. programs. Colin Gray, for example, argues that the weapons acquisition process in the Soviet Union is not driven "by a determination to overcompensate for US programs that could threaten Soviet maintenance" of an assured destruction capability. Instead, he says, Soviet programs are driven "by some combination of a doctrinal imperative to improve Soviet war-waging/war-winning ability and a bureaucratic defense-industrial momentum."[29] This almost certainly underestimates the extent to which Soviet policymakers react to U.S. actions.

Arms race stability remains a useful concept even though the action-reaction theory of the arms race on which it was originally based has been found wanting. There is more to the arms race than action-reaction. And analysts are not limited to the extreme views that the action-reaction phenomenon explains everything or nothing at all. In some cases, weapons undoubtedly constitute a reaction to action by the other side, although other factors must be adduced to give a complete explanation of why a particular weapon was developed.

Concern about arms race stability must, however, be kept in perspective. Among the many failings of the movement for a nuclear freeze in the United States was a tendency to view all technological innovation, all strategic and tactical nuclear modernization, as equal candidates for freezing. From the viewpoint of crisis stability, the U.S.-Soviet balance of the early to mid-1980s could be improved (for example, by deploying single-warhead, mobile ICBMs and more Trident submarines).

Improving Arms Race Stability

A number of the measures pertaining to crisis stability are relevant to arms race stability as well. Harold Brown and Lynn Davis, for example, have assessed a number of different arms control proposals, from modification of SALT II to restructuring the nuclear forces of the United States and Soviet Union and establishing overall equivalence. As normally understood, the notion of improving arms race stability requires arms control agreements in order to increase predictability about the forces of the two sides. Brown and Davis have noted that every arms control proposal they analyzed provided "greater confidence about the characteristics and size of the nuclear force postures of each side than would exist in the absence of an arms control agreement."[30]

As with crisis stability, cooperative measures may usefully be supplemented by unilateral ones. A decision by one side to constrain ASAT technology, for example, could help prevent an arms competition in that class of weapons.

The Emerging Debate:
Defenders versus Stabilizers

Two views stand out in the emerging policy debate. One of the most important cleavages between them centers on the idea of stability. The first view emphasizes strategic defense. The debate over the SDI is at times confusing because advocates and analysts often assign different meanings to the term. At the broadest (and least plausible) level is President Reagan's vision of a perfect defense against ballistic missile attacks on the population of the United States. At the narrowest (and most plausible) level are technologies deployable in the near term that, by altering the exchange ratio, could (in principle and at a high political and economic cost) create uncertainty in the mind of Soviet planners and make them question the effectiveness of a first strike against ICBMs and other military targets. Depending on who is speaking and what is being discussed, the debate over strategic defense may refer to virtually any point along a continuum anchored at either end by these two extremes. The discussion of defenders here will focus on those located on the Reagan–perfect defense end of this continuum. Although references to stability are sometimes made by proponents of defense (who, after all, favors instability?), there is a tendency for this group to deemphasize or even denigrate the goal of stability.

The second view emphasizes strategic stability as a goal and seeks to achieve it by reducing the vulnerability of offensive forces. Although the vulnerability of such forces could in principle be reduced by ballistic missile defense (BMD), the group I will be describing clearly prefers mobile ICBMs to the alternative of BMD of fixed ICBMs.

In sum, there are important disagreements between defenders and stabilizers.

Defenders

The contempt that advocates of SDI have for stability as an overarching goal in the contemporary international environment is perhaps clearest in a 1986 speech by Fred Charles Iklé, under secretary of defense for policy. He decried the fact that "for many people in the free world . . . the word 'stability' sums up the goal of Western strategy." Criticizing previous administrations for believing that the United States and the Soviet Union shared a goal of arms stability, Iklé argued that the strategic balance resulting from the SALT process "is inherently unstable."[31]

This is so, he argued, because the continuation of an international order based on mutual vulnerability assumes that two "psychologically incompatible" elements can coexist for the indefinite future. One of these is "a relationship of trust, fidelity to agreements, and self-restraint to protect the interests of the opponent." The other is "a ceaseless struggle to maintain strategic offensive forces, decade after decade, that could totally destroy the opponent." Iklé argued that Soviet leaders were incapable of adhering to a U.S.-designed stability based on mutual vulnerability. Such stability is an illusion.

There is an alternative to this "illusory" stability. According to Iklé, "President Reagan's speech of March 1983 sought to lift the spell of this illusion. *Instead of trying to impose stability through a permanent nightmare, his initiative on strategic defense shows the road to a safer future* [emphasis added]."[32] Iklé emphasizes the point that after the ABM Treaty of 1972, many in the United States persisted in believing that the Soviets had accepted the U.S. concept of mutual vulnerability. As subsequent years passed, however, the actions of Soviet leaders—weapons deployed and command bunkers built, among others—suggested that the SALT tutorials given by U.S. negotiators had failed. The Soviets, by this view, emphatically rejected the concept of strategic stability.

Colin Gray has summed up this position succinctly. There is, he has written, no Soviet acceptance of "the idea that some weapons and operating practices promote stability, and that other weapons and practices promote instability." In short, the Soviets are serious about nuclear war; the Americans are not. He sees no evidence that would support the view of many in the United States that a stabilized military structure is possible.[33]

Defenders share with the antinuclear Left a distaste for nuclear deterrence. They share with the Right a belief that the Soviet record of the past fifteen years suggests that the Kremlin seeks something more than a world of offensive weapons deployed in a stable configuration. The overriding national objective, then, is the development and deployment of a strategic defense of the United States.

On arms control, defenders in the Reagan administration have linked reductions in strategic offensive forces to forward movement (at a brisk pace) on SDI. Defenders in the administration have sought to expand the scope of testing of elements of strategic defense beyond that allowed in the traditional (narrow) interpretation of the ABM Treaty.

In 1985, the administration struck at the heart of the stabilizers' agenda by proposing a ban on mobile ICBMs. The purpose of this proposal is still unclear, although mobile missiles do create an especially acute dilemma for defenders. Deterrence (and, hence, stability) would have to be preserved during a transition to a defense-dominant world. And arms control negotiations would presumably continue, if for no other reason than to simplify the task of defense by reducing the threat on the other side. Soviet mobile missiles create problems on both of these fronts; they complicate U.S. targeting for strategic deterrence and pose obstacles to verifying compliance with an arms reduction regime.

On the other hand, U.S. mobile missiles would increase the survivability of the ICBM force and the stability of deterrence (which is exactly why stabilizers favor them). Some analysts believe that the administration views the small, mobile missile as a possible competitor to deployment of an initial layer of BMD for ICBMs. Whether this is an accurate perception, the mobile missile ban is a graphic illustration of the different approaches taken by defenders and stabilizers.

Defenders seek to move as rapidly as possible to a defense-dominant world. It was perhaps this mind-set that led President Reagan and his top civilian (although not military) advisers to contemplate at Iceland the elimination of ballistic missiles. The most reliable elements of the existing structure of nuclear deterrence would have been scrapped while the right was maintained to move forward with strategic defenses that are at present largely hypothetical.

Stabilizers

Despite Soviet-American differences over doctrine and objectives, stabilizers view stability as an achievable goal. The Scowcroft commission report, for example, stated that "whether the Soviets prove willing or not stability should be the primary objective" of U.S. arms control and strategic force modernization efforts.[34]

In one of the most explicit and systematic discussions of stability, Senator Albert Gore, Jr. (D–Tennessee) enumerated three possible strategic goals.[35] The first of these, superiority, he dismissed as unobtainable. The second, parity or equality, he dismissed as potentially dangerous because with "equal" forces, one side can still possess a first-strike advantage. It is, thus, to the third goal—stability—that Gore turned. (The most important goal is having an assured retaliatory capability within the context of a stable Soviet-American relationship. This, in turn, is a function of survivable forces on both sides. *Stability* is often used as a shorthand term for this set of relationships.)

Gore embraced the Scowcroft definition, which seeks to eliminate first-strike incentives. "The means for achieving this relationship," he said, "is to reduce the ratio of accurate warheads on one side to weapons that are targeted on the other side. Stated another way, our objective is to increase the price to attack to the aggressor."

The immediate policy objective was to proceed with Midgetman in hardened mobile launchers (HMLs). Calculations publicized by Senator Gore suggested that a force of small ICBMs on HMLs on military reservations of 5,000 square miles would force the Soviet Union to use its entire force of strategic warheads to destroy the Midgetman force. Similarly, a report by Congressman Aspin, chairman of the House Armed Services Committee, concluded that to destroy one Midgetman, the Soviets would have to use between three and seventeen warheads.[36] These analyses suggest that mobile ICBMs in HMLs would deprive the Soviets of a major class of targets that are typically supposed to be the focus of a first strike.

Importantly, this can be done unilaterally. Beyond basic notions of deterrence, the Soviet Union is not required to share precise American concepts of stability in order for the price of a first strike to be substantially increased by deployment of Midgetman. Because concern over ICBM vulnerability has been a major preoccupation of U.S. arms planning and arms control negotiations for the past fifteen years, removing this problem unilaterally would be a considerable achievement.

Many stabilizers support nuclear deterrence through offensive threats as unavoidable in the contemporary world. Mutual societal (as opposed to weapons) vulnerability is viewed as a fact of life.

On arms control, stabilizers oppose the Reagan administration's proposed ban on mobile ICBMs. (Some stabilizers would welcome a ban on mobile MIRVed ICBMs such as MX on railroad cars and the SS-24, but they argue passionately in favor of deployment of single-warhead systems such as Midgetman and the SS-25.) On the ABM Treaty, stabilizers tend to favor the traditional or narrow interpretation of the treaty.

Stabilizers see no realistic alternative to an offense-dominant world and hence seek unilaterally to reduce the vulnerability of ICBMs and some command and control assets. Some stabilizers also want to pursue CBMs to help avoid or to contain crises. Negotiated arms reductions are favored, although stabilizers would be interested in preserving, at every point on the reductions curve, a stable configuration of forces with minimum incentives for a first strike.

Conclusion

The idea of stability that was put forward in the 1950s and 1960s continues to play an important role in the debate over strategic nuclear weapons. In important respects, the stabilizers discussed in this chapter base their arguments on what might be called the classical notion of stability. The logic of the case for keeping R&D on SDI at a modest level while emphasizing reducing the vulnerability of ICBMs and command assets is quite convincing. The combination of these measures may preserve arms race stability in defensive systems for a time while significantly improving crisis stability by minimizing incentives for a first strike.

Although stabilizers have logic on their side, it is not clear how they will fare against defenders at the political level. If the American public is led to believe that SDI is likely to make possible a population defense of the United States, support for defenders may be strong. The political challenge for stabilizers is to place their call for new weapons (such as Midgetman) and for restraint on SDI spending in a context that can attract political support. This will necessitate arguing in favor of deploying new, stabilizing weapons and arguing against simplistic visions of a perfect defense.

As is true of many other sensible ideas that lie in the middle of ideological spectrums, offensive stability as a goal is unlikely to generate the passions of either the left-wing (disarmament) or right-wing (SDI) visions of a nuclear-free world. But the case must be made, for until we have a better idea of what strategic defenses can contribute to international security, nuclear deterrence based on offensive threats is the only security regime on the horizon. Improving the stability of deterrence is one of the most important objectives in world politics.

Notes

1. Thomas C. Schelling, "Surprise Attack and Disarmament," in his *The Strategy of Conflict* (New York: Oxford University Press, 1960), p. 232.

2. *Report of the President's Commission on Strategic Forces* (Washington, D.C.: Government Printing Office, April 1983), p. 29 (cited henceforth as Scowcroft commission).

3. Colin S. Gray, *Nuclear Strategy and National Style* (Lanham, Md.: Hamilton Press, Abt Books, 1986), pp. 133–168. George W. Rathjens and Jack Ruina, "The Real Issue in the Geneva Talks," *New York Times*, August 3, 1986.

4. Alexander L. George and Richard Smoke, *Deterrence in American Foreign Policy: Theory and Practice* (New York: Columbia University Press, 1974), p. 20.

5. See, for example, Bernard Brodie, *Strategy in the Missile Age* (Princeton: Princeton University Press, 1959); Albert Wohlstetter, "The Delicate Balance of Terror," *Foreign Affairs* 37 (January 1959): 211–234; Schelling, *Strategy of Conflict*.

6. Brodie, *Strategy in the Missile Age*, p. 303.

7. Lawrence Freedman, "The First Two Generations of Nuclear Strategists," in *Makers of Modern Strategy: From Machiavelli to the Nuclear Age*, ed. Peter Paret (Princeton: Princeton University Press, 1986), p. 757.

8. Secretary of Defense McNamara gave an operational definition of assured destruction: "In the case of the Soviet Union, I would judge that a capability on our part to destroy, say, one-fifth to one-fourth of her population and one-half of her industrial capacity would serve as an effective deterrent," Robert S. McNamara, *Statement before the Senate Armed Services Committee on the Fiscal Year 1969–73 Defense Program and 1969 Defense Budget* (January 2, 1968), p. 50. For a succinct summary of U.S. nuclear strategy, see Donald M. Snow, *Nuclear Strategy in a Dynamic World: American Policy in the 1980s* (University: University of Alabama Press, 1981), chap. 3.

9. Albert Carnesale et al., *Living with Nuclear Weapons* (New York: Bantam Books, 1983), p. 203.

10. Department of Defense, *Annual Report: Fiscal Year 1981* (Washington, D.C.: Government Printing Office, 1980), p. 69.

11. John D. Steinbruner, "National Security and the Concept of Strategic Stability," *Journal of Conflict Resolution* 22 (September 1978): 414–415.

12. Ashton B. Carter, "Assessing Command System Vulnerability," in *Managing Nuclear Operations*, ed. Ashton B. Carter, John D. Steinbruner, and Charles A. Zraket (Washington, D.C.: Brookings Institution, 1987), p. 577.

13. Steinbruner, "National Security," pp. 420–422.

14. Carter, "Assessing Command System Vulnerability," p. 607.

15. Bruce B. Blair, *Strategic Command and Control: Redefining the Nuclear Threat* (Washington, D.C.: Brookings Institution, 1985).

16. Ibid., p. 294. Emphasis added.

17. Scowcroft commission, p. 6. In the Carter administration, this type of strategy was called a "countervailing" one. For an argument that a countervailing strategy represents an appropriate middle way between assured destruction and war winning, see Robert C. Gray, "The Reagan Nuclear Strategy," *Arms Control Today* 13 (March 1983).

18. Harold Brown and Lynn E. Davis, *Nuclear Arms Control Choices*, in *SAIS Papers in International Affairs*, no. 5 (Boulder, Colo.: Westview Press, 1984), p. 42. For an interesting discussion of possible restrictions on weapons tests, see Sidney D. Drell and Theodore J. Ralson, "Restrictions on Weapon Tests as Confidence-Building Measures," in *Preventing Nuclear War: A Realistic Approach*, ed. Barry M. Blechman (Bloomington: Indiana University Press, 1985), pp. 86–98.

19. The word *possibly* should be emphasized here, for it is not yet clear what kinds of restraints are feasible or desirable. For an excellent survey of the issues, see Ashton B. Carter, "Satellites and Anti-Satellites: The Limits of the Possible," *International Security* 10 (Spring 1986): 86–98.

20. For an interesting discussion of arms control and command system vulnerability, see Michael M. May and John R. Harvey, "Nuclear Operations and Arms Control," in *Managing Nuclear Operations*, pp. 703–735.

21. Barry M. Blechman, "Containing the Threat of Nuclear Terrorism," in Blechman, *Preventing Nuclear War*, pp. 59–62.

22. Richard K. Betts, "A Joint Nuclear Risk Control Center," in ibid., pp. 65–85.

23. The decision of the Reagan administration resulted in large part from congressional pressure in support of Midgetman. The administration also announced plans to study deployment of MX missiles on railcars. For a discussion of the legislative origins of Midgetman, see Robert C. Gray, "Congress, Arms Control, and Weapons Modernization," in U.S., Congress, House, Committee on Foreign Affairs, *Congress and Foreign Policy: 1983*, 98th Cong. 2d sess. 1984, pp. 86–109. See also the discussion of stabilizers later in this chapter.

24. Carnesale et al., *Living with Nuclear Weapons*, p. 203.

25. Robert S. McNamara, "The Dynamics of Nuclear Strategy," in *Nuclear Strategy, Arms Control and the Future*, ed. P. Edward Haley, David M. Keithly, and Jack Merritt (Boulder, Colo.: Westview Press, 1985), p. 81.

26. Jerome H. Kahan, *Security in the Nuclear Age: Developing U.S. Strategic Arms Policy* (Washington, D.C.: Brookings Institution, 1975), p. 264.

27. See, for example, the explicit action-reaction view set forth by George Rathjens and Jack Ruina in "BMD and Strategic Instability," *Daedalus* (Summer 1985): *Weapons in Space, Volume II*, p. 252.

28. For a succinct summary of the challenge to the action-reaction hypothesis, see Lawrence Freedman, *The Evolution of Nuclear Strategy* (New York: St. Martin's 1981), pp. 347–348. For a case study illustrating the utility of employing a multidimensional approach, see Ted Greenwood, *Making the MIRV: A Study of Defense Decision Making* (Cambridge, Mass.: Ballinger, 1975).

29. Gray, *Nuclear Strategy*, p. 149.

30. Brown and Davis, *Nuclear Arms Control Choices*, p. 33.

31. The speech was given in February 1986. An article based on it was published as "The Idol of Stability," *National Interest* (Winter 1986–1987): 75–79.

32. Ibid., p. 78.

33. Gray, *Nuclear Strategy*, p. 145.

34. Scowcroft commission report, p. 3. Emphasis added.

35. Senator Gore set forth his analysis in a series of speeches on the Senate floor from November 4, 1985, to November 22, 1985. The argument here can be found in *Congressional Record*, November 5, 1985, pp. S 14770–771.

36. Les Aspin, "Midgetman: Sliding Shut the Window of Vulnerability," House Armed Sevices Committee mimeo., February 10, 1986.

II
Strategic Nuclear Relations

4
Assured Coercion: Managing the Defense Transition

Stephen J. Cimbala

U.S. deterrence and arms control policies are caught between past—the comfortable certainty of mutual assured destruction—and future—the security of mutual assured survival. MAD depends on the certainty of offensive retaliation by U.S. forces after absorbing a Soviet attack. It also assumes the Soviets can respond with comparable effectiveness to a U.S. attack. Mutual assured survival offers to transcend the paradox of mutual assured destruction; in this view, the peace is maintained by the ability to destroy and be destroyed. Assured survival invites the deployment of highly competent defenses (relative to the offenses that will oppose them) and a gradual build-down of offensive forces. The ultimate destination, for advocates of assured survival in the Reagan administration, has been described as a world disarmed of superpower strategic offensive forces.[1]

Advocates of both views acknowledge a lessening of consensus among American political leaders and defense analysts about nuclear policy and strategy. A working elite consensus on assured destruction has broken down, and a new one has not replaced it. Meanwhile negotiations with the Soviet Union on near-term and longer-range arms control issues cannot be delayed if they are to be productive.

Among the necessary sparks for arms control combustion is the need to define a clearer concept of the interim between assured destruction and whatever is going to take its place. It may be assured survival if defenses can be made much more competent than offenses. But there are various forms of assured survival, offered by persons inside and outside the Reagan administration. Wherever we end up, a transitional concept of interim management should be designed to focus U.S. strategic deterrence and arms control efforts.

Such a concept is described below, but it is offered only provisionally. The true test of any tool is whether it is meaningful to those who must use it. Abstract elegance counts for very little if it leads to elegant destruction of civilization. A transition or interim concept must also depart substantially from present designs. Present designs are clearly not working, but they must not be ignored or circumvented.

There are several requirements for a concept that will move us from arms control impasse to arms control progress. First, the concept must not make arms control into a totem. It must serve the interests of U.S. foreign policy as much as it serves the interests of some abstract good attributed to it by theorists.[2] Second, the concept must not assume identical, or even parallel, motives on the part of the United States and the Soviet Union. Neither deterrence nor arms control demands purified participants. Third, although identical motives are not necessary, there must be common ground on basic expectations about strategic intentions and capabilities of the two sides.

A concept that fulfills these requirements might be given many names. Pinning labels is less important than getting the ingredients correct. The correct ingredients are clear enough. The concept should contribute to a U.S.-Soviet deterrence and arms control regime that improves crisis stability, arms race stability, and strategic stability.[3] Crisis stability is the degree to which both sides' retaliatory forces are so configured that they discourage preemption. Arms race stability prevents the two sides from deploying quantities or types of forces that motivate the opponent to match and surpass with comparable or better systems. Strategic stability (or basic stability) obtains when both have survivable second-strike forces that can inflict unacceptable damage against the opponent even after absorbing the worst-case attack.[4]

A transitional concept fulfilling these requirements is defined as *assured coercion*. This concept should be adopted as a focus for U.S. deterrence and arms control efforts whether the Soviets follow suit or not. Assured coercion means that through all phases of any crisis or war, whatever the opponent does, the United States will at least preserve the capability to threaten destruction of the opponent's cities and to pursue war termination under the most tolerable conditions possible. The appropriate forces and war plans will contribute to these objectives and not be sized or calibrated by the number of targets they can destroy or the total megatonnage they can deliver. Studies by the Office of Technology Assessment and other U.S. governmental agencies have made clear that a major strategic war between the superpowers would leave their societies incoherent and chaotic and their citizens killed in unprecedented numbers. Politicians faced with crisis countdowns will know what this means, even if analysts struggle over how much is enough.

Assured coercion is not identical with assured destruction. Assured destruction has been described by its creators, including former Pentagon aids Alain Enthoven and K. Wayne Smith, as a guideline for force sizing and budgetary constraint.[5] Assured destruction was the reaction by former secretary of defense Robert S. McNamara to the distortion of his "no cities" doctrine, first suggested in 1962, into a counterforce hubris policy for increments to U.S. strategic land-based missiles (ICBMs).[6] It is an overstatement to say, as some do, that McNamara reached for assured destruction only for budgetary reasons. He came to believe in the concept after being persuaded that racing the Soviet Union to deploy unlimited counterforce capability was strategically self-defeating.[7]

Assured destruction established the very important principle that more is not necessarily more deterring when dealing with incomprehensible levels of devastation. But it defaulted at the very point where it should have been most insistent: when deterrence fails and war begins. Assured destruction thus mandated abstemious disregard for ABM or BMD. According to some of its most influential adherents, it offered no meaningful distinction between uninhibited countercity exchanges and war prevention. Assured destruction advocates, including McNamara, did acknowledge that the United States might not retaliate against cities first in the event of war. But the capability to destroy cities during a short war of few exchanges became the sufficient, rather than part of the necessary, condition for deterrence.[8]

For assured destruction forces to guarantee deterrence, it was not thought necessary for U.S. strategic C^3 to be preserved very long after war began.[9] The purpose of the strategic forces was to inflict decisive retaliation quickly. Only if war could be conceived as a protracted or extended series of exchanges over many days would a command system be required that could survive dedicated attacks against it. Thus the U.S. strategic force superiority of the 1960s was marred by the apparent lack of very survivable command and control for those forces, if some expert assessments can be believed.[10] This command vulnerability is not a serious problem if the war ends within minutes after it has begun and both sides' arsenals are quickly exhausted and their societies virtually destroyed.

Limitations of assured destruction became apparent to policy planners in the 1970s. President Nixon issued National Security Decision Memorandum 242 (NSDM-242) in 1974, and it was followed by subsequent clarifications of new declaratory and employment policies by Secretary of Defense James R. Schlesinger.[11] The changes brought about by Secretary Schlesinger recognized the impact of U.S.-Soviet strategic parity and the need for limited options short of all-out retaliation. In some instances the capability for selective strategic nuclear response and flexible targeting might be more deterring, according to his reasoning, than less credible threats to unleash the entire arsenal.[12] The Carter administration reviewed U.S. strategic targeting policy and reached similar conclusions. PD-59 (Presidential Directive 59) has been reported as acknowledging a need for U.S. forces and C^3 that can provide selective options and a capability to respond with more variations of delayed, as well as prompt, attacks.[13]

The Reagan administration applied similar logic to the problem of flexible options and extended conflict as had the Carter administration, if reports about the classified Defense Guidance and National Security Decision Directive (NSDD)-13 are reliable.[14] But the Reagan continuation of the drift from assured destruction took one important detour. While additional options were sought and both survivable and enduring command and control received declaratory emphasis, policy planners were trumped by the president's March 23, 1983, speech launching the SDI.[15] The president called for defenses that could make strategic offensive forces "impotent and obsolete." This meant a redefinition of the terms of superpower arms competition rather than its regulation according to criteria of stability based on offensive retaliation.[16] Ultimately the Reagan strategic concept as explained by Ambassador Paul Nitze would reduce offensive forces to negligible deployments and substitute mutually protective defenses using nonnuclear weapons.[17]

For the Reagan concept to be realized, much would depend on the capacity of active defenses to protect cities as well as retaliatory forces. In the near term, city protection was not likely to be very meaningful. Offensive retaliation based on assured destruction, plus countervailing against Soviet attacks in proportion to their destructiveness, remained the basis of the U.S. deterrent. And the assured destruction–countervailing deterrent was for the most part based on a short war concept rather than on an expectation of exchanges that continued over days or weeks.[18] Although the Carter administration gave lip-service to the recognition that war might be protracted, it called for capabilities far less than those required to provide extended war deterrence. This was probably judicious. The administration was still far from having the capability for flexible targeting that Secretary Schlesinger had called for when the Democrats took over the White House in 1977. It would be enough to increase options in the Single Integrated Operational Plan (SIOP) to provide for target coverage and "withholds" against certain (however temporary) sanctuaries. PD-59 was really an acknowledgment after the fact that the Carter administration had implemented the Schlesinger doctrine rather than inventing a new doctrine of its own. Certainly the change in employment policy (targeting) was more evolutionary than revolutionary.[19]

Assured coercion begins with the recognition that assured destruction was a valuable and valid pivot for U.S. deterrence and arms control, given U.S. capabilities and those of the Soviets for most of the 1960s and 1970s. What is needed is a replacement for assured destruction that preserves what was essential and modifies what was ephemeral. The essential component of assured destruction was the recognition that in superpower nuclear conflict, absolute levels of destruction are more compelling than relative outcomes once more than a few weapons are exchanged. Policymakers will be motivated to avoid war if at all possible by this recognition. Any modification of this policy (assured destruction) that makes relatives into absolutes and absolutes into relatives would make deterrence weaker.

It happens nevertheless that the superpowers might blunder into war despite their recognition that both might lose. If a crisis gets out of control and deterrence fails, preemption might be chosen as a worst-case alternative by either side. It also happens that the dynamics of mutual alarm, as Thomas Schelling has described them, could cause each side to overcompensate during alerts. A very "prudent precaution" by the United States could result in "overreaction" by the Soviet Union until one party decided to cross the threshold to war.[20] The strategic command and control systems of the superpowers are to some extent mutually interdependent; each watches what the other is doing and has tightly coupled its warning and attack assessment systems to the other's retaliatory forces.[21] Thus wars with no advantage for either side might break out; deterrence would be carried into war itself, or war would become genocide with no discernible stopping point.

Assured coercion implies recognition of the possibility of war however much we are motivated to prevent it. The United States has come part of the way toward assured coercion and away from assured destruction in the Schlesinger amendments and the declaratory policies of PD-59. The Reagan declaratory policies take a sidestep. They offer assured survival or assured denial of the opponent's capability to attack rather than retaliation against its values and forces. No one knows whether assured survival will eventually come to pass, but it will not offer a near-term prospectus for U.S. deterrence and arms control policies. Something else must fill in, building on the policies of the Nixon, Ford, and Carter administrations and their not-always-consistent adoptions of assured destruction.

This recommended building block is assured coercion; it calls for forces and commanders that can contribute to war termination by protracted coercion. This does not express any particular relish for protracted war. Quite the opposite is intended by the concept: the longer the war goes on, the harder it will be to terminate. In order to terminate superpower nuclear conflict once it begins, the United States will need fighting forces and coercive forces. Coercive forces are those withheld from the early stages of conflict to be used against cities or other highly valued civilian and military targets that might provide a basis for ending the war.

Assured coercion values survivable forces and commanders not because of the revenge they can take against their opponents but because of the further destruction that they can do after the first exchanges of weapons have transpired. The value of these coercive forces is that they can promise to do more damage, and to things presumably more valuable, than those already destroyed. These judgments are highly subjective. Reading the minds of Soviet leaders about the things they value most highly is speculative for even the most knowledgeable Soviet experts in academic and governmental circles. The Soviets themselves may not know until the scenario unfolds. Some studies assert with confidence that the Soviets value their leadership and force survivability more than they value the survivability of their population, but it is never clearly explained whether this valuation (if true) is instrumental (you must save the forces and commanders so that they can retaliate and save the population) or inherent in Soviet ideology.[22] Soviet efforts to protect their leadership and population from the effects of nuclear and conventional war are motivated by unique geopolitical predicaments and their perception of the correlation of forces at a particular time.[23]

But assumptions must be made regarding the value of attacking forces, cities, and commanders (among other things) early or later in war. Assured coercion borrows from assured destruction the notion that the most inherently valued component of a society is its population. This is true in a truistic sense: there is no society of any kind with most of its people dead or incapacitated. But it is also true in a more subtle sense. Beyond a level of destruction that is not exactly certain but can be guessed at by Kremlin oligarchs, Soviet citizens will have less motivation to obey and more to revolt. When there is so much destruction of one's society and habitat that one has little or nothing to lose by ignoring or usurping authority, revolution or apathy is highly probable as a reaction. Soviet rulers must know this better than anyone else.[24] Thus it is at least a valid starting point that assuredly coercive forces should hold as many Soviet citizens at risk after the two sides have exchanged counterforce attacks as the numbers of U.S. citizens jeopardized in similar fashion.

Thus it might seem a crude calculus, but it represents estimates that surviving leaders will have to make. They may not be "fortunate" enough to see everything vaporized in one massive firestorm. They may be compelled to bargain, to arrange terms, to negotiate about the condition under which millions of additional citizens will die or be spared. The survivors may envy the dead, but leadership has responsibilities that cannot be subverted by slogans. It will be the task of unfortunate American statesmen in the postattack period, after the early and almost automatic exchanges of weapons, to calibrate their subsequent attacks based on expectations of Soviet and U.S. incentives to continue or quit.

Assured coercion would thus modify assured destruction for the purpose of recognizing that war may be protracted and must be terminated. Contributions of the Nixon-Ford-Carter policies are positive in this regard. But in another way they are destructive of the transition from assured destruction to assured coercion. This other way involves the apparent consideration given under PD-59 and NSDD-13 (respectively, Carter and Reagan policies) to destruction of the opponent's political and military leadership early in war.[25]

At least one essential clarification is required here. We are not discussing countercombatant attacks against division, front, and army commanders (in the U.S.-NATO case) that might have tactical and operational rationales in conventional war.[26] Instead Carter and Reagan declaratory policies apparently contemplated, and contemplate, selective targeting of the highest levels of Soviet political and military leadership, including paramilitary and security forces. Chess players will recognize this as an attempt to achieve an elegant solution; cost-benefit analysts or game theorists might term it efficient. But it is deceptively efficient and elegant. If we are assuming that the United States is planning early attacks against the Soviet leadership, the precise location and identification of those leaders and their communications during war will not be certain. U.S. reconnaissance and communication assets, some based in space, might be vulnerable to present or future generations of Soviet ASAT weapons that reduced U.S. capability to monitor leaders' comings and goings. Moreover, there is some evidence that Soviet leaders are well protected compared to their U.S. counterparts. They have some 1,500 to 2,000 command bunkers for the highest political and military leaders and have made other arrangements to protect key personnel and industries, to an extent far exceeding any U.S. effort.[27]

Thus U.S. "decapitation" attacks could result in Soviet responses that left the United States worse rather than better off. Of course, the Soviet Union may attack the U.S. command system anyway, but they must recognize, as U.S. analysts do, that the benefits are uncertain. What matters is not the physical things that they can destroy, such as command posts, communications links, and U.S. leadership. What is much more important for Soviet planners is whether they understand correctly how the U.S. system is organized to fight nuclear war. As Paul Bracken has noted, a successful Soviet attack on the U.S. command system could increase, rather than reduce, their level of destruction that the United States is able to inflict in retaliation. This could happen because there are many rather than one or a few triggers when the command system is poised to retaliate.[28] This is certainly its likely condition during a superpower crisis. Under generated alert conditions, a Soviet attack on the U.S. command structure could increase the rate at which de facto control over nuclear response cascaded downward through the military command system into middle management and below. Soviet decapitation of the top of the pyramid could preclude the survival or reconstitution of any coherent U.S. leadership with which to negotiate war termination, even surrender on terms the Soviet Union later found to be acceptable.

There is some irony in the fact that both countervailing strategies of the Carter administration and the prevailing strategies attributed to Reagan depend upon some capability for active defense that the United States does not possess. Whether the abstract logic of these declaratory strategies and operational adjustments to the SIOP make possible greater degrees of offensive damage limitation is not enough. Soviet advantages in ICBM throw weight compared to U.S. deployments suggest that the United States begins any quest for offensive counterforce equivalence at a disadvantage that may be insurmountable. More important, however, even counterforce matching will not rescue U.S. society and strategic command and control from their vulnerability. There may be no feasible deployments in this century that provide societal survivability; the reason for the lack of C^3 protection has more to do with American policymakers' emphases on almost automatic and preformatted retaliatory options.

Assured destruction has been jeopardized since it was first promulgated by pressures from military leaders and presidents. Military leaders wanted attacks against the opponent's military forces to occur promptly after war began. Delayed attacks might suffice for city targeting; cities' infrastructures were immobile, although with sufficient warning, citizens might be evacuated. But Soviet forces would (it was frequently assumed) have to be attacked and destroyed as soon as possible. This was termed damage limitation by American strategists: destroying the residual forces of the attacker so that its follow-on attacks would be less successful.

If military leaders sought counterforce–damage limiting options, presidents wanted more control over the character and pace of nuclear response. President Kennedy learned during the Cuban missile crisis that presidential orders could be reshaped or misconstrued during their progression through the chain of command.[29] Standard operating procedures and the intellectual ethos of political and military bureaucracies could countermand flexibility assumed to be available by civilian policymakers. Kennedy's experience during the Bay of Pigs might have been equally valuable if less apocalyptic. The Bay of Pigs apparently taught him the limits of reliance on lower levels of the bureaucracy, including military and intelligence experts, without providing for devil's advocates who can dispute prevailing consensus.[30]

Both the assumed limitations on presidential grasp and the perceived military necessity for prompt attacks on Soviet military targets created pressure for force structures and command systems that provided for rapid and massive response. The early war might be the only war; Soviet forces had to be attacked quickly, and the presidential chain of command might not last very long in practice or might be prone to unintended delegations of authority. U.S. civilian policymakers and their military advisers thus imparted the most flexibility to the portion of U.S. strategic retaliatory forces that had to be used quickly: the land-based missiles that would attack Soviet missile silos, command bunkers, and other time-urgent targets (time urgency refers here to the need to attack a target quickly, before it can be activated and used).

True, the United States during the 1960s also deployed highly competent strategic submarine (Polaris, later Poseidon) forces for attacking Soviet cities, and this sea-based force now carries the greater number of survivable warheads. The submarine force was an assured destruction force rather than an assured coercion force, however. Although it provided some additional survivability for the U.S. strategic triad of land-based missiles, bombers, and submarine-launched missiles, it could not be used for flexible targeting and made uncertain contributions to multiple exchange wars. Three characteristics of the strategic submarine force (SSBN) limited its capabilities. First, firing a single SLBM would reveal the position of the boat, making its destruction possible. Second, SLBM reentry vehicles lacked the yields and accuracies necessary to attack many of the hardest targets that U.S. planners might want to strike in retaliation. Some residual counterforce is useful for assured coercion, although it is not necessary or desirable to match Soviet *preattack* counterforce capabilities. Third, and most significant, the ability to communicate between the submarines and the national command authorities (NCA: the president, the secretary of defense, and/or their successors) was uncertain after the outbreak of war. Communications with patroling submarines were clear enough in peacetime to preclude accidental or unauthorized launch, but wartime communications connectivity was described by expert analysts as likely to fail rapidly.[31]

The immediate isolation of submarines from NCA instructions would not preclude U.S. retaliation. Severed or disturbed communications could prevent central political or military authorities from changing strike plans during the initial stages of any conflict. In short, the high probability of postattack-severed connectivity meant that the strategic submarine force (at least prior to the late 1970s) was a revenge, not a coercive, force. Carter and Reagan programs have made some improvements in the command and control of strategic submarines, at least at the level of improved hardware.[32]

These limitations prevented the SSBN force from fulfilling any requirement for selective postattack coercion. The submarines might use their weapons in large salvos against some counterforce or countercommand targets, but mostly they would be used against vulnerable industrial areas and other targets in and near cities.[33] Although the SSBN force will become more capable of carrying out counterforce options in the 1990s when the Trident II (D-5) missile is deployed aboard Trident and Poseidon submarines, these additional capabilities will be a mixed blessing.

Counterforce-capable SSBNs assigned to carrying out prompt missions are neither necessary nor desirable from the standpoint of assured coercion. They purchase survivable coercive capability at too high a price: the price of adding to the U.S. capability for preemption.[34] Trident II missiles on Trident or Poseidon submarines are not primarily useful in the later stages of war but in the early attacks against military targets; one can assume that SIOP planners do not want to waste most of the sea-based hard target capability on cities. This might appeal to those favoring city avoidance and military destruction, but that distinction is probably more important to U.S. planners than it is to their Soviet counterparts. Cities will be spared to the extent that they are by Trident and Trident II attacks because the combination of Trident II and other systems is expected to defeat the Soviet Union, not to coerce it.

A coercive strategy would emphasize the deployment of slow rather than prompt counterforce capabilities. Cruise missiles aboard submarines and surface ships and those delivered by bombers are admirably suited to the postattack counterforce needs of U.S. deterrence. They are comparatively inexpensive, can be launched from many platforms, and above all are slow compared to ballistic missiles—characteristics necessary for the counterforce component of an assured coercion force. This component should provide for proliferation of aim points, making surprise attack against it more difficult for any opponent. It should provide for flexible adaptation for the largest possible number of delivery modes. It should take advantage of opportunities for concealment or stealth. It has been noted with some justice that cruise missiles are not totally without drawbacks. Verification of their deployments for arms control agreements presents formidable problems for policy planners. The trade-off between verification difficulties and slower counterforce is regarded as desirable from an assured coercion perspective. There are very few counterforce targets in the Soviet Union that the United States would have to destroy immediately, compared to the effects of delayed attacks against those same targets, unless the United States were striking first.[35]

The distinction between an assured coercion force and counterforce first-strike force could break down if U.S. counterforce capabilities exceeded the level of sufficiency needed to destroy those Soviet forces capable of attacking after the Soviet Union absorbs retaliation by the United States. In other words, U.S. forces that can deny the Soviet Union the countermilitary effectiveness of its third-strike forces have accomplished whatever can be accomplished by counterforce capabilities after deterrence fails. Other U.S. forces will still hold Soviet cities at risk. This point is extremely important and has received only partial clarification in policy debates. Paul H. Nitze, for example, argued in influential contributions to strategic policy debates during the 1970s that the United States would be deterred from retaliating after a Soviet counterforce first strike. Soviet forces surviving U.S. retaliation would be much more capable of destroying the remaining U.S. counterforce targets compared to the U.S. capability to destroy those of the Soviet Union.[36]

Assured destruction advocates denied that postattack counterforce balances mattered very much. At the level of human suffering, this is certainly so. At the level of strategic planning, Nitze had a point. If the Soviets expected that they would survive any U.S. retaliation with an aggregate surplus of countermilitary potential compared to that of the United States, they might be bolder in a crisis than they otherwise would be. Nitze also recognized that this was a scenario-dependent analysis; much would depend on the stakes and interests involved for both sides. But there were analytical deficiencies. The vulnerability of the U.S. command structure made Nitze's projections too optimistic; the undoubted caution of the Politburo at the moment of truth made his analyses more pessimistic than reality. I do not doubt that Nitze understood both limitations of his force models. His purposes included a political bull's eye, which he saw as awakening public apathy about the strategic balance. What is interesting for our purposes is the way that Nitze chose to define that balance: not in preattack static indicators but in dynamic counterforce exchange models.

What Nitze and other advocates of vastly improved U.S. prompt counterforce capabilities have not done is to make the case more convincingly for fast as opposed to slow counterforce. The more prompt counterforce weapons the United States deploys, the more the Kremlin must wonder just what the United States is aiming at. Deterrence is something that works if it works in the minds of

Soviet leaders rather than American strategists. In this regard, Soviet leaders (Andropov, Chernenko, and Gorbachev) have provided interesting data in their reactions to U.S. and NATO deployments of Pershing II and cruise missiles in Europe. Of course, they launched a propaganda campaign to get Europeans to object to the missile deployments. Their serious arms control proposals for intermediate nuclear forces at Geneva made clearer their priorities. Cruise missiles were initially viewed as not welcome but tolerable; Pershing II had to come out. The United States and the Soviet Union almost reached an agreement to this effect during the now-famous walk in the woods,[37] and eventually signed the INF Treaty. Pershing IIs were seen by Soviet leaders as accurate weapons designed to strike at their command bunkers within ten minutes from launch in West Germany. They are perceived not as weapons of retaliation but as weapons for preemption.[38]

Several U.S. administrations have created the same dilemmas, in divergence between U.S. intentions and Soviet understanding of those intentions, in their attempts to deploy the MX/Peacekeeper ICBM. Deploying the MX in a non-survivable basing mode makes it vulnerable to Soviet attacks and invites them to perceive it as a first-strike weapon. Their incentive to attack it early in war before the United States must "use it or lose it" is increased. At this writing, it is doubtful that any survivable basing mode exists for the MX that can carry a majority in Congress, although new proposals are still made.[39] No case for additional prompt counterforce as opposed to slow counterforce can succeed if it creates extra incentives for Soviet planners to attack American prompt counterforce more promptly. Trident II might then be justified if some of the target coverage planned for MX were transferred to it in the 1990s, but the size of the Trident II force would still be an issue if its purposes are coercive-retaliatory as opposed to preemptive.

A new great debate has developed since President Reagan announced his commitment to a program for research, development, and possible deployment of a U.S. BMD system. Two panels appointed by the administration to study the feasibility of this SDI concluded that defenses were feasible and would contribute to deterrence stability.[40] Critics inside and outside the government disputed the president's stated objective of making nuclear offenses obsolete, although they expressed more positive appraisals of limited defenses that protected retaliatory forces.[41]

The cases for and against BMD have been summarized elsewhere.[42] Two points deserve clarification relative to earlier discussion. First, the administration's own strategic concept requires that BMD be survivable and "cost effective at the margin."[43] Ambassador Nitze has indicated that if a U.S. BMD system cannot meet these criteria, it should not be deployed. Second, an American missile defense program is dependent for its success on how the Soviets react to it—a point obviously related to the first.

Survivable and cost-effective U.S. missile defenses will require some adjustments in prevailing thinking about counterforce. This refers to prevailing thinking about declaratory, employment, and force acquisition policies for offensive counterforce systems. Until now, it has been assumed that the United States needs offensive systems that are adequate to fight counterforce duels with their Soviet counterparts. We have also assumed that counterforce imbalances favoring the Soviet Union in certain categories will leave the United States subject to coercion at the margin. Although more theoretical than practical, these suppositions about U.S. vulnerability to coercion have been important in motivating the acquisition of more prompt hard target capabilities. Missile defenses complicate the process of estimating relative susceptibility to coercion.

The more plausible near-term deployment of any U.S. BMD system will emphasize point defense of military and other hard targets rather than area defenses of cities. It may turn out that, given reasonable investments by the Soviet Union in offensive force modernization, no defense of cities can be deployed that meets the criteria of the U.S. "strategic concept."[44] Point defenses are more feasible, but they raise difficulties that are not acknowledged by some of their proponents. They would provide added survivability for strategic forces provided two assumptions held. First, offenses would have to slow their rate of qualitative and quantitative growth until defenses caught up. Second, from then on, defenses would have to be marginally cost-effective, understood to mean that the marginal increment required to destroy each attacking reentry vehicle should not be more expensive than the marginal increment required to destroy either the target being defended or the defense itself. If these assumptions cannot be made, the case for active defenses is weaker. It is not self-evident that defenses provide the most cost-effective improvements in crisis and arms race stability; they may or may not.

Missile defenses could contribute to a coercive strategy provided they created added protection for strategic forces without providing protection for cities, under the conditions described in the preceding paragraph. This is not the concept of the administration, which includes defenses so competent that offenses are eventually nullified. Defenses that are competent are improbable in our lifetimes. More immediate dilemmas lie in proposals to deploy missile defense systems in space, using kinetic or directed-energy kill mechanisms to attack ballistic missiles in their boost or earliest phase of flight.[45]

At least two problems must be addressed if space-based missile defenses are to support a coercive strategy of retaliation rather than a strategy of counterforce exhaustion. First, any missile defense system with boost phase intercept capabilities threatens the opponent with some urban damage denial. The system might not preclude all retaliation, but it could prevent a coherent retaliatory strike and thus confer on its possessor a potential first-strike capability. Second, this mission ambiguity of space-based defenses is complicated by the imminent threats against satellite survivability posed by ASATs already deployed or developed by the superpowers.[46] ASATs already have significant capabilities against satellites in low earth orbit, including some important U.S. meteorological and reconnaissance satellites.[47] More capable ASATs will undoubtedly be deployed in the future unless they are limited by treaty. If deployments are not limited, both super-powers may have to deploy defense satellites to defend the ballistic missile in-terceptor satellites. Readers can imagine where this leads, since the attacker will attempt to create countermeasures to fox the defense, and so on. Long before there are wars in space, the superpowers may create new requirements for traffic control, legal regimes dealing with space object travel, and com-munications snafus that make the divestiture of AT&T appear prosaic.

Since even very crude BMD weapons based in space could be much more effective for ASAT missions, their early testing and deployment will signal a threat to the survivability of the opponent's early warning and communica-tions satellites. Thus BMD deployments, depending on how they are perceived, could create crisis instability rather than reduce it.[48] Clearly there is an im-perative for arms control to establish boundaries around the deployments of BMD and ASAT in the near future, whatever is to be decided about the longer term. Absent arms control, U.S. BMD deployments will simply race Soviet of-fensive countermeasures and may create incentives for them to consider preemp-tion rather than retaliation. That choice will not be our preference but it may be forced upon us by the competitive deployment of space-based ASAT satellite defenses and BMD systems that invite attack on themselves. The assured coercion–delayed retaliation strategy could be helped by BMD, however, under the proper conditions. If BMD increased significantly the proportion of U.S. slow counterforce that survived a first strike, thus providing additional inven-tives for policymakers to ride out an attack and not launch on warning, then it would contribute something very important. It may be that future technologies for BMD and strategic air defense (against air breathing threats, including bombers and cruise missiles) can accomplish this significant increment in sur-vivable slow counterforce. It would also be salutary if BMD could contribute to more survivable strategic C^3, which would guarantee responsive control over U.S. forces even after absorbing a "worst-case" first strike. Currently this cannot be guaranteed.[49] But these potential contributions would have to be weighed against the negatives if BMD contributed to instability or arms races in other ways. We simply do not know enough about these trade-offs now.

Stable deterrence has been provided by assured destruction, but assured destruction has become ragged at the edges. Even some of its advocates have wandered into the dangerous terrain of potentially preemptive counterforce. Assured coercion returns to the essentials of assured destruction, which was designed to retaliate assuredly, for that is indeed the basis of deterrence. But it need not mean that retaliation must take place as quickly as possible and against time-urgent military and command targets. The Scowcroft commission contended that, for the Soviets, their missile silos, command bunkers, and other war-fighting targets are most valued by them.[50] This might be misunderstood. Those targets are valuable to the United States as well as to them. If they are destroyed as rapidly as possible, especially the command targets, the Soviet Union has nothing to lose. Escalation control and war termination become impossible. It was the strength of assured destruction that it wanted to prevent war by making threats credible. Threats to destroy cities certainly are, and will remain so. It is the weakness of assured destruction that when push comes to shove, it might not be believed because the punishment could be disproportionate to the crime. Having figured this out, NATO European allies have expressed some disbelief in U.S. willingness to retaliate against Moscow in response to attacks on Paris.

Assured coercion explains it better without requiring different forces that may threaten the opponent's deterrent, thereby provoking first strikes. Assured coercion regards cities as valuable as long as they are held hostage but not actually attacked. It would argue for preserving that capability as far into war as is needed to end it. No war termination of this kind can be as good as wars that are successfully prevented. The important argument is about how to prevent war. One school of thought wants to replace the present environment with a defense-dominant one. Another wants to cling to assured destruction because it has seemed to work, although our understandings of why are not always clear or consensual. A third school wants to amend assured destruction into countervailing and prevailing strategies for winning counterforce wars. The alternative presented here offers another choice.

Notes

1. U.S. Department of State, "The Strategic Defense Initiative," *Special Report*, no. 129 (June 1985).

2. On this issue as it applies to space-based weapons, see Colin S. Gray, "Space Arms Control: A Skeptical View," *Air University Review* 37, no. 5 (November–December 1985): 73–86.

3. These concepts are very well explained in Leon V. Sigal, *Nuclear Weapons in Europe: Enduring Dilemmas, Present Prospects* (Washington, D.C.: Brookings Institution, 1984), pp. 8–10.

4. Ibid., p. 9.

5. Alan C. Enthoven and K. Wayne Smith, *How Much Is Enough? Shaping the Defense Program 1961–69* (New York: Harper & Row, 1971).

6. Lawrence Freedman, *The Evolution of Nuclear Strategy* (New York: St. Martin's Press, 1981), pp. 246–247.

7. Fred A. Kaplan, *The Wizards of Armageddon* (New York: Simon and Schuster, Touchstone Books, 1983), pp. 320–324, discusses development of McNamara's skepticism about damage limitation strategies.

8. See Robert S. McNamara, *The Essence of Security: Reflections in Office* (New York: Harper & Row, 1968), for McNamara's recollections. Background and perspective are provided by William W. Kaufmann, *The McNamara Strategy* (New York: Harper & Row, 1964).

9. Paul Bracken, *The Command and Control of Nuclear Forces* (New Haven, Conn.: Yale University Press, 1983), passim.

10. Bruce G. Blair, *Strategic Command and Control: Redefining the Nuclear Threat* (Washington, D.C.: Brookings Institution, 1985); Desmond Ball, "Can Nuclear War Be Controlled?" Adelphi Papers No. 169 (London: International Institute for Strategic Studies, Autumn 1981).

11. Desmond Ball, "Counterforce Targeting: How New? How Viable?" *Arms Control Today* 11, no. 2 (February 1981), reprinted with revisions in John F. Reichart and Steven R. Sturm (eds.), *American Defense Policy* (Baltimore: Johns Hopkins University Press, 1982), pp. 227–234.

12. Lynn Etheridge Davis, "Limited Nuclear Options: Deterrence and the New American Doctrine," in Christoph Bertram (ed.), *Strategic Deterrence in a Changing Environment* (Montclair, N.J.: Allenheld, Osmun and Co., 1981), pp. 42–62.

13. Leon Sloss and Marc Dean Millot, "U.S. Nuclear Strategy in Evolution," *Strategic Review* (Winter 1984): 19–28.

14. Peter Pringle and William Arkin, *SIOP: The Secret U.S. Plan for Nuclear War* (New York: W.W. Norton, 1983), passim; Jeffrey Richelson, "PD-59, NSDD-13 and the Reagan Strategic Modernization Program," *Journal of Strategic Studies* 6, no. 2 (June 1983): 125–146.

15. White House, *The President's Strategic Defense Initiative* (Washington, D.C.: Government Printing Office, January 1985).

16. Paul H. Nitze, "On the Road to a More Stable Peace," in U.S. Department of State, *Current Policy*, no. 657, February 20, 1985, explains the administration's strategic concept.

17. Ibid.

18. Although the declaratory countervailing strategy called for protracted war fighting, capabilities to implement the strategy lagged. See Sloss and Millot, "U.S. Nuclear Strategy"; Colin S. Gray, *Nuclear Strategy and Strategic Planning* (Philadelphia: Foreign Policy Research Institute, 1984); Aaron L. Friedberg, "The Evolution of U.S. Strategic 'Doctrine'—1945 to 1981," in Samuel P. Huntington (ed.), *The Strategic Imperative: New Policies for National Security* (Cambridge, Mass.: Ballinger, 1983), pp. 53–99.

19. Ball, "Counterforce Targeting": Sloss and Millot, "U.S. Nuclear Strategy"; Christopher I. Branch, *Fighting a Long Nuclear War: A Strategy, Force, Policy Mismatch* (Washington, D.C.: National Defense University Press, 1984).

20. Thomas C. Schelling, *Arms and Influence* (New Haven: Yale University Press, 1966), pp. 106–107 and passim.

21. This is not the same as purely "accidental" war. See Paul Bracken, "Accidental Nuclear War," in Graham T. Allison, Albert Carnesale, and Joseph S. Nye, Jr., *Hawks, Doves and Owls: An Agenda for Avoiding Nuclear War* (New York: W.W. Norton, 1985), pp. 25–53. On the subject of wars beginning as a result of mistaken perceptions, see Robert Jervis, *Perception and Misperception in International Relations* (Princeton: Princeton University Press, 1976).

22. President's Commission on Strategic Forces (Scowcroft commission), *Report* (Washington, D.C.: Government Printing Office," April 1983).

23. Raymond L. Garthoff, "Mutual Deterrence, Parity and Strategic Arms Limitation in Soviet Policy," in Derek Leebaert (ed.), *Soviet Military Thinking* (London: Allen

and Unwin, 1981), pp. 92–124. See also Benjamin S. Lambeth, "How to Think about Soviet Military Doctrine," in Douglas J. Murray and Paul R. Viotti (eds.), *The Defense Policies of Nations* (Baltimore: Johns Hopkins University Press, 1982), pp. 146–163.

24. Sensible comments on this appear in Robert J. Art, "Between Assured Destruction and Nuclear Victory: The Case for the 'MAD-Plus' Posture," *Ethics* 95, no. 3 (April 1985): 497–516. See also Robert Jervis, "Why Nuclear Superiority Doesn't Matter," *Political Science Quarterly* 94, no. 4 (Winter 1979–1980): 617–633. Art and Jervis agree on mutual assured destruction as the basis of stability, but they differ on the utility of flexible nuclear targeting.

25. Ball, "Counterforce Targeting"; Sloss and Millot, "U.S. Nuclear Strategy"; Richelson, "PD-59."

26. This distinction appears in Richelson, "PD-59" and is reminiscent of an earlier proposal by Bruce M. Russett for a countercombatant deterrent.

27. On the Soviet command structure, see Harriet Fast and William F. Scott, *The Soviet Control Structure* (New York: Crane, Russak, 1983).

28. A point emphasized by Bracken, *Command and Control of Nuclear Forces.*

29. Graham T. Allison, *Essence of Decision: Explaining the Cuban Missile Crisis* (Boston: Little, Brown, 1971).

30. Irving L. Janis, *Groupthink: Psychological Studies of Policy Decisions and Fiascoes* (Boston: Houghton Mifflin, 1982), pp. 14–47, esp. pp. 40–44.

31. Communications with the U.S. SSBN force are discussed in Blair, *Strategic Command and Control*, pp. 198–201.

32. For perspective, see Richard L. Garwin, "Will Strategic Submarines Be Vulnerable?" *International Security* 8, no. 2 (Fall 1983): 52–67.

33. An example for the European theater is provided in Geoffrey Kemp, "Nuclear Forces for Medium Powers," in Bertram, *Strategic Deterrence*, pp. 116–189.

34. See Robert S. Norris, "Counterforce at Sea: The Trident II Missile," *Arms Control Today* (September 1985): 5–10. For counterpoint, see the article by Walter B. Slocombe, "Why We Need Counterforce at Sea," pp. 10–12, in the same issue.

35. Counterforce targets include nuclear and conventional forces and perhaps military headquarters that support those forces (also termed C^3) targets. On the difference between counterforce strategies designed to destroy capabilities and those to influence the intentions of the opponent, see Richard N. Rosecrance, "Strategic Deterrence Reconsidered," in Bertram, *Strategic Deterrence*, esp. p. 19.

36. Paul Nitze, "Assuring Strategic Stability in an Era of Detente," *Foreign Affairs* 54 (1976): 207–233. Both counterforce advocates and critics have frequently missed two important points about the Nitze scenario and its offspring. First, postattack counterforce discrepancy would be important only if the war could be terminated rapidly on some terms acceptable to both sides. Second, for the first to happen, survivable C^3 have got to be preserved on both sides, creating conflict between military and political logic under the most extreme tensions.

37. Raymond L. Garthoff, *Detente and Confrontation: American-Soviet Relations from Nixon to Reagan* (Washington, D.C.: Brookings Institution, 1985), p. 1031; Strobe Talbott, *Deadly Gambits* (New York: Alfred A. Knopf, 1984), provides extensive background.

38. Garthoff, *Detente and Confrontation*, p. 1031. Former Soviet Defense Minister Ustinov referred to the Pershing II as a "nuclear first-strike weapon," *Pravda*, July 31,

1983, p. 4. Soviet studies of command and control stress the importance of avoiding enemy preemption: for example, Army Gen. P. Lushev, "The Art of Command and Control," *Sovetskoye voyennoye obozreniye* (January 1983): 9–12 (translations by the U.S. Air Force).

39. Targeting silo-based MX may not be as easy as pessimists imagine. See Barry R. Schneider, "Soviet Uncertainties in Targeting Peacekeeper," in Schneider, Colin S. Gray, and Keith B. Payne (eds.), *Missiles for the Nineties* (Boulder, Colo.: Westview Press, 1984), pp. 109–134.

40. Defensive Technologies Study, *The Strategic Defense Initiative* (Washington, D.C.: Department of Defense, April 1984), unclassified summary.

41. Union of Concerned Scientists, *The Fallacy of Star Wars* (New York: Random House/Vintage Books, 1984).

42. See, for example, Freeman Dyson, *Weapons and Hope* (New York: Harper Colophon, 1985), pp. 73–84.

43. Nitze, "On the Road to a More Stable Peace."

44. Office of Technology Assessment, *Ballistic Missile Defense Technologies* (Washington, D.C.: Government Printing Office, September 1985), presents a balanced assessment of BMD technology prospects and expresses little optimism about eventual, comprehensive city protection.

45. Department of Defense notional multilayered BMD system is illustrated in Keith B. Payne, *Strategic Defense: Star Wars in Perspective* (Lanham, Md.: Hamilton Press, 1986), p. 93.

46. Office of Technology Assessment, *Anti-Satellite Weapons, Countermeasures and Arms Control* (Washington, D.C.: Government Printing Office, September 1985).

47. Paul B. Stares, *The Militarization of Space: U.S. Policy, 1945–84* (Ithaca, N.Y.: Cornell University Press, 1985), pp. 150–156.

48. According to the U.S. State Department, SDI is designed to improve deterrence rather than to replace it: "Successful SDI research and development of defense options would not lead to abandonment of deterrence but rather to an enhancement of deterrence and an evolution in the weapons of deterrence through the contribution of defensive systems that threaten no one." U.S. Department of State, *The Strategic Defense Initiative*, Special Report No. 129 (June 1985), p. 5.

49. U.S. strategy choices and their relationship to defense capability levels are summarized in Office of Technology Assessment, *Ballistic Missile Defense Technologies*, pp. 290–291. Current U.S. countervailing strategy requires at least survivable C^3.

50. Scowcroft Commission, *Report*, p. 6.

5

The Soviet Arms Control Compliance Record

Gary L. Guertner

A rms control negotiations and occasional treaty successes (eleven bilateral agreements since 1963) have become the keystone in Soviet-American relations. The danger of nuclear war, spiraling arms competition, and domestic politics has worked to maintain their centrality, even in an administration that has often sought to downgrade the importance of arms control in favor of strategic modernization programs and a tough stance against Soviet policies. The major thrust of the anti–arms control faction in the Reagan administration and Congress has rested on Soviet noncompliance with existing arms control agreements. The Soviets, it is argued, cannot be trusted, have cheated in the past, and plan to do so in the future. Arms control is a one-way street that leads only to Soviet advantages while lulling Americans into a false sense of complacency.

This chapter examines the extensive debate over arms control compliance issues during the Reagan administration. Is arms control a viable process? Can it remain a critical component in Soviet-American relations? How accurate are the administration's charges of Soviet noncompliance? To answer these questions, this study will focus on the three agreements that have played the most important regulatory function in the Soviet-American strategic relationship: SALT I, SALT II, and the ABM Treaty. Soviet noncompliance will be measured against three competing images in the public debate about whether the Soviets honor their commitments: deliberate cheating, bureaucratic structure and process, and conflicting interpretations of treaty obligations. Which of these images one accepts quite clearly affects the desirability of entering into agreements with the Soviets in the future.

The data will be drawn primarily from the congressionally mandated White House reports on Soviet noncompliance and the political debate surrounding those reports. Public Law 99-145 (FY 1984 Arms Control and Disarmament Act) requires the president to submit classified and unclassified reports by December 1 of each year. While a complete evaluation of Soviet noncompliance

An earlier version of this chapter appeared in *Political Science Quarterly*.

is impossible when limited to unclassified data, even those with access to both reports have not always been able to reach a consensus on the scope of Soviet violations. Conflicting interpretations divide members of Congress and members of the arms control bureaucracies within the executive branch despite their access to classified data and analysis.

This should not be surprising. Noncompliance is a conclusion drawn from the analyses of complex monitoring activities by the intelligence community and comparing Soviet behavior against treaty obligations. Intelligence data may be ambiguous relative to the legal complexities of treaty language. Intelligence ambiguity and legal complexity are hardly the characteristics of a process that cuts cleanly through rigidly held political and ideological views of the Soviet Union or arms control. Perceptions that the United States is letting its guard down through arms control negotiations is certain to push the noncompliance debate to the front of the arms control agenda.

This assessment is designed to cut through the noncompliance debate, isolating what may be known from the often misleading political debate and selective intelligence leaks from beaureaucratic insurgents bent on scoring political points at strategic times (for example, negotiating compromises or ratification debates). The purpose is neither to indict nor apologize for Soviet practices. The real questions are whether strategic arms control is a viable process through which U.S. security interests can be served and whether existing or more intrusive means of verification will result in a more quiescent opposition to future Soviet-American arms control regimes.

The compliance debate has become a central part of Soviet-American relations for two reasons. First, the Reagan administration has linked future treaties to Soviet acceptance of more intrusive (a code word for on-site inspection) means of verification, as found in the INF Treaty. The more ambitious is the proposal—50 percent reductions in strategic forces, or zero ballistic missiles—the more elaborate is the verification regime. Second, the Reagan administration has built a case for Soviet noncompliance and has adopted it to the principle of proportionate response. Proportionate response is based on a principle of international law that recognizes the right of one party to take action against the other in response to a material breach of an agreement. The administration has argued that since the Soviet Union has breached several existing arms control agreements, including its political commitment to honor the unratified SALT II Treaty, the United States has the right to abandon its own pledge not to undercut SALT II and to take compensatory steps to protect its security. In practice this has led to the abandonment of SALT II weapons ceilings and a more permissive interpretation of the ABM Treaty, combined with an open debate on the virtues of abrogating that treaty in favor of extensive testing and deployment of spaced-based BMD. Such radical departures from these agreements leave the administration with a political and legal responsibility to establish beyond a reasonable doubt that new departures are based on solid evidence of Soviet noncompliance. The administration position is captured in image 1:

Image 1: The Soviets engage in a well-orchestrated strategy of noncompliance to gain unilateral military advantage over the United States.

Testing this thesis requires careful examination of specific U.S. allegations, a comparison of noncompliant with compliant behavior, and an assessment of comparative military gains and losses that may result from decisions to comply or push beyond legitimate treaty boundaries. Military gains can be assessed against three specific criteria:

1. Does it contribute to a deployed military capability or alter the strategic balance?
2. Does it improve a breakout capability by shortening deployment schedules?
3. Does it undermine the predictability of Soviet strategic modernization programs?

Image 2: Soviet bureaucratic politics and standard operational procedures (SOPs) create an environment of resistance, subjective interpretation, and imperfect oversight of arms control obligations.

Image 3: Charges of Soviet noncompliance stem from genuine differences of interpretation of treaty language and obligations.

The strength and validity of image 1, on which the Reagan administration has based its case for Soviet noncompliance, can be tested against images 2 and 3. Both tend to see a more compliant pattern of Soviet behavior. For this reason, as well as their close functional relationships, images 2 and 3 will be examined together.

Image 2 incorporates bureaucratic politics and the SOPs followed by the Communist party, the Soviet military, and the strategic forces research and development infrastructure during the development, testing, and deployment phases of strategic weapons. Within many of these organizations and their sub-bureaucracies, the saliency of arms control concerns is almost certainly lower than are the broad priorities of Soviet defense policy.

The tone from the top can also set the overall standards for officials responsible for ensuring the compliance of their subordinate organizations. Leonid Brezhnev established a loose constructionist standard in his statement to Richard Nixon during the 1972 Moscow Summit when he indicated that everything not expressly prohibited by SALT I was permitted.[1] Unlike their American counterparts, Soviet bureaucracies lack the highly developed legal sieve through which their decisions on what may be permitted must pass. The process of legal counsel available to the U.S. State Department, Arms Control and Disarmament Agency, Department of Defense agencies, and congressional oversight committees is far more centralized in the Soviet Union and may often be more restricted by Soviet walls of secrecy and compartmentalized systems of information. It is well established that Soviet lawyers, most of whom are attached to the Treaty and Legal Administration of the Foreign Ministry, serve the post facto role of legitimizing party decisions and less the watchdog function of their American counterparts. Such a system is prone to exploit the gray areas, and its actions may result in de facto violations but not in the sense that they are coherent policies or preplanned Politburo decisions to gain military advantage. Actions may be the result of subjective and uncoordinated bureaucratic players.

It is also worth noting that Soviet bureaucratic routines may have gone through a period of either reduced oversight or competitive interpretations by rival factions during the last years of Brezhnev's life and the long period of maneuvering for succession that lasted until Gorbachev consolidated his power. The most serious compliance issues—Krasnoyarsk, encryption, and the SS-25 mobile ICBM—occurred near the end of the Brezhnev era. Raising arms control compliance issues in the face of a highly competitive party structure and during the early, most combative period of the Reagan administration could not have seemed wise or proper to most self-interested Soviet bureaucrats.[2]

Image 3 is far less complex and assumes that considerable room for disagreement can develop from nearly any contractual agreement. To use a domestic analogy, tens of thousands of American lawyers earn comfortable livings from contractual disputes between parties who discover that agreements that seemed clear-cut grow ambiguous in practice.

Soviet writings available in the West have not attempted to share arms control compliance guidelines that may be available to responsible bureaucrats. Soviet general attitudes toward monitoring have been discussed, however, and their basic principles vary considerably from those found in American discussions. For American negotiators, monitoring Soviet activities and verifying compliance is the vital substitute for mutual trust. Effective verification distinguishes the arms control process from the more utopian calls for world disarmament.

The Soviets themselves are concerned with verification, but they approach the problems with the traditional Russian passion for maintaining secrecy from the prying eyes of a hostile world. The basic principles spelled out by the Soviets argue that the means of verification must be "limited," "in no way prejudice the sovereign rights of states," should not be built upon the principle of "total mistrust," and should take into account the deterrence effect of the risk of detection by modern, sophisticated intelligence capabilities.[3]

To Soviet elites, the mutually agreed upon national technical means of monitoring Soviet territory and exchanges of previously classified data during SALT I and II were intrusive, if not revolutionary. One Soviet official is said to have remarked of these provisions, "There goes 400 years of Russian history."[4]

It would be no surprise, then, to discover that decision makers were more faithful to tradition than to the demands for sharing military information.

Determining when the political decisions were made that set disputed programs in motion is critical to this analysis. Certainly the decision dates for the three major issues would have preceded the signing of SALT II. Both parties attempted with great success to protect strategic modernization programs from arms control restrictions. How Soviet bureaucracies responded after 1979 is unknown. This period was the last chance to align programs with treaty obligations through what has been described by Dimitri Simes as an "informal" interagency process.[5] This process, whether formal or informal, would have taken place in the midst of both a growing succession struggle in the Communist party of the Soviet Union (CPSU) and deteriorating Soviet-American relations. During this period, the CPSU's Politburo struggled to sustain the pretense that a faltering trio—Brezhnev, Andropov, and Chernenko—were functioning national leaders. This struggle is difficult to reconcile with preplanned cheating and deception directed from the top.

It was clear even before the Reagan victory in 1980 that SALT II was not going to be ratified. The period between 1980 and the spring of 1982—when both sides pledged not to undercut the provision of the SALT II treaty—may have been a decisive phase inside the Soviet government for arms control compliance issues. Strict constructionist positions that went beyond "reasonable" Soviet interpretations of treaty obligations would have found a poor reception in the midst of competitive oversight produced by the struggle for successive party leadership.

The transformation of treaty language into actions by rival Soviet decision makers through self-interested bureaucracies during a period of growing U.S. hostility certainly played a role in Soviet compliance behavior. The precise mechanics of Soviet decision making are unknown in the West, but some general propositions can be explored on the basis of what is known about broader issues in the nuclear weapons decision-making process.

While there is widespread agreement that the Politburo is the center of political decision making in the Soviet Union, the complex machinations that take place beneath that body are clouded in secrecy. For example, the agenda for the Politburo is prepared by the party Secretariat, an administrative body that normally includes at least three Politburo members. Does this overlapping membership mean that many issues have been effectively resolved and decisions drafted in advance of Politburo meetings? Does the Secretariat represent just one of many potential sources of influence? Are the overlapping members divided among themselves over basic issues?[6]

A second organization, the Defense Council, also has a membership drawn from the Politburo. From fragmentary evidence in Soviet sources, this body appears to review or coordinate defense-related activities, including military development and arms control.[7]

The Military-Industrial Commission, a state organization controlled by the Presidium of the Council of Ministers, appears to have major responsibilities in weapons research and development and in controlling the system of scientific and technical information serving the defense sector. As a clearinghouse for technical information, the commission could play an important role in the internal arms control compliance debate. It is also worth noting that like the party Secretariat and the Defense Council, the Presidium includes Politburo members. The overlapping but not necessarily identical membership was intended to strengthen Politburo oversight and control. In practice it also gives rival party members access to powerful bureaucratic resources that can be mobilized in times of domestic or foreign policy crises.

The state Ministry of Defense has the primary responsibilities for the design and production of weapons and military equipment. The Soviet General Staff is subordinated directly to the minister of defense for the coordination of all the various service programs and activities. All evidence indicates that the General Staff of the armed forces is an extremely important player in arms control decision making. Its members are the major source of information for the Defense Council and represent a mediating body between top political leadership and the military. The General Staff has played an active, if not central, role in arms control negotiations through participation with the Defense Council, Politburo, and direct representation on the SALT and START delegations.[8]

The Ministry of Foreign Affairs has administrative responsibilities for the actual conduct of arms control negotiations, thus creating yet another layer of bureaucracy with possible compliance oversight responsibilities. Treaty compliance debates may pass through all or only selected participants in these and other complex Soviet organizations. We do not know the precise mechanics of Soviet arms control compliance. What is clear, however, is that rival factions in the party have access to complex bureaucratic machinery managed by self-interested organizations. One of the lessons to be learned is that U.S. negotiators should not resolve arms control deadlocks by falling back on ambiguous language that may later be exploited by Soviet domestic or bureaucratic factions.

The Charges

In January 1984, the administration sent to Congress the first in a series of mandated reports that concluded that there had been an "expanding pattern of Soviet violations" of arms control agreements. The administration submitted three follow-on noncompliance reports (in February and December 1985 and in January 1987), and the Arms Control and Disarmament Agency has published two additional reports of its own (in October 1984 and February 1986).[9]

The number of violations and the language used to characterize them have gone through considerable change (table 5–1). These changes suggest interagency

Table 5–1
President's Reports to Congress on Soviet Noncompliance with SALT I, SALT II, and the ABM Treaty

		Conclusions			
Issues	*Treaty*	*January 1984 Report*	*February 1985 Report*	*December 1985 Report*	*March 1987 Report*
Impeding verification by encryption of missile test telemetry	SALT II	Violation	Violation	Violation	SALT I
SS-25 as a violation of the one new-type ICBM provision	SALT II	Probable violation	Violation	Violation	and
Ban against SS-16 testing, production, or deployment	SALT II	Probable violation	Probable violation	Probable removal of SS-16 equipment	SALT II deleted;
Strategic nuclear delivery vehicles exceed the 2,504 cap	SALT II	—	—	Violation	U.S. no
Impeding verification by concealing the association between an ICBM and its launcher	SALT II	—	—	Violation	longer bound by
Use of dismantled SS-7 sites for support of SS-25	SALT I	—	No violation	Violation	these
Reconfiguration of one Yankee SSBN for use as a cruise missile carrier	SALT I	—	No violation	—	limits
Krasnoyarsk radar	ABM	Almost certainly a violation	Violation	Violation	Violation
Development of mobile ABM system or components	ABM	—	Potential violation	Potential violation	Potential violation
Concurrent testing of ABM and SAM components	ABM	—	Probably has violated	Probably has violated	Probably has violated
Aggregate ABM activities provide base for territorial defense	ABM	—	May be preparing	May be preparing	May be preparing
Tested a SAM system or component as an ABM	ABM	—	—	Insufficient to assess	Insufficient to assess
Rapid reload of ABM launchers	ABM	—	—	Ambiguous situation	Ambiguous situation

conflict over the strength of new evidence and some new interpretations of old data. The president's reports to Congress conclude that there is "a pattern of Soviet noncompliance," although the body of these reports contains ambiguities that may not support such a conclusion. For example, their language and categories make it nearly impossible to aggregate data in any "clear pattern." The reports discuss "issues," "violations," "probable violations," "likely violations," "potential violations," and two questionable "cases" where the Soviets were found to be "in compliance." These categories are subdivided into classified and unclassified "issues."

The specific discussions of issues and violations are equally confusing. The December 1985 report, for example, lists six issues of concern about the ABM Treaty. Issues 1–5 end with the finding that the "USSR may be preparing an ABM defense of its national territory." Issue 6 is titled "ABM Territorial Defense" and simply repeats the closing lines and several arguments of the previous five issues as a separate issue. Adding to the confusion is the fact that the case for possible Soviet noncompliance with the prohibited development of a territorial ABM defense is based on issues 1–5. Only issue 1, the Krasnoyarsk radar, is listed as a violation. The remaining four issues are labeled, respectively, "potential violation," "probably has violated," "insufficient to assess," and "ambiguous situation." The March 1987 noncompliance reports centers on these ABM Treaty issues. SALT II was deleted from the report as part of the policy ending U.S. adherence to the SALT limitations.

The March 1987 report also introduced a new element in the efforts to assert that the Soviets were preparing a nationwide missile defense system. Three new Soviet radars were reportedly under construction on the western borders of the Soviet Union. The Defense Department contended that these new radars were redundant with existing radars and appeared to be part of a missile tracking capability for an ABM system. State, ACDA, and the CIA did not fully support this interpretation, pointing out that the radars seemed to be replacements for radars deployed in the 1960s. One radar could be intended to provide warning of attack by U.S. Pershing II missiles deployed in the Federal Republic of Germany. Whatever their purpose, these radars are among the first legally deployed systems that defense officials have attempted to associate with a major treaty violation. Skeptics believe that the issue may have more to do with administration efforts to break out of ABM constraints on SDI testing than with actual Soviet behavior.[10]

These examples of the administration's noncompliance reporting to Congress, and the interagency conflicts responsible for producing the often vague language with which they are written, illustrate why the debate has often been confusing and frustrating to those who seek corrective actions. Confusing data and multiple categories of noncompliance have been amplified inaccurately by members of Congress and the news media. Cautious or inconclusive language were often collapsed into a single measure of Soviet duplicity. Analysts look in vain for any two sources that have cited the same number of Soviet violations. Part of the problem has been a failure to examine carefully what Soviet military incentives might be in a deliberate cheating scenario and how those same objectives may be affected by uncontested Soviet compliance with the major provisions of SALT I, SALT II, and the ABM Treaty.

The Evidence

Table 5–2 summarizes the six issues on which the administration has concluded violations have occurred. Competing images and the potential military significance of Soviet noncompliance will be limited to these issues.

Encryption of ICBM Test Data

Image 1: Encryption is the coding of radio transmissions or telemetry from a test missile to its control stations.[11] These test data are a vital part of all research and development programs. They are essential to the testing party in determining whether a system meets operational requirements and to an arms control partner in verifying compliance with treaty commitments. Neither party wishes to reveal more information than is required by specific treaty provisions. In the case of SALT II, encryption is allowed except when it "impedes" verification. How much encryption shields sensitive test data while communicating treaty compliant data is determined by the testing party. The failure of the SALT II treaty to establish clearly how and when encryption impedes verification left an ambiguity that the Soviets have fully exploited.

The United States has accused the Soviets of heavily encrypting telemetry broadcasts during tests of their SS-24 and SS-25 ICBMs, as well as a new SLBM, the SS-N-20. These practices impede U.S. verification of Soviet compliance with the SALT II Treaty. The president's reports to Congress concluded that Soviet concealment activities presented special obstacles to maintaining existing arms control agreements and undermined the political confidence necessary for concluding new treaties.[12]

Images 2 and 3: The Soviets reportedly began encrypting signals from their missile tests in the mid-1970s when they learned through espionage of the sophistication of U.S. satellite monitoring capabilities. The technological capabilities for encryption devices demonstrated prior to SALT II required a long lead time for production and deployment aboard test missiles.[13] The issue from within the responsible Soviet bureaucracies was what modifications would be required in Soviet encryption capabilities and practices after SALT II.

Part of this difficult and technical question has to do with the relationship between legal encryption and the SALT II obligation not to impede verification.

Table 5–2
Competing Images of Soviet Noncompliance

Issues[a]	Image 1: Military Significance of Deliberate Cheating			Image 2: Bureaucratic Culture and SOPs	Image 3: Conflicting Interpretations of Treaty Obligations
	Strategic Balance, Stability	*Breakout Potential*	*Undermines Predictability*		
Encryption of test data	No significance at SALT II levels	Marginal depending on other monitoring capabilities	Yes	Tradition of secrecy Complex encryption capabilities standard on all test missiles Compliance oversight difficult in complex compartmentalized bureaucracies	Other means of data collection available Treaty requires minimal uncoded signals No collection from third country territory
SS-25 as a second new-type ICBM	Potentially stabilizing with mobile basing and single warhead	No impact with single warhead	No	Loose constructionist approach to complex treaty language	SS-25 falls within SALT compliant boundaries
SNDV ceiling exceeded	No significant impact at SALT II levels	No significant impact at SALT II levels	No	No final agreements on bomber dismantlement/conversion SOPs	Soviet ceilings fall within agreed limits U.S. failure to ratify SALT II changes Soviet obligations

Krasnoyarsk radar	Significant only as part of a territorial defense	Contributes to more rapid deployment of territorial defense	Yes	Definition influenced by logistical and geographic problems of construction	Implied guilt, Soviets willing to negotiate issue
Launcher/ICBM association	No significance	Marginal at existing launcher/warhead ceilings	Yes	Vague issue; poor oversight of test SOPs	Agree on treaty provision/may disagree test SOPs are a violation
Activities at old SS-7 sites	No significance at SALT II levels	No	No	Considerable savings to use old infrastructure for new mobile missiles	Disagree there is a violation
					Define "facilities" differently from U.S.
					Issue is not applicable to mobile ICBMs

aThese six issues were the confirmed violations listed in the president's reports to Congress.

Monitoring missile telemetry, like satellite photography, includes a high degree of overlap between its verification and intelligence-gathering functions. What we would like to learn about Soviet missiles and what SALT II requires the Soviets to give us are two separate and often controversial issues.

The Soviets have never agreed that access to telemetry is necessary for verification. They maintain that other national technical means are capable of verifying the relationship between Soviet ICBMs and treaty obligations.[14] When this issue came up during the SALT II negotiations, the Soviets resisted. Eventually they gave in to U.S. pressure but with the proviso that it not require them to alter existing practices. American negotiators rejected this line, noting that encryption was already hampering the intelligence gathering (it became "verification" after the treaty) of provisions then under negotiation.[15] The final compromise was based on the limited data required to verify the new-type ICBM provision. Neither side would engage in "deliberate" denial of telemetric information "whenever" such denial impedes verification of compliance. A total ban on encryption was unacceptable to the Soviets. A specific list of data requirements would have opened far too much discussion of U.S. intelligence techniques and procedures. The vague compromise in treaty language has resulted in persistent U.S. charges of Soviet noncompliance.

The fact that the Soviets encrypt data to a substantial degree is troubling but does not automatically constitute a violation. As the staff report to the SALT II Treaty pointed out, no criteria for determining when encryption impedes verification were ever established.[16] Nor have subsequent negotiations at the SCC, established by the ABM Treaty as a forum for regular discussion and resolution of verification problems and disputes, been successful in working out specific procedures. For example, during a series of twenty ICBM test flights, must data be transmitted in the clear from all twenty tests? Some tests? How many tests? How many data? The SCC has become deadlocked on the issue. Soviet negotiators have asked U.S. officials to explain what aspects of verification have been impeded. The United States has refused to present the Soviets with a model of treaty-compliant behavior because such specifics might compromise U.S. intelligence capabilities.[17] The dilemma is an exact replay of the original—and unfortunate—SALT II compromise that failed to specify what data were required to verify Soviet compliance.

The Soviet leadership is unlikely to modify existing test procedures as long as the United States refuses to discuss the details of what it considers adequate compliance. It would be difficult for them to reconcile U.S. demand with the position apparently taken by their technical specialists and the military that "other means" of verification are available to determine the very selective performance data that the United States is entitled to have under existing treaty provisions.

An additional complication arises from the extensive deployment of U.S. monitoring stations on the territories of its allies. The Soviet Union has never accepted third-country monitoring sites as legitimate "national technical means."[18] In practice this means that they need not respect limitations on interfering with the operations of such stations and may believe that early boost phase (first 100 kilometers) telemetry can be totally encrypted.

The SS-25 ICBM

Image 1: In an attempt to limit the development and deployment of new, more capable ICBMs, the provisions of SALT II permit each side to test and deploy just one "new type." For the United States this was the MX; the Soviets designated the SS-25 as their new missile. By almost any definition except one, the SS-25 ICBM is a second new missile, and not, as the Soviets claim, a permissible follow-on to the SS-13. The one exception may be the SALT II definition of "new type."

This compliance controversy has grown out of a combination of complex treaty provisions and inadequate monitoring capabilities for those provisions. For example, both sides wished to maintain the right to modernize their existing missile inventories (for example, new warheads and improved guidance systems). Exactly when a new or modernized missile became a new type was spelled out in detail. Treaty language defines a new type as any missile that would change an existing missile's fuel type, number of stages or, by 5 percent or more, its length, largest diameter, launch weight, or throw weight. An additional provision precludes the deployment of a new single-warhead ICBM if the warhead weight is less than half the overall throw weight. The intention of the latter provision was to prevent the sudden emergence of multiwarhead missiles.

When the United States first detected testing of the missile in early 1983, American intelligence concluded that it was a new type based on estimates of its dimensions, throw weight, and warhead weight. U.S. officials concede, however, that their data base on the SS-13 is poor and incomplete.[19]

Images 2 and 3: The first problem that image 1 or 2 analysis encounters with the SS-25 ICBM issue is in establishing an accurate accounting methodology. Administration reports claim:

The SS-25 is an illegal second new-type ICBM.

The weight of its warhead is less than 50 percent of its total throw weight (thereby posing an illegal threat of a MIRV-capable ICBM).

The Soviets have encrypted vital data during its test flights.

The Soviets conceal the relationship between the SS-25 ICBM and its launcher.

The Soviets have used "remaining facilities" at former SS-7 ICBM sites to support SS-25 activities.

Does the SS-25 represent one or five violations, or is it one issue that violates five provisions of SALT I and II? The most serious issue is the missile's legality as a modernization or follow-on to the SS-13 rather than a second, illegal new-type ICBM. This issue rests on a controversial Soviet definition of throw weight. They have argued at the SCC in Geneva that a device, which normally would be considered part of a missile's throw weight, is attached to the SS-13 missile's third stage. The United States has not included this device in its estimates of SS-13 throw weight. The results have been a consistently undervalued throw weight for the SS-13, which in turn has produced an SS-25 data base that exceeds the SALT II 5 percent provision for ICBM modernization. The Soviets, as a result of this alleged SS-13 testing procedure, claim that the throw weight of the SS-25 is actually less than that of the SS-13.

The second SS-25 violation, the testing and deployment of a single reentry vehicle that weighs less than 50 percent of an ICBMs total throw weight, has also been denied by the Soviets. They have argued that during testing, they have attached a heavy instrumentation package that increases the missile's throw weight and thereby decreases the reentry vehicle's percentage of the total throw weight. According to the Soviets, when a deployed SS-25 is tested without this package, the missile complies with the treaty.[20] The Soviets commonly test operational missiles, and, depending on their degree of encryption or alternate U.S. monitoring capabilities, this part of the controversy could eventually be resolved.

Krasnoyarsk Radar

Image 1: Krasnoyarsk could be remembered by historians as the central Siberian birthplace of the late Soviet leader, Konstantin Chernenko. Instead its notoriety in the West is the result of the Krasnoyarsk Radar Station and consensus violation of the ABM Treaty.

Discovered by U.S. intelligence in 1983, the radar's single face looks across 6,000 miles of Soviet territory toward the northern Pacific. When completed, the radar will have the appearance and capability of other Soviet early warning radars already operational along the Soviet periphery. These radars comply with the ABM Treaty because they are located on the edge of Soviet national territory and are sited outward. The Krasnoyarsk location, if not its function, however, violates the intention of the ABM Treaty to restrict radars, especially large phased-array radars capable of legitimate early warning and prohibited ABM battle management missions. Restricting radar locations was the best solution to the problems of limiting a technology with both legitimate and proscribed missions. Radars are especially sensitive ABM components because they play a critical role and require a long lead time for construction if the Soviets planned to develop a territorial defense in violation of the ABM Treaty.

Images 2 and 3: The Soviets have countered U.S. claims of noncompliance by asserting that the radar is a treaty-compliant space-tracking station, and this will become clear to U.S. observers when the radar begins operations. The issue underlines the great difficulties in negotiating functional limitations on versatile technologies. Even so, the Soviets have tacitly admitted doubts on the strength of their position by offering to stop construction at Krasnoyarsk if the United States will do the same at Thule, Greenland, the site of a nearly thirty-year-old early warning radar currently undergoing extensive modernization, which some former U.S. officials have argued is also a violation of the ABM Treaty.[21] Whether the Soviets have raised the U.S. radar at Thule as an analogy to defend themselves or to find a face-saving compromise is uncertain. The larger issue is why and how the decision was made to locate the radar at Krasnoyarsk.

Krasnoyarsk fills the last gap in the Soviet early warning radar system. Difficult lessons may have been learned from Soviet experience with earlier radar construction. Building along the northern periphery of the Soviet Union may have been more expensive and more difficult than imagined. They may also have discovered that in actual operation, these radars had a narrow field of vision. Filling the last gap in northeastern Siberia may have required two radars distant from existing rail or road networks. A decision to build on the periphery of the existing Soviet logistical support base could have seemed appropriate, even logical, to those involved during the declining years of Brezhnev and the ascendancy of the Reagan administration.

Even the most extreme loose constructionist model of Soviet compliance decision making has difficulty in accommodating an expenditure as large as Krasnoyarsk. Nevertheless, if the conditions described above are valid, the gambit may have seemed worth the risk, particularly if it were not accompanied by a larger scheme to break out of the ABM Treaty. Any such long-range plan, if it existed at all, would most probably have been devised within the bureaucratic subculture (party-military hardliners, for example) rather than by an enfeebled Politburo undergoing the first of three leadership successions in almost as many years. The ABM Treaty, however, makes no provisions for such practical problems or internal political friction. The radar is the most convincing issue in the president's noncompliance reports.

Exceeding the Strategic Nuclear Delivery Vehicle Limits of SALT II

Image 1: This complex issue arises from the logical and reasonable assumption that the 1982 mutual pledge to abide by the major provisions of the SALT II Treaty includes some numerical ceiling on the deployed numbers of strategic nuclear delivery vehicles (SNDV). U.S. ratification of the treaty, however, was the only means of activating the specified SNDV ceilings. Without ratification, no explicit agreement exists on the numerical value of a launcher ceiling.[22] The United States has used 2,504 as the aggregate number to which the Soviets have politically committed themselves because that number was in effect in 1979 when the SALT II Treaty was signed. In its December 1985 noncompliance report, the administration concluded that the Soviets were in violation by exceeding that number. The administration's case is based on Soviet activities between September 1981, when the United States informed the Soviets that it would not seek to ratify SALT II, and the 1982 mutual political commitment to abide by the treaty. During this period, the Soviet Union deployed additional SNDVs, and those activities continued through 1984 and 1985, including the destruction of older SS-11 launchers and silos as new SS-25s were deployed. Bear H cruise missile–carrying bombers were also deployed, but older bombers were not destroyed in sufficient numbers to compensate. The net effect was to maintain their SNDV count at a level slightly above the 2,504 ceiling claimed as binding by the United States.[23]

Images 2 and 3: Whether the Soviet Union has violated the implicit SALT II limits on SNDVs depends on how the data are interpreted for strategic bomber forces. The procedures for dismantling or converting bomber aircraft to aerial refueling tankers have been drafted but not completed by the SCC. The lack of specific agreement on bomber dismantling procedures, combined with uncontested Soviet compliance with the dismantlement of other strategic weapons, raises serious questions about the strength of the U.S. case. The president's reports fail to note that as new Soviet strategic systems have been deployed, older systems (nearly 1,300) have been retired.[24] Missile silos have been destroyed; missiles and submarines have been cut up according to SALT II procedures.

The Joint Chiefs of Staff have also reported that the tail sections of fifteen Bison bombers were cut off as the Soviets deployed new Bear H cruise missile carriers.[25] At issue are approximately thirty Bison bombers that were converted to aerial fuel tankers but that the United States still counts as operational bombers.[26] The Soviets, while not publicly stating their case, may believe that these newly converted tankers are no longer SALT accountable and in the same category as other Bison tankers that were formally exempted from SALT II limits. Even with the unresolved tanker issue, the administration claims that the Soviet SNDV ceiling varied between 2,504 and 2,540 during 1985, with the most recent figure set at 2,520–sixteen over the U.S. claimed ceiling.[27] If the drafted bomber-tanker conversion procedures were signed at the SCC, the SALT-accountable Soviet limits would drop to 2,490, or fourteen below their permitted limits. If an alleged violation can be resolved at the SCC through formal agreement on bomber dismantlement and conversion procedures already in draft form, its credibility in the image 1 cheating scenario is substantially reduced.[28]

Launcher and ICBM Association

Image 1: SALT II prohibits "deliberate concealment measures which impede verification by national technical means," including activities that conceal the association between an ICBM and its launcher during testing. For example, is a missile being launched from a silo or a mobile launcher? Precision is required for counting launchers, identifying them, and differentiating them from launchers of missiles that are not limited by the treaty—SS-20 mobile, intermediate-range missiles, for example.

The administration's December 1985 compliance report added this issue for the first time. Without spelling out the details, the report concludes that the SS-25 test series have violated SALT II provisions by concealing the relationship between the missile and its launcher.[29] A statement by the Soviet government that the SS-25 has a mobile launcher has not been judged sufficient to relieve the Soviets of their obligation to allow the United States independent access to make its own judgment on the issue.

Images 2 and 3: This is the fourth issue involving the SS-25 ICBM. The concealment of the relationship between the missile and its launcher described under image 1 would have potential military significance if the Soviets had declared their intent to deploy the SS-25 in silos. A case could then be made that perhaps the Soviets might attempt covert deployment of mobile missiles. However, since the Soviets have not only declared but have already deployed the SS-25 on mobile launchers, which are presumably distinguishable from other Soviet mobile launchers, the issue has no military relevance.

The degree to which Soviet SOPs at the SS-25 test range may violate concealment prohibitions in SALT II represents a principle worth calling to the attention of Soviet leaders, but it is not an issue that would have likely been directed or controlled from the top. Image 2 offers the most likely explanation of Soviet actions. Responsible bureaucrats may have attempted to conceal something. They could just have easily assumed that U.S. satellites could see burn marks and debris associated with missile launchers from silos or test pads.

Use of Remaining Facilities at Former SS-7 Sites

Image 1: Soviet activities at some former SS-7 ICBM sites became the single SALT I issue to be upgraded from "no violation" to "violation" in the December 1985 report. SALT I prohibited the use of certain facilities remaining at dismantled or destroyed ICBM sites in order to prevent the rapid reactivation of old sites. Construction activity during 1984 and 1985 at retired SS-7 sites was judged to be incorporating remaining facilities in support of the deployment and operation of new SS-25 mobile ICBMs.

SALT I and the procedures for dismantling ICBMs negotiated in the SCC established two major criteria for determining whether the use of a structure remaining at any former SS-7 sites would be a violation. For this purpose, "structure" must meet the definition of a "facility," and the "facility" must be used for storage, support, or launch of ICBMs.[30]

The administration's December 1985 compliance report and the 1986 ACDA report found the Soviets in compliance with their destruction and deactivation of SS-7 missiles and launch sites. However, both reports concluded that a number of surviving facilities were being used in support of SS-25 mobile ICBMs.

Images 2 and 3: This fifth and final issue related to the SS-25 ICBM is the one issue most clearly explained by image 3. There is a sharp disagreement between the parties over this SALT I issue. The Soviets maintain that any remaining facilities at former SS-7 ICBM sites used in support of SS-25 activities are legal because the provision did not apply to mobile missiles. Even when mobile missiles are brought into the debate, it can be argued that the SS-25 is being deployed in self-sufficient support bases similar to SS-20 intermediate-range missiles. Remaining SS-7 facilities are treaty compliant and support construction and logistical functions for the SS-25 bases but not for "storage," "support," or launch of ICBMs. Even if the issue were more ambiguous than it seems, powerful forces in the Soviet bureaucracy would find it attractive to cut costs by integrating as much existing infrastructure as possible into Soviet strategic modernizations programs.

Military Significance of Noncompliance Issues

The available evidence supports conclusions that vary significantly from official noncompliance reports to Congress. One important test of images 2 and 3 is to assess the military significance of each charge. Is there a pattern? Does that pattern suggest a well-orchestrated strategy of noncompliance to gain unilateral military advantage over the United States? If Soviet activities have resulted in no significant military advantages, the case for alternative interpretations of the evidence becomes more compelling.

Table 5–3 summarizes the military significance of the six "confirmed" violations. Together these violations suggest no clear pattern that strengthens Soviet strategic posture in any one of the three criteria for significant military behavior. Soviet behavior can be explained through a combination of political, technical, and legal motivations. The violations described here are such blatant acts that they cannot be called cheating in the usual sense of clandestine activities to gain a military advantage or strategic surprise. Even if the Soviets were exploiting the plausible denial that often results from vague treaty language and imperfect monitoring capabilities, the military benefits are marginal in comparison with the political damage to overall Soviet-American relations.

Table 5–3
Military Significance of Soviet Noncompliance

Issues[a]	Strategic Balance, Stability	Breakout Potential	Undermines Predictability
Encryption of test data	No significance at SALT II levels	Marginal depending on other monitoring capabilities	Yes
SS-25 as a second new-type ICBM	Potentially stabilizing with mobile basing and single warhead	No impact with single warhead	No
SNDV ceiling exceeded	No significant impact at SALT II levels	No significant impact at SALT II levels	No
Krasnoyarsk radar	Significant only as part of a territorial defense	Contributes to more rapid deployment of territorial defense	Yes
Launcher/ICBM association	No significance	Marginal at existing launcher/warhead ceilings	Yes
Activities at old SS-7 sites	No significance at SALT II levels	No	No

[a]These six issues were the confirmed violations listed in the president's reports to Congress.

For example, the long-term military significance of encrypting missile flight test data depends largely on the degree to which other intelligence methods—including ground-, sea-, or space-based radars—can, as the Soviets imply, gather required data. Telemetry is the most reliable means of making firm estimates, and total encryption would undermine the ability of the United States to predict the direction of Soviet strategic modernization programs. On the other hand, it is difficult to reconcile U.S. claims that encryption has impeded verification of treaty-selected performance characteristics with the detailed official descriptions of Soviet missiles and with the precise data required to refute Soviet claims that the SS-25 is a legal follow-on to the SS-13 rather than a new-type ICBM. Former secretary Caspar Weinberger, for example, described the SS-25 in precise terms—it is 10 percent longer, 11 percent larger in diameter, and has 92 percent more throw weight than the SS-13.[31]

Technical and operational procedures seem to be at the heart of the SS-25 issue. Recent Soviet activities are difficult to explain in terms of duplicity or deception. Why, for example, in the midst of a controversy over the SS-13/25 relationship, would the Soviets resume test flights of old SS-13s if they were deliberately cheating or attempting to obscure the technical relationships between the two missiles?

From the administration's point of view, the Soviets have violated the SALT II limitation of one new missile type. Ironically the military significance of the SS-25 may be in the interest of both the United States and the Soviet Union. Strategic modernization trends toward less vulnerable, smaller, single-warhead ICBMs have been advocated by many U.S. government officials and defense analysts, including the president's Scowcroft commission.[32] The United States should be pushing the Soviets in precisely this direction, just as many are pushing for a new U.S. mobile missile—the Midgetman. Strategic stability in the form of fewer incentives to launch a first strike could be strengthened by mobile ICBM deployments in combination with reductions in the Soviet SS-18 ICBM force.

Perhaps the most significant SS-25 issue is the throw weight of its warhead. If, as the United States claims, it is less than 50 percent of the total weight of the reentry vehicle, a limited breakout capability would result in the capability to deploy a multiple warhead version. Such engineering and packaging games would not affect the strategic balance unless the Soviets attempt to deploy forces above SALT II limits or until arms control agreements bring strategic nuclear force levels down to at least 50 percent below their current levels. Even then, the survivability of U.S. forces would depend as much on their deployment modes as marginal numerical advantages by either side. In any event, there will be adequate time for the United States to respond if future Soviet tests of deployed SS-25s confirm the American throw-weight estimates.

Two additional SS-25 issues described in the president's reports seem less serious. The military significance of Soviet efforts to conceal the relationship between the SS-25 missile and its launcher would have potential military significance if the Soviets had declared their intent to deploy the SS-25 in silos. A case could then be made that perhaps the Soviets might attempt covert deployment of mobile missiles. However, the Soviets have not only declared but have already deployed the SS-25 on mobile launchers, which are presumably distinguishable from other Soviet mobile launchers. The issue has little military relevance, but left unresolved, a precedent could be established that undermines the U.S. capability to predict the direction of Soviet strategic modernization programs if future Soviet test practices do not clearly show U.S. intelligence a single launcher and missile association.

The military significance of Soviet actions at former SS-7 ICBM sites is negligible as long as they remain within SALT I and SALT II ceilings. The only measurable advantage is the savings that result from using existing roads and facilities to support SS-25 bases.

There is far less ambiguity in Soviet radar deployments; Krasnoyarsk is an illegal radar site. The best test of its military potential is to assess its capabilities against the deliberate Soviet ABM breakout thesis. There are at least four functions that Krasnoyarsk could perform: early warning (legal), satellite tracking (legal), ABM battle management (illegal), and ASAT battle management (illegal). According to a 1985 CIA assessment, the radar is not well designed for ABM battle management because its single face (unlike the legal four-sided battle management radar near the Moscow ABM complex) looks in the wrong direction to detect the northern trajectories of U.S. ICBMs and their warheads against which the radar would have to guide interceptor missiles.[33] Moreover, the radar is not hardened against nuclear effects, and there are no interceptor missiles, associated radars, or other ABM-related items near the facility. The CIA report, as well as former secretary of defense Harold Brown, conclude that the radar is a violation but not a military threat.[34] In fact, the administration's noncompliance reports indirectly make the same case through their inability to confirm that other suspected ABM violations—such as mobile components and dual-capable air-missile defense radars—are valid, much less linked in any way to the Krasnoyarsk facility. The case for a creeping Soviet territorial defense or breakout from the ABM Treaty requires clear evidence of a more systematic effort, including hundreds if not thousands of radars, sensors, and ICBM interceptors, all of which require long lead times for construction and deployment as part of a credible territorial defense.

Finally, and by all accounts, the issue of Soviet strategic nuclear delivery vehicles in excess of SALT II ceilings has little military significance and does not, when combined with the destruction patterns of Soviet strategic forces and the unresolved bomber-tanker conversion procedures, support the case for concerted cheating to gain strategic advantage. The numbers in dispute rest on the bomber conversion issue. These bombers, when converted to refueling tankers, will support a modernized Soviet bomber force, but their numbers are too small to undermine the predictability of Soviet force modernization or to challenge the strategic balance.

Conclusions

The marginal military gains from Soviet activities described under image 1 and other plausible models of Soviet behavior assessed under images 2 and 3 support the conclusion that the Reagan administration's attacks against the major pillars of the existing arms control regime—SALT I, SALT II, and the ABM Treaty—exceed the principle of proportionate response. At the same time, those in the United States who have consistently argued the case for Soviet noncompliance are aided by Soviet counterparts who are equally anxious to exploit every treaty ambiguity. The result is a political climate in which images of Soviet cheating and actual Soviet bureaucratic behavior are natural allies in fomenting protracted compliance debates that threaten the Soviet-American arms control regime.

If the image of Soviet bureaucratic politics and standard operating procedures described here has even marginal validity, the SCC has been an ingenious device to cut through the highly secretive and compartmentalized Soviet bureaucracy, confronting political leadership formally and directly with U.S. concerns about compliance behavior. The SCC functioned in this manner during the Nixon, Ford, and Carter administrations.[35] This is not to suggest that all issues were resolved smoothly or that the Soviets, when confronted with U.S. concerns, pleaded guilty or confessed. Behavior, however, often did change over time, demonstrating the relationship between the SCC and the Soviet leadership's active intervention to alter bureaucratic SOPs.

The Reagan administration has been far more critical of the SCC. the number of noncompliance issues has risen dramatically, along with a much greater tendency to discuss them publicly rather than at the SCC. SCC negotiators have experienced a greater degree of frustration and more dead ends, as in the case of encryption. Its function as a continuing negotiating forum for resolving SALT and ABM Treaty disputes will produce fewer visible results when and if image 3, differences in interpretations of treaty obligations, or image 1, preplanned deception to gain military advantages, is at work. Image 3 requires complex and often protracted negotiating that matches that of the original treaty. Image 1, to which the administration has gravitated, threatens not only the SCC but the entire arms control regime—present and future.

Soviet behavior is not the only, and perhaps not even the most, critical variable. Powerful forces in the administration have consistently made it clear that strategic modernization programs ("supply-side arms control" as former assistant secretary of defense Richard Perle has quipped) are the top priority. Since 1983 the president's SDI has introduced yet another new, if not revolutionary, strategic challenge that U.S. negotiators have been required to protect at the negotiating table. Support for both offensive and defensive modernization programs has been made easier by the administration's frontal assault against Soviet compliance with their arms control obligations.

There are important lessons in these events if arms control is to have a role in future Soviet-American relations. For the Soviets, it would be a mistake to dismiss all of the allegations against their compliance record as propaganda from unregenerate hawks. The Reagan administration has struck a sympathetic nerve in the American public because mistrust of the Soviet Union is widespread, if not a fundamental part of American beliefs. Arms control, though widely supported, always walks a fine line between public fears of nuclear war and Soviet intentions. Loose constructionist compliance behavior will have to give way to something closer to the U.S. legalistic or tight constructionist views of treaty obligations if arms control is not to be supplanted by unilateral military responses to Soviet threats.

The Soviets can respond to U.S. concerns only if Washington establishes politically realistic standards of compliance. Unfortunately, American domestic politics have produced three competing standards.[36] First, within the most enthusiastic wing of the arms control community, there is often an implicit acceptance of ambiguity or even of minor violations as long as they have no military significance. By contrast, legalists argue that all violations are important, and the degree to which parties adhere to the provisions of a treaty is an important measure of their goodwill and trustworthiness. Precise language strictly adhered to is fundamental to treaties between states.

The Carter administration was split by these two factions just as the Reagan administration has become divided between legalists and a third and increasingly dominant faction, the skeptics, for whom no degree of arms control verification can buy more security than unilateral defense programs. For skeptics, suspicion is the basis for action. The Soviets must prove the absence of noncompliance, because even compliance with provisions of a treaty can be interpreted as sinister. The skeptics' influence can be found in many of the ambiguous conclusions of the administration's compliance reports. The most recent example is the internal debate that followed the discovery of three new but treaty-compliant radars. Although these radars were located at legal sites, several administration officials wanted their existence cited as evidence of a Soviet program to construct an illegal territorial ABM defense system.

The loose constructionist school is politically unacceptable in the United States. On the other hand, the skeptics demand standards of evidence that could be satisfied only by levels of intrusive verification that are as unacceptable to many Americans as they would be to the Soviets. By default, the legalist standard survives as a measure most likely to be accepted by both American and Soviet officials. It is also the standard best suited to deal effectively with all three images of Soviet compliance behavior.

Precise treaty language, reduced levels of complexity, and ambiguities resolved by more intrusive means of verification and a strongly supported SCC are reasonable standards to incorporate in future treaties. Cheating at the margin will always be possible, but cheating to the degree that one side gains a significant military advantage before the other responds is difficult and risky. Soviet nuclear weapons are not produced by cottage industries. Their components, production, testing, and deployment require massive infrastructures that are visible to U.S. intelligence. For the Soviets to break out of treaty obligations with programs that suddenly and dramatically alter the strategic balance would require something close to a total U.S. intelligence failure.

The prospects for intelligence failures, no matter how slight, have and should always be hedged by robust research and development programs, which provide both insurance against cheating and incentives not to. Russian history from Potemkin Village to the bomber and missile gap controversies of the late 1950s and early 1960s is filled with examples of deception to conceal weakness, not strength. Military strength is the one symbol on which the Soviets have rested their superpower status. They wear it proudly for all its cost and sacrifice. Examples of strategic surprise that have revealed Soviet strength are limited mostly to wartime experiences such as the battle of Stalingrad, won by counterattacks by massive reserves unknown to the Germans. In war, however, deception need work only once for a short period. Protracted deception required for breaking out of an existing arms control regime with significant military capabilities is much more difficult and extremely dangerous when compared to the political and military benefits the Soviets could gain through a more stable strategic environment that results from arms control. Cheating also wastes the considerable political capital the Soviets have invested in the process of negotiating treaties in the first place.

Multiple explanations for Soviet actions and marginal military benefits from the Reagan administration's cheating scenarios do not justify the U.S. decision to abandon SALT and threaten the ABM Treaty. The danger in these trends stems from long gaps between old and new treaties that may be filled by destabilizing offensive or defensive actions by one or both parties. An arms control failure at the end of costly strategic modernization programs and in spite of a strong U.S. negotiating posture would leave the Reagan administration with a dubious legacy and confront its successors with formidable obstacles on the path of Soviet-American relations.

Notes

1. Described in Raymond L. Garthoff, *Detente and Confrontation: American-Soviet Relations from Nixon to Reagan* (Washington, D.C.: Brookings, 1985), p. 300.

2. Evidence of the SS-25 became available by 1983 and of the Krasnoyarsk radar in 1983. Encryption practices were common prior to SALT II; they stopped but resumed again with tests of the SS-25 and the SS-NX-20—a sea-based missile. The Soviet radar was well underway when first discovered. Construction probably began in 1980 or 1981. This is not considered to be an intelligence failure. With finite resources, it is axiomatic that one will not find what one is not looking for.

3. V. Issraelyan, *Final Record of the 119th Meeting,* document CD/PV119 (Geneva: Committee on Disarmament, March 31, 1981), pp. 16–17.

4. Quoted in Thomas Wolfe, *The SALT Experience* (Cambridge, Mass.: Ballinger, 1979), p. 261.

5. Arnold Horelick (ed.), *US-Soviet Relations: The Next Phase* (Ithaca: Cornell University Press, 1986), p. 160.

6. This section draws on Scilla McLean (ed.), *How Nuclear Weapons Decisions Are Made* (New York: St. Martin's, 1986), chap. 1.

7. Ibid., p. 10.

8. The important role of the military at SALT I is illustrated by American accounts of the rigorous reaction shown by Soviet military members of the delegations when U.S. negotiators gave their civilian counterparts data on Soviet strategic forces. That information was not to be shared with unauthorized civilians.

9. The president's reports to Congress cover compliance issues for all Soviet-American arms control treaties in force. Only SALT I, SALT II, and ABM Treaty issues are examined here.

10. Described by Michael Gordon in *New York Times,* December 19, 1986, p. 6.

11. For a detailed study of the technical aspects of monitoring arms control compliance, see Allan S. Krass, *Verification: How Much Is Enough?* (Lexington, Mass.: Lexington Books, 1985).

12. *Soviet Noncompliance* (Washington, D.C.: U.S. Arms Control and Disarmament Agency, February 1986), p. 11.

13. Krass, *Verification,* p. 188, n. 28.

14. I am grateful to Arnold Horelick on this point. See also "Explaining Soviet Compliance Behavior: Conference Digest," mimeo. (Stanford University, February 14, 1986), p. 53. For discussion of "other ways" to derive data on Soviet ICBMs, see Krass, *Verification,* p. 189, n. 41.

15. James A. Schear, "Arms Control Treaty Compliance: Buildup to Breakdown?" *International Security* 10, no. 2 (Fall 1985): 163.

16. John Pike and Jonathan Rich, *Soviet Compliance with SALT II and the ABM Treaty,* Report by the Federation of American Scientists, March 7, 1984, p. 7.

17. Described by Jack Mendelsohn, "Reagan's Proportionate Response Policy: Sense or Nonsense?" *Arms Control Today* 16, no. 1 (January-February 1986): 7–11.

18. Krass, *Verification,* p. 187, n. 28.

19. Schear, "Arms Control," p. 166; Pike and Rich, *Soviet Compliance,* pp. 8–10.

20. Mendelsohn, "Reagan's Policy," p. 8.

21. Legal and technical issues are described by former ACDA staff member Peter Zimmerman in *Los Angeles Times,* November 23, 1986, p. E:5.

22. The Soviet Union declared that as of the date of signing SALT II, it possessed 1,398 ICBM and 950 SLBM launchers and 156 heavy bombers. Since the SALT II levels of 2,400 and 2,250 are applicable only "upon entry into force" of the treaty, this total of 2,504 is considered to be the implicit limit on Soviet SNDVs.

23. ACDA, *Soviet Noncompliance,* pp. 8–9.

24. *Joint Chiefs of Staff Military Posture Statement, FY 1987* (Washington, D.C.: Department of Defense, 1986), p. 19.

25. Ibid., p. 19.

26. *New York Times,* November 24, 1985, p. 18.

27. ACDA, *Soviet Noncompliance,* p. 9.

28. The administration confirmed in a letter to Congressman Lee Hamilton (D–Indiana) that no effort has been made to complete bomber dismantlement and conversion procedures at the SCC. This raises an important consideration: how much has the Reagan administration been responsible for creating the Soviet record of compliance?

29. ACDA, *Soviet Noncompliance,* pp. 11–12. One can only speculate on the specifics of this issue. A reasonable scenario is the deployment of an SS-25 mobile launcher near a test silo or launch pad, resulting in U.S. monitoring uncertainties about which launching mode was actually used.

30. Ibid., p. 13.

31. Secretary of Defense Weinberger, during a briefing for NATO defense ministers in Brussels. *Los Angeles Times,* October 30, 1985, p. 16.

32. *Report of the President's Commission on Strategic Forces* (Washington, D.C.: Government Printing Office, 1983), pp. 9–21.

33. See Michael Gordon's report, "CIA Is Skeptical That New Soviet Radar Is Part of an ABM Defense Report," *National Journal,* February 9, 1985, pp. 523–526.

34. Ibid., p. 525.

35. Questions about Soviet compliance began surfacing publicly in 1975. According to a 1978 Department of State report to Congress, the United States raised eight different issues in the SCC, six of which were resolved. Two other issues were unresolved due to ambiguities in the agreements themselves. See Mark M. Lowenthal and Joel S. Wit, "Politics, Verification and Arms Control," *Washington Quarterly* 7, no. 3 (Summer 1984): 117, 125.

36. I am indebted to Glenn C. Buchan for these typologies. See his "The Verification Spectrum," *Bulletin of the Atomic Scientists* 39, no. 9 (November 1982): 16–19.

6

New Technologies and the 1990s: The Strategic Implications of the Advanced Cruise Missile

David S. Sorenson

T he October 1957 launch of Sputnik I caused considerable anxiety in the United States since the feat dramatically demonstrated the Soviet capability to deliver nuclear weapons against U.S. targets. In 1983 the United States deployed the Pershing II missile in West Germany, placing it six minutes away from its Soviet targets. The strong Soviet reaction to this act, culminating in the INF Treaty, suggested that similar anxiety was felt in Moscow as it had been felt in Washington twenty-six years earlier. These are only two of a number of cases where one of the two rivals in the postwar superpower competition developed a new weapon (or modified an old one) that increased the insecurity of the rival camp. More recently, the SDI and comparable SDI-like experiments in the Soviet Union have had similar effects. In this chapter some possible influences of another important weapons development, the advanced cruise missile (ACM), will be examined with respect to how it may affect Soviet and American nuclear doctrine once these missiles are deployed.

U.S. and Soviet Strategic Nuclear Doctrine

Several summary points may be made about the strategic concepts and developments guiding the use of central strategic systems by both superpowers.[1] First, both sides have emphasized offensive power in preference to homeland defense against a nuclear attack. In this sense, deterrence through the threat of punishment is stressed over deterrence through the threat of denial, with active defense limited to antibomber systems, and even this capability is relatively minimal in the United States. Although the Soviet Union has invested more effort in bomber defense and possesses a minimal ABM system, neither side can effectively limit damage from a nuclear attack.

I am grateful to the Mershon Center, Ohio State University, for supporting this project with a 1986 Mershon Center National Security Award. Valuable research assistance was provided by Ellen L. Hamann, and helpful editorial suggestions were given by Don Snow.

Second, both sides have configured their strategic nuclear forces around land-based ICBMs, SLBMs, and long-range aviation (bombers, aerial refueling capacity, and bomber-launched nuclear munitions). Each side, however, has a different balance among the three components; in fact important asymmetries exist between the superpowers in each category. The Soviets have a larger portion of yield in their ICBM force, and the United States concentrates its force efforts in the bomber and SLBM areas.

Third, both sides have acted in ways that suggest a mutual interest in preserving rival retaliatory capacity: avoiding the development of systems and doctrines that would deny the relative security of the SLBM and bomber forces (relative to ICBMs). This point must be made carefully; both sides have bomber defenses, and work continues on ASW, though there is no indication of a pending major breakthrough in this latter area that could threaten the security of the deployed SLBM force. Both sides also have the capacity to attack C^3I sites in ways that could cripple or paralyze retaliatory ability. But neither side has developed a major capacity for surprise attack against either of the "secure" legs of the triad (bombers and SLBMs) or against ICBMs that would deny at least some human time for decisions to scramble bombers and communicate emergency war messages to deployed SSBNs.

Fourth, until recently, both sides had agreed to place limits on the elements of their strategic forces that were agreed upon in the SALT accords. There has been some controversy about mutual compliance with strategic arms control agreements, but neither side has formally renounced the whole SALT package.

Fifth, the dominance of the ballistic missile as a strategic weapon will probably be challenged by emerging technology in the air-breathing portion of the triad. During the 1960s and 1970s, ballistic missiles emerged as the primary means of delivery strategic weapons because, in both their land- and sea-based modes, they offered several important advantages over bomber aircraft, the original strategic delivery system. Ballistic missiles were very fast, they were cheaper to manufacture and operate than were aircraft, and, when operated from silos or submarines, they were less vulnerable to attack. And there was not, and is not now, any real defense against a major ballistic missile attack. Their incorporation into military arsenals was aided by developments in solid fuels and improved inertial guidance systems. As a result, manned bombers have remained a small portion of the Soviet force, and in the United States, bombers dropped from 465 in 1970 to 280 in 1986.[2] Interest in cruise missiles (CMs), stimulated initially in the late 1940s, also dropped until the mid-1970s, when the present generation of CMs came under development.

The strategic ballistic missile has its limitations, though. Once fired, it cannot be destroyed in flight. The guidance system on current models cannot be altered once the weapon is launched, and they cannot thus be retargeted once fired. Missile accuracy may be degraded by problems ranging from those encountered during launch to weather. By the mid-1970s, the relative invulnerability of silo-based ICBMs was challenged by improvements in warhead guidance. Silo-based ICBMs may be superseded by mobile missiles, but there are problems here too, including high cost, public opposition in the United States, and limited mobility for the Soviet Union during its harsh winters (except possibly for rail-mobile models). Additional problems include the BMD potential in SDI (and its Soviet counterpart) that could compromise the ability of ICBMs to reach their targets.

Such problems and limitations suggest that the ballistic missile may wane in relative importance as the next century approaches. Even a limited BMD, Fred Hoffman notes,

> would make the ballistic missile less militarily useful and less politically useful to the Soviet leaders, it would lead them to look for other ways to accomplish their objectives. I think their first recourse would be to think about and perhaps move to aerodynamic systems.[4]

Guertner and Snow make a similar point, claiming that "thousands of Soviet air-launched cruise missiles could be deployed years ahead of United States ballistic missile defenses."[5] It should not be surprising, therefore, that a renewed interest in the strategic cruise missile has developed in both superpower camps during the past decade.

Cruise Missiles: An Old Idea Cast Anew

Like most other current defense technologies, the CM has been around a long time; ideas for "flying bombs" date back to World War I.[6] In the United States interest has continued since the late 1940s, when, inspired by the German V-1 "buzz bomb," American scientists began to develop a series of CMs. The 1946 design for the Snark, for example, called for a 30-ton vehicle guided by stellar inertial means with a circular error probability (CEP) of 1.4 nautical miles.[7] Its 3,000–5,000 nautical mile range would have given it the capacity to reach targets in the Soviet Union from bases in Maine. A subsequent design, the Hound Dog, demonstrated the possibility of supersonic CMs, with a speed potential of Mach 1.6 and a range of 800 kilometers. The U.S. Navy's Regulus improved on this performance with a range of 1,000 nautical miles and a speed of Mach 2. The U.S. Air Force's Navaho, a missile as large as a fighter plane, reached Mach 3 in 1958, and the navy's planned Triton of the 1950s was designed for a 12,000 nautical mile range, a speed of Mach 3.5, a radar map-matching guidance system, and a CEP of 600 feet.[8]

These early designs were plagued with technical and bureaucratic problems. They were often unstable in flight (if they took off at all) and were frequently troubled with guidance problems; for example, a wayward Snark that disappeared during a 1956 test was discovered in Brazil in 1982. Early intercontinental versions that could have potentially replaced the manned bomber were the subject of some anxiety by SAC bomber crews, who favored the short-range Hound Dog carried by the B-52 bomber, which could possibly extend the life of this aircraft in the face of threats to it from long-range ballistic missiles.[9] As a result of such problems, interest in most forms of CM faded in the late 1960s and early 1970s, but these early models did demonstrate CM potential, including supersonic-plus speed and intercontinental range, capacities that may appear on the advanced CM of the 1990s.

The present generation of American CMs is based on lessons learned from past mistakes, coupled with some important advances in guidance and propulsion, and it is believed that Soviet designs are based on imitations of basic U.S. technology. The development of miniaturized turbo jet and turbofan engines has resulted in a relatively inexpensive and light propulsion system, which has allowed a major size reduction of present CMs from earlier generations. The most important development, though, has been the terrain contour matching (TERCOM) technology, which allows the missile to guide itself over land by matching the terrain altitudes that it overflies with a computerized "map" containing its projected course to target. The system matches the actual course with the programmed course during the flight, and under proper conditions the missile can fly precisely to its target, correcting for deviations along its flight path, and permitting CEPs of around 100 meters.[10] The accuracy of comparable Soviet systems is shrouded in some secrecy, but the most recently deployed Soviet CM, the AS-15, is reportedly accurate enough to be used against hard targets.[11]

CMs are currently deployed in three modes: air launched from bombers (ALCM), from submarines (SLCM), and ground launched from truck-like vehicles (GLCM). The ground-launched versions are designed for theater operations and are unlikely in the near future to be upgraded to intercontinental capacity. The U.S. SLCM has been limited by the SALT II Protocol to a range of not greater than 600 kilometers but could be increased with relative ease to that of the ALCM—around 1,500 nautical miles. Even with a 600-kilometer range, the SLCM puts some Soviet coastal assets within its range, though it is not counted in any arms control pact as a strategic weapon. The same is true for the Soviet SLCM, which, while not as accurate as the U.S. SLCM (around 25 feet CEP after a 400-mile flight), still puts all U.S. coastal targets at risk, including a number of bomber bases and SLBM facilities.[12] Since so many more potential U.S. targets are located within range of present Soviet SLCMs, the United States is obviously more vulnerable to this non-SALT-accountable weapon system.[13]

The present generation of CMs is not without limitations and problems. Because they lack true intercontinental capacity, all require a separate launch vehicle to carry them partway to their targets. In the case of ALCMs, bomber aircraft must either penetrate defended airspace or at least approach such airspace before launching, making them vulnerable to antibomber defenses and raising the the potential risk of losing a large number of ACMs if only few bombers are lost. The SLCM does not face problems of such magnitude now, but the submarine carriers will become vulnerable to improved ASW capacity as they approach enemy coastlines—and possibly most susceptible to ASW as they close in to reach deep inland targets. The shorter range of SLCMs is a special problem for the United States, given that outside the Pacific coastal region of the Soviet Union, much of the ocean littoral is frozen much of the year and, so far as is known publicly, SLCMs do not have ice penetration capacity.

CMs also lack adequate penetration speed in their present versions. While the Soviets are reported to be working on a supersonic SLCM, the SS-NX-24, they do not now have one deployed with such capacity, nor does the United States.[14] CMs were once thought to be so difficult to detect with their small size and low-altitude flight profiles that high speed was believed unnecessary. But advances in look-down-shoot-down antiaircraft capacity have made them easier to detect and intercept, and now their limited speed makes them quite vulnerable to fighter aircraft.

In 1984 the Defense Department decided in the light of these problems (plus some contractor difficulties) to cease production of the present-generation CM. In the succeeding years, development has reportedly been accelerated on the follow-on weapon system, the ACM.

The Advanced Cruise Missile

It is difficult to describe in any detail a weapon program so shrouded in secrecy as the ACM. Some information has been released, however, and areas of likely improvement can be extrapolated from knowledge about the deficiencies of present systems. Five such areas of improvement can be identified: increased speed, increased range, incorporation of "low observable" (stealth) technology, improved guidance, and multiple warhead capacity.

Speed increases would not require any major new technological advances; the CMs of the 1950s, after all, had the potential speeds of up to Mach 3, far above the subsonic capacity of present CMs. Speed improvements can come from technical developments, including more powerful engines, improved aerodynamics, and better fuel management. In fact, speed can be boosted at the terminal attack phase of the CM flight by simply adding a high-thrust booster while preserving the range advantages of lower speed,[15] as well as the flexibility of decision time that lower speed allows.[16]

Intercontinental range was incorporated in models built or designed decades ago. While the ranges of ACM models have not been released, recent hearings before congressional committees describe the range of the ACM as greater than the present ALCM, though unspecified.[17] It would not be unreasonable, though, to expect ranges in excess of 3,000 nautical miles, and perhaps much more.

Speed and range improvements can be made possible by several changes, including lighter weight and improved propulsion. Technological development of the advanced tactical fighter (ATF), expected to be deployed in the 1990s, can produce useful spinoffs for the ACM. For example, advanced materials, replacing steel and aluminum, are expected to reduce the weight of the ATF by half, and similar improvement can be expected in the ACM area. Turbine engine development is expected to lead to thrust-to-weight ratios of around 20:1 (now about 10:1), and this, along with digital electronic fuel controls, can bring dramatic improvements in fuel usage. The latter technology alone is expected to result in a 40 percent fuel savings at supersonic speed over present designs.[18] Range may also be improved by the simple addition of expendable external fuel tanks in launch situations where the ACM is not fired from a confined space such as a torpedo tube or rotary launcher on a bomber.

Developments in low observable (or "stealth") technology (LOT) in bombers and fighters can be easily transferred to the ACM. Various sources indicate the radar cross-section (RCS) of the ACM is smaller than present versions because of the incorporation of LOT, including advanced radar-absorptive material in the airframe, reduced infrared signature from the engine exhaust, and turbulence reduction and masking designed to make the vehicle almost invisible to both radar and infrared detection. The engine air inlet, for example, may be made flush to the fuselage and extended only for Mach-plus flight.

Some of these technological advances (power and weight, for example) will allow the ACM to fly at much higher altitudes than present versions, and this means that much greater ranges are possible (high-altitude flight through thinner air provides a substantial reduction in fuel consumption over the present flight altitudes in the hundreds of feet). Greater power would also allow lower altitudes during penetration because the present CMs' tendency to "sky out" after crossing ridge lines can be corrected with additional power to overcome and vector down the lift occurring after climbing an incline.

Guidance will also be improved in the ACM models through the use of carbon dioxide laser radar technology for improved target homing.[19] In addition, the incorporation of very high-speed integrated circuitry (VHSIC) design to provide rapid target recognition and protection from electronic countermeasures will add greatly to the ACM's guidance capacity.[20] Future advances in VHSIC technology and the ultimate development of gallium-arsenide chips might permit close to zero CEPs, along with computer improvements that can enhance map data processes to improve TERCOM.[21] Guidance for the ACM could come from external sources as well, specifically from satellites. The global positioning system (GPS), scheduled to become operational in the late 1980s, is an eighteen-satellite navigation system expected to provide highly accurate guidance for both aircraft and missiles, and the Soviet GLONASS is expected to give similar capacity.[22] This system could improve accuracy and also offer a solution to one of the more vexing problems of TERCOM: its inability to provide guidance over flat surfaces like the ocean or the plains of the Soviet and American heartlands.

Satellite guidance for the ACM would also potentially offer another advantage: retargeting during flight. Surveillance of enemy territory could monitor such moving targets as mobile missiles and aircraft and provide real-time information to attacking ACMs in order to direct them in flight toward new target coordinates.

Delivery of multiple warheads must also be considered a possibility for the ACM, though there is no indication in the sparse public literature that such a feature is being planned. Even present CM models can carry payloads with the weight and size of multiple nuclear warheads. The navy Tomahawk carries one nuclear warhead with a weight of 270 pounds or a conventional warhead weighing 1,000 pounds and taking up more than twice the space in the forward part of the missile. Of course, the additional weight and size might require a sacrifice in range, but external expendable fuel tanks could compensate for the additional weight of multiple warheads.

A MIRVed ACM would reduce greatly the cost of delivering warheads and would require fewer penetrations of hostile airspace in order to deliver the required number of weapons for the desired target coverage. The guidance task would not be especially difficult, involving a track overflying multiple targets and delivered time-delayed weapons on them.

Strategic Implications of ACMs

There are five areas where the ACM will have an important impact: reduced attack warning time, greater ease of targeting, greater ambiguity as to strategic weapons characteric, greater problems for arms control efforts, and greater uncertainty for strategic defense programs.

Reduced Attack Warning Time

The preservation of attack warning time helps stabilize superpower nuclear relations, especially in crises. Each side may decide that the loss of such time necessitates an automated warning-and-response weapons launch system because the human decision time required to initiate retaliation would be impossibly short should attack times in tens of minutes or less become possible.

There have already been major reductions in attack warning time, from hours in the bomber era to minutes in the missile age. At the present time, though, there is probably just enough warning time in the face of a ballistic missile attack to permit launch before arrival of at least some portion of the retaliatory force. For example, an attack by Soviet ICMBs against U.S. ICBMs would allow about twenty to twenty-five minutes in which to launch manned bombers and to communicate with SLBM carriers before the ICBMs arrived. Similarly a SLBM attack on airfields would allow perhaps fifteen minutes' warning time for the launch of ICBMs in retaliation even if bombers and SLBM communications were lost. These kinds of calculations were reportedly a factor in the Scrowcroft commission report of 1983, which reduced the Reagan administration's alarm over the so-called ICBM window of vulnerability.[23] Adequate warning time is important largely because attack responses take time with launch safeguards in place. The president, for example, must authorize a launch decision for American nuclear systems; should he not be able to do so, the decision is delegated to some other human decision maker in the chain of command. Presumably the Soviet Union has a similar system. The reasons for this human link are fairly obvious. The decision to launch is, after all, a political one to be made by the president or the general secretary of the Communist party or their delegates. It is also probably true that only humans can ask the right questions in the face of an alert, so to shorten attack response time by moving to automation may increase the probability of failure—either failure to warn when an attack is underway or launching on a false warning.

But when warning time is reduced to a few minutes, the capacity of human decision making becomes compressed to the point where automation becomes more tempting. And even if the final launch decision is left in human hands, the number of safety control functions that are designed to avoid accidental or unauthorized launches might be reduced to save response time.

The ACM is one of several technologies on the near-term horizon that threatens the available warning time for both the United States and the Soviet Union. A low-observable ACM obviously reduces and potentially eliminates warning time, particularly if fired over a short distance—say, from a submarine. Even a long-range ACM can do the same, given the greater freedom of its flight patterns. Evasive flight paths through ground clutter would make ACMs difficult to detect at all, and even after detection, the target of the missile might be difficult to determine. Because of this, the ACM will place a number of potential targets such as SSBN bases, air defense facilities, C^3I, and bomber bases at even greater risk than they are now under. Warning time for such targets is likely to be even less than the short time currently available in the event of SLBM strikes.

Greater Ease in Targeting

Nuclear weapons have long been associated with indiscriminate damage. From the earliest days of the atomic age, large-yield weapons delivered from relatively imprecise platforms were able to destroy only large areas but incapable of selecting out smaller targets. Cities thus became important targets for their war-related industrial value, at least for U.S. planners. Technology gradually made it possible to target ICBM silos and other hardened facilities, and targeting doctrine began to deemphasize urban areas. Despite improvements in guidance and reductions in yield, it is still considered impossible to attack targets near population areas without inflicting tremendous collateral damage. Since many important military-related targets are located close to or in urban areas in both the United States and Soviet Union, destroying such targets is difficult for a number of reasons—not the least of which is the moral dilemma of killing many civilians in order to destroy a single site. Advances in guidance and warhead design expected in ACMs may solve this dilemma because they may combine high accuracy and either low-yield nuclear weapons or conventional strategic warheads to produce much less collateral damage than was incurred during U.S. and British bomber raids during World War II.[24] It can be argued that such precision makes counterindustrial targeting more practical as a "war termination" objective.

The kind of accuracy and low yields required for counterindustrial targeting may also allow selective population targeting, which has taken on the term *ethnic targeting*. Colin Gray, among others, has suggested that the "captive" peoples of the Soviet Union are basically non-Russian and that in the event of a general superpower nuclear war, the "freedom" of these "captive peoples" could be accomplished by destroying the Soviet Russian elite.[25] William Lee has pondered the possibility that the Soviets too might consider such selective targeting of "ruling groups" in the United States while sparing the general population.[26]

Selective population targeting may or may not be a strategically sound idea. Such discrimination may be very difficult at the operational level; after all, neither the Soviet nor the American leadership elite may be in their offices when the threat of attack arrives, and the top political leadership is very unlikely to remain in known places if the attack threat is high. Moreover, if one purpose of nuclear destruction is to persuade the leadership of targeted nations that further pursuit of violence is fruitless, the point of the message will be lost on dead leaders. There is, in other words, little point in killing leaders in an attack if the purpose of that attack is to get them to surrender or at least negotiate. And with respect to more general ethnic targeting, (against "Great Russians," for example), Quester argues that this would amount to genocide— killing people chosen, perhaps, on the basis of their language.[27] And even highly accurate weapons would have to carry high-yield weapons to blanket ethnic areas, especially if the prime ethnic area is "Great Russia." The spread of contamination from Chernobyl is only the latest reminder that radiation cannot be confined to particular areas.[28]

Even if the concept of selective targeting is strategically or ethically questionable, the ACM makes it more possible to contemplate such strikes. Given the proximity of Washington to the Atlantic Ocean, U.S. leadership is especially vulnerable to such an attack because a supersonic ACM fired from a Soviet submarine could reach targets in Washington in only a few minutes. Moscow is obviously less vulnerable to such an attack but certainly not impervious to it. A supersonic-plus GLCM could, for example, reach Moscow in around two hours from the West German border or slightly more than one hour from the Barents Sea. If stealth capacity prevents early detection, this warning time could be reduced to the point where at lest some leadership targets are vulnerable. If counterleadership targeting becomes technically feasible, the value of a surprise preemptive attack becomes greater.

Arms Control Implications

The present generation of CMs already has a reputation for complicating arms control between the United States and Soviet Union. They are small and easy to conceal, making agreement on verification rules difficult. They are dual-use weapons, capable of both conventional and nuclear roles and of both strategic and theater roles, so they are difficult to categorize into weapons types. This complicates arms control because definitions of the weapons to be controlled must be made before limits can be negotiated. The variety of launch platforms for the ACM, including submarines, surface ships, and fighter planes, further confuses arms control efforts, again because arms control has required a strict definition of each platform before limits can be established. As Alton Frye has written,

> Long-range SLCMs could constitute a vast loophole in any arms reduction agreement, and insisting on their deployment without restraint may kill such an accord. An enormous number of such missiles might be deployed on existing submarines and ships. And such missiles would be much more difficult to keep track of than ALCMs or ground launched cruise missiles, which can be verified to some extent with already agreed-upon counting rules and by monitoring distinguishing characteristics of the platforms.[29]

SALT II used a minimalist approach to the CM problems of the 1970s. It limited the GLCM and SLCM only in range in the protocol, and overall numbers of ALCMs were not limited. Limits were placed on the ALCM carriers such that no ALCM delivery system could exceed an average of twenty-eight ALCMs and that none of the bombers deployed at the time of the treaty could carry more than twenty ALCMs. Furthermore aircraft carrying ALCMs were to be counted as MIRV launchers and had to carry distinctive features known as functionally related observable differences (FRODS) that were supposed to be unique to their mission as CM carriers.[30]

Beyond this, progress in definition for purposes of verification proved difficult. Distinctions as to type (nuclear, tactical, conventional, strategic, and so on) are quite elusive, since most U.S. and Soviet CMs use the same basic airframes for all their models. Although the present U.S. ALCM is distinct, antiship CMs and longer-range SLCMs and GLCMs appear almost identical. Range is also difficult to define because CMs are designed to fly long distances in evasive patterns. The question that arises is defining range: some set distance? the flight time until fuel runs out? or something else? Furthermore, verification of compliance on any range limitation would be extremely difficult. Flight test telemetry would be hard to read since it would be sent over short distances at low altitude. Surveillance of test results might also be difficult since the weapons would undoubtedly be tested in unpredictable locations and the full flight, even if caught by surveillance satellite, could not probably be monitored in its entirety.

Escalation Control Problems

One important component of present American deterrence doctrine is the phased control of violence escalation. This concept dates back at least to the days of flexible response in the 1960s; it refers to a graduated phasing in of successive levels of violence should initial responses fail to halt Soviet aggression. For example, if conventional force fails, it gives way to theater and then strategic force levels. Although there is no doctrinal pause between theater and strategic weapons, there are distinctions at each level with respect to weapon types, and indeed these weapons types, with their own distinct qualities, are the basis of the differences of conventional, theater, and strategic forces. Conventional forces are by definition nonnuclear; theater forces are designed to operate theater-range weapons that, like conventional forces, are oriented around a force-destruction mission outside the homeland of either superpower; strategic forces are homeland targeted.

Should war between the superpowers actually break out, this graduated response might well not occur. It is designed, though, to provide the United States with a credible action to varying Soviet threat levels should the Soviets choose to escalate and offering a higher cost for each level if the previous stage fails. It offers a choice of response designed to maximize, across the spectrum of violence, a means of meeting the two requirements of deterrence: its likelihood and its vast cost, which should outweigh even the most optimistic assessment of gain from aggression. Deterrence threats must, in other words, be both possible (thus believable) and as terrible (thus outweighing expected attack benefits). And the instruments for deterrence at both levels must be clear, it is assumed, to the potential attacker.

There has always been some ambiguity between force-level categories. But as Kincade points out with respect to even the present generation of CMs, this weapon system makes category distinctions ever murkier.[31] CMs can deliver anything from a conventional warhead against a ship to a large-yield thermonuclear device against a city, and ship-busters may be identical to city-busters in appearance.

The extended range of the ACM complicates this serious problem. Long-range CMs can also be equipped for theater and strategic missions and indeed can be stationed on the same platforms that might also carry conventional CMs. Further confusion may arise should a recent Office of Technology Assessment proposal be adopted, calling for the use of B-52 and FB-111 bombers in delivering conventional ordnance (possibly including ACMs) against deep-strike Warsaw Pact targets in Europe.[32] This makes force assessment very difficult at each level.[33] Perhaps more important, it makes the control of escalation difficult to carry out and difficult to perceive correctly. The hoped-for message that the distinct first phase will be followed by a worse second phase of violence may be quickly lost on the target of that violence as that target watches CMs flying from all kinds of launch platforms with unknown payloads and heading for unknown targets. Would a flight of ACMs coming from Great Britain, for example, be headed for Moscow, for a tank concentration in Poland, or something else? Could Soviet leaders wait to find out? Or would they escalate at the moment they first detect a CM attack from American launchers? And if American leaders correctly understand that such a response could occur or even believe that it is likely, would they be able to take advantage of the supposedly lower-risk use of a conventional weapon like the conventional CM in accordance with escalation doctrine? The commonality of CMs, in other words, may emerge as a sort of self-deterrent against the use of the weapon because it might resemble too much a nuclear weapon, risking a nuclear response.

Missile Defense Problems

The Reagan administration is supporting a major research program designed to test the feasibility of a high-technology missile defense, the SDI. The Soviet Union has been working on a similar research program for a number of years and in fact may be ahead of the United States in some aspects of technological development. The American program operates under a broad charter that designates a variety of missile defense problems that SDI is intended to address in terms of feasibility studies. But despite the breadth of that charter, the real emphasis of the program is on defense against ballistic missiles in general, especially the ICBM. The head of the SDI organization, General James Abrahamson, has stated as much:

> I think it is too early to say that we can clearly identify technologies now within our research program that have a high confidence that we can solve the cruise missile problem. However, one of my responsibilities, and I would like to emphasize it is a secondary responsibility, is to identify which of the technologies, as we go forward, might be applied to other threats such as the cruise missile and other air-breathing threats. At this point we feel that the ballistic missile

is the most dangerous and certainly the most destabilizing and the thing that arrives the fastest that puts us in a hair-trigger situation. When the submarine launched ballistic missiles can arrive in only from five to six minutes from off our coasts, that is the most destabilizing and the most dangerous of the threats that we face.[34]

He noted that CMs will be a destabilizing threat in the future and that SDIO is not ignoring the problem, despite the emphasis on BMD. Much SDI work encompasses space-based systems oriented toward detecting, tracking, and ultimately destroying a ballistic missile or its ejected warheads along its flight path. The three (or more) layers of SDI are boost phase, midcourse intercept, and terminal intercept. The first two layers are useful only for BMD and would depend largely on weapons and detection systems based in space. The terminal phase might involve technology appropriate to CM defense but only if the weapons and pointing and tracking equipment associated with them are oriented toward a low-flying, air-breathing vehicle and not a warhead descending quickly from space.

The defense problems associated with the CM more approximate those involved in air defense against more traditional weapons—bombers, for example. The United States has relatively little experience in this area and has invested little effort in the task compared to the Soviets, who have one of the world's most extensive air defenses. This leads to questions of what might happen if the Soviets were to turn to the CM as a way to defeat what they may see as an inevitable U.S. SDI oriented against ballistic missiles. The United States could thus invest a tremendous effort in erecting a space-based anti-BMD system only to see the Soviets develop a major CM effort to fly under this SDI. A Soviet CM effort would probably be accompanied by an effort to upgrade their already substantial air defense efforts to handle U.S. ACMs, and the United States would then face a potential disadvantage since it lacks organizational experience in the air defense area by comparison.

The CM problem suggests that strategic defense, now heavily oriented toward the defense of ballistic missiles, might be reoriented around concepts more traditionally associated with air defense—perhaps much more concentration on coastal threat detection and interception, more ground-based air defense weaponry emphasizing coverage of both likely penetration routes and targets, and, with respect to submarine-launched CMs, more emphasis on ASW and large-area surveillance. In other words, the concept of air defense needs to be upgraded to CM characteristics rather than CM defense becoming an adjunct part of SDI with its emphasis on BMD.

Conclusions

The ACM is already on the deployment horizon in both the United States and the Soviet Union. Its performance parameters will surpass the already formidable capability of currently deployed CMs and will complicate the strategic issues posed by these weapons. Deterrence based on the security of some of the strategic arsenal may now be challenged by this new technology, as will present thinking about arms control limits on CMs. Developments in strategic defense areas may be rendered obsolete or inefficient by ACM technology.

This technology is advancing at a pace that could well lead to deployment of the ACM before the strategic and tactical problems raised in this chapter have been addressed. Thus the 1990s may resemble the 1980s in the sense that emerging technology may produce weapons before strategic justification can emerge to guide such weapons through their development and deployment phases.

Notes

1. The term *central strategic systems* is used here in conformity with the SALT II strategic weapons categories.

2. John M. Collins, *U.S.-Soviet Military Balance: Concepts and Capabilities, 1960–1980* (New York: McGraw-Hill, 1980); *Soviet Military Power, 1986* (Washington, D.C.: Department of Defense, 1986), p. 34. The number of U.S. strategic bombers rises to 320 in 1986 if the FB-111 is counted.

3. Brent Scowcroft, "Strategic System Development and New Technology: Where Should We Be Going?" Adelphi Papers, No. 197 (London: International Institute of Strategic Studies, Summer 1985), p. 7.

4. Testimony of Fred Hoffman, *Department of Defense Authorization for Appropriations for Fiscal Year 1986*. Hearings before the Committee on Armed Services, U.S. Senate, 99th Cong., 1st sess., 1985, p. 3667.

5. Gary L. Guertner and Donald M. Snow, *The Last Frontier: An Analysis of the Strategic Defense Initiative* (Lexington, Mass.: Lexington Books, 1986), p. 90.

6. A good history of these early efforts may be found in Kenneth P. Werrell, *The Evolution of the Cruise Missile* (Maxwell AFB: Air University Press, 1985).

7. CEP is a measure of weapon accuracy. Its number represents the radius of a circle into which half of the number of repeated weapon shots would fall.

8. Ibid., chap. 4; Ronald Huisken, *The Origins of the Strategic Cruise Missile* (New York: Praeger, 1981), chaps. 2–4.

9. Huisken, *Origins,* p. 18.

10. A useful discussion of cruise missile guidance is found in Kosta Tsipis, "Cruise Missiles," *Scientific American* 236 (1978): 20–29. See also John Toomay, "Technical Characteristics," in Richard K. Betts, *Cruise Missiles: Technology, Strategy, Politics* (Washington, D.C.: Brookings Institution, 1981), pp. 36–40.

11. *Aviation Week and Space Technology,* March 31, 1986, pp. 21–22.

12. *Department of Defense Authorization for Appropriations for Fiscal Year 1986,* Hearings before the Committee on Armed Services, U.S. Senate, 99th Cong., 1st sess., 1985, pp. 3860–62.

13. Alton Frye, "Strategic Synthesis," *Foreign Policy,* no. 58 (Spring 1985): 25.

14. *Department of Defense Authorization,* p. 3862.

15. Myron Hura and David Miller, "Cruise Missiles: Future Options," *U.S. Naval Institute Proceedings* 112/8/1002 (August 1986): 52.

16. George Quester raises the question of whether the time frame for decisions on the use of ballistic missiles is even remotely adequate, given their rapid flight times. See Quester, *The Future of Nuclear Deterrence* (Lexington, Mass.: Lexington Books, 1986), chap. 11.

17. *Department of Defense Authorization,* p. 3696.

18. *Aviation Week and Space Technology,* June 23, 1986, pp. 48–51.

19. Ibid., pp. 3696, 3668.

20. Hura and Miller, "Cruise Missiles," p. 53.

21. Stephen M. Millett, "Deterrence in the High-Technology Era: A Speculative Forecast," *Air University Review* 37 (May–June 1986): 30–31.

22. See Paul Stares, "U.S. and Soviet Military Space Programs: A Comparative Assessment," in Franklin A Long, Donald Hafner, and Jeffrey Boutwell (eds.), *Weapons in Space* (New York: W.W. Norton, 1986), pp. 127–146; Kurt Gottfried and Richard Ned Lebow, "Anti-Satellite Weapons: Weighing the Risks," in ibid., pp. 147–170.

23. President's Commission on Strategic Forces, *Report* (Washington, D.C.: Government Printing Office, April 1983), pp. 7–8.

24. Millett, "Deterrence," makes a similar point with respect to counterforce targeting on pp. 34–35.

25. Colin S. Gray, "Nuclear Strategy: A Case for a Theory of Victory," *International Security* 4 (Summer 1979): 68–69. Gary Guertner notes that a U.S. counterforce strike could have the effect of destroying much of the greater Russian population, given the location of most Soviet ICBM silos. See Gary L. Guertner, "Perceptions of Soviet Strategic Vulnerability" (paper presented at the Annual Meeting of the International Studies Association, Los Angeles, March 1980), pp. 4–5, 26.

26. William T. Lee, "Soviet Nuclear Targeting Strategy," in Desmond Ball and Jeffrey Richelson (eds.), *Strategic Nuclear Targeting* (Ithaca: Cornell University Press, 1985), p. 91.

27. Quester, *Future,* pp. 178–179.

28. The BRAVO 15 MT test in 1954 spread radiation levels of 800 rads, a lethal dose, over 140 miles from ground zero. Samuel Glasstone and Philip J. Dolan, *The Effects of Nuclear Weapons* (Washington, D.C.: Department of Defense, 1977), p. 437.

29. Frye, "Strategic Synthesis," p. 25.

30. *The SALT II Treaty,* Hearings before the Committee on Foreign Relations, U.S. Senate, 96th Cong., 1st sess., 1979, p. 19. A MIRVed ACM would obviously be a complication.

31. William H. Kincade, "Arms Control: Negotiated Solutions," in Richard Betts (ed.), *Cruise Missiles: Technology, Strategy, Politics* (Washington, D.C.: Brookings Institution, 1981), p. 315.

32. *Aviation Week and Space Technology,* September 1, 1986, p. 183.

33. Kincade, "Arms Control," p. 317.

34. *Department of Defense Authorizations,* p. 3980.

III
Conventional Military Relations

7
NATO: Coping with New Challenges

Gale Mattox

D espite the doomsayers, NATO is not poised to slip into an abyss and vanish in the near future. It has survived forty years of periodic crises and can be expected to dominate the organization of Western defense policy into the next century. This is not to deny the seriousness of issues now confronting the Western allies or to minimize the potential challenges they pose to the alliance. This is also not to say that there will not be change, even substantial change, in the structure of U.S.–West European defense policy in the years ahead, particularly if the nature of perception of the nature of the Soviet threat changes.

If one is to believe the strictest Europeanists, NATO will soon be replaced by a vibrant European Defense Community, which will eventually assume the present U.S. defense guarantees. This scenario is, however, highly unlikely for several reasons; foremost is the propensity not to alter the status quo, particularly a status quo that has proved so successful since 1949. Furthermore, the existing political and economic circumstances in Europe would make an independent European defense unlikely, if not impossible. Finally, despite those who charge otherwise, there has not been such a dramatic change in the perceived threat and therefore fundamental needs of the alliance members to prompt drastic change.

But it cannot be denied that the alliance has been strained by several issues in the past few years, and those issues can be expected to challenge it in the future. First, there have been a number of challenges to long-held assumptions about the requirements of European defense. Will the possibility of Gorbachev-inspired reforms alter the perception of the Soviet threat, and thereby the basis of the Western defense structure in the postwar era? The U.S.-Soviet negotiations in Geneva, and to a lesser extent in Vienna and Stockholm, also raise the issue of defense requirements and structure. Does the agreement most recently struck between the United States and Soviet Union eliminating whole

The views expressed are solely those of the author and do not reflect the views of the U.S. government or any institutional affiliation.

categories of INF weapons with ranges from 300 to 3,400 miles portend an eventual change in the ultimate U.S. nuclear guarantee of European security? If, as most analysts agree, the result of the INF agreement is a shift in emphasis from nuclear to conventional, policymakers will confront a number of dilemmas in dealing with the Soviet "challenge" to the West.

Second, on out-of-area issues, the persistent Middle East conflicts and the recent resurgence of terrorist attacks have driven a wedge at times between Europe and the United States. Will these issues erode allied relationships and isolate the United States? What is the role for NATO or even U.S. allies in the resolution of those conflicts?

Third, transatlantic trade problems have strained West-West relations in a number of areas, including traditional trade issues and also East-West technology transfer. With the threatening onset of protectionism in the West and the heightened Soviet interest in obtaining Western technology, both of these areas can be expected to challenge Western policymakers to come up with more innovative solutions.

Finally, the U.S.–West European relationship has undergone a substantial transformation since World War II from one of unequals militarily, politically, and economically, with the United States clearly predominant, to a relationship of near economic and political equals. With the expected withdrawal of U.S. INFs, maintenance of an acceptable military balance will require more effort on the part of the Europeans. These changes in the power balance have been reflected in closer consultation on a range of issues within NATO and increased European participation. There has also been a notable increase in foreign policy coordination among West Europeans, both within the European Community and in the Western European Union (WEU). While official U.S. policy supports these European initiatives, does it hold the potential to threaten the long-term U.S. commitment to NATO? Is Europe either prepared or willing to assume more responsibility for its defense?

This chapter will concentrate its attention on the issues affecting U.S.-European defense policy: strategy and arms control, out-of-area operations, trade and economic relations, and the structure of U.S.-European defense. All of these areas may be expected to confront the NATO allies with difficult issues affecting the future direction of the NATO alliance and the security of its members.

Strategy and the Dilemmas of Arms Control

A major issue in the Atlantic Alliance today is defining the most appropriate strategy to continue to provide a necessary deterrent to the East. Although the prevailing strategy has proved successful since 1949, it is the result of incremental change in the real or perceived balance of forces and fundamental policy shifts at critical junctures. The alliance has again reached a juncture at which change, desired or not, will be necessary. Those who argue that nuclear deterrence has served the alliance well since the origins of NATO often fail to recognize the iterations the strategy has undergone over the years. Change has been and will continue to be part of the process of constructing an adequate defense of the West.

But the success of change is dependent on the way in which alliance decisions are taken. As supporters of the proposed NATO multilateral force (MLF) discovered in the 1960s, it is not always an easy process to strike agreement between disparate views and security needs of all alliance partners.[1] A nuclear deterrent strategy has protected the European continent for forty years, and those who advocate its immediate replacement with a purely conventional defense in the near future are ill advised. It is clear, however, that there are factors encouraging discussion of nonnuclear options. The most pressing of these is the recent U.S.-Soviet arms control agreement to eliminate all intermediate (INF) and short-range (SRINF) intermediate nuclear weapons (approximately 300–3,400 mile range) in Europe.

In examining the implications of an INF agreement, it is important to recognize what it will not mean. It will not mean the elimination of all U.S. nuclear forces in Europe; over 3,000 warheads on aircraft, short-range, and battlefield weapons will remain.[2] Also, the United States has made it clear that there will be no change in its strategic nuclear guarantee. Both of these factors suggest that future European defense will continue to have a nuclear component. A final factor reinforces this conclusion; there is every indication that at least some U.S. conventional forces will remain on the Continent as a sign of American commitment. The U.S. administration continually points out these factors, and the Europeans almost as regularly question them.

For this reason, it is as important for the United States to understand why Europeans are disconcerted as a result of gleaned perceptions (or misperceptions) as it is for the Europeans to recognize that the United States has no intention of backing away at this point from its commitment to Europe. Foremost, since 1983 and the announcement of the SDI, the U.S. president has persistently underscored (without European consultation) his intention to move into a nonnuclear world, most recently during the Moscow summit. While a laudable long-term goal and certainly one shared by many or even most Europeans, there has not yet been a clear sense of an acceptable alternative means of defense, particularly to the ultimate U.S. strategic nuclear guarantee. Even before the 1983 speech, the strategic parity codified in the SALT II agreement between the superpowers prompted discomfort among Europeans who had assumed U.S. strategic superiority to have deterrent value in and of itself. The 1979 NATO decision to modernize INF was a result of this discomfort.

Europeans have also been disconcerted by the repeated threats by the U.S. Congress to force troop withdrawals if the Europeans were not more financially forthcoming.[3] Any shift to greater reliance on conventional forces confronts the Europeans with two commodities in short supply: the funds for the expensive and necessary high-tech conventional weapons and draft-age personnel to fill out the required forces. Even beyond these issues is the suspicion that these U.S. actions are steps down the road to the end of U.S. extended deterrence in Europe.

Historically there have been attempts by the Congress to reduce the U.S. commitment in Europe, usually prompted by economic concerns. This was true in the late 1960s and early 1970s when the Mansfield amendments legislating troop withdrawals were often only narrowly defended. The later efforts by Senators Ted Stevens (R–Alaska) and, more specifically, Sam Nunn (D–Georgia) were aimed at forcing a greater financial contribution from the Europeans. Congresswoman Patricia Schroeder (D–Colorado) has more recently taken a somewhat different approach in a series of congressional hearings held in mid-1988. She has called for the American troop commitment to be tied to the U.S. trade deficit with Europe. For European military planners, the U.S. debate can be confusing and dismaying.

The U.S.–West European relationship is complex and multifaceted. The needs of each of the partners are also often contradictory. Certainly there is an inherent contradiction in the European need to exert independence on the one hand while at the same time seeking reassurance that the United States will not withdraw its forces, a visible sign of its commitment to European security. The Europeans often become especially unsettled in the face of comments by public officials such as former secretary of state Henry Kissinger. In a speech at Palais d'Egmont in Brussels to a group of European officials, Kissinger challenged the reliability of the American strategic nuclear guarantee and chastised the Europeans for not recognizing the uncertainty of the guarantee and doing enough in their own behalf.[4]

A contradiction is also apparent in the French posture.[5] While intent on maintaining their separate nuclear *force de frappe*, the French were also the most vehement proponents of the INF stationing, viewed as a broadening of the U.S. presence. Obviously the U.S. presence reinforces and could act as a firebreak for the independent French. On the one hand, they do not want to participate officially in the integrated NATO military command with its dependence on the United States. On the other hand, the French defense strategy appears to presuppose a U.S. presence in Europe.

A final example of contradiction in the past few years is clearly the U.S. advocacy of sharp reductions in nuclear weapons and eventually their abolition. From the time of the INF double-track decision[6] in 1979 to the deployment of GLCMs and Pershing IIs in 1983, there was a tremendous popular debate over whether to deploy. The U.S. as well as official Western European position strongly supported deployment. But for West European governments that argued against the nonnuclear movement opposed to INF, the later U.S. arguments for eliminating an entire class of nuclear weapons in the INF agreements had a familiar ring. The single largest challenge to NATO in the future will be redefining the role of nuclear weapons versus conventional.

The debate has already begun. The move to flexible response (NATO document MC 14/3) in 1967 was one step along the way, and the next iteration will move even further from the ultimate nuclear threat without going beyond it. The wide debate over the question of no first use advocated by four prominent Americans[7] and the nervous German retort[8] made the inevitability of a shift clear. The primary point made by the Americans that the debate was necessary to force conventional improvements was not lost on the Europeans.

Most recently there have been reports of a restructuring of the process by which NATO will arrive at the decision to use nuclear weapons. But how many, and how will the future rounds of arms control affect the U.S. posture? Will the British and French forces eventually replace the U.S. commitment, or will their role become gradually destabilizing?[9] What will be the German role in the future? How will the Germans react to overtures from the East, particularly those from East Germany?[10] Again the contradictions are apparent; a European nuclear policy is inconceivable without German input and yet hard to imagine as part of any independent force given not-so-distant European history. Yet a reduction in the U.S. forces in Europe or even the perception of a less adamant U.S. commitment can be expected to force answers to all these questions.

While not abolishing the U.S. nuclear guarantee ensured by the continued presence of short-range and battlefield nuclear weapons as well as U.S. commitment of strategic forces, the increased dependence an INF Treaty is expected to prompt on conventional forces confronts the United States and its allies with a number of uncomfortable dilemmas.[11] Above all, most Western countries are grappling with significant economic problems that undermine a serious commitment to increased budgets for conventional forces. As one observer commented when discussing the potential impact of SDI for a European defense initiative, "the government's fears about decoupling and zones of unequal security might not be fulfilled in missile-defence itself—but the financial squeeze on conventional defence, combined with the strains a forthcoming era of missile defence would put on Flexible Response, would certainly heighten concern about unequal security on the conventional level."[12] This lack of resources is compounded by the expected shortfall in manpower over the next few years that will make increases in force numbers impossible.[13]

The challenge to NATO will be to orchestrate the inherent contradictions in the competing needs of its members in order to devise a doctrine responsive to the future requirements of the alliance.[14] If the United States remains committed to drastic reductions and then abolition of nuclear weapons in the near future, as discussed at the superpower summit in Iceland, closer consultation and coordination with the allies will be urgently required. The Reykjavik meetings considerably unnerved European officials who assure their publics of the U.S. nuclear guarantees. While a nonnuclear world is clearly attractive in the abstract, it is not now or in the near future to the advantage of the United States or Europe to move away from U.S. extended deterrence without a consensus in Europe on an acceptable and defined alternative. Anything less than intensive involvement by the allies will prompt the opposite from its desired goal, resulting in an increasingly less stable rather than stable world.

Out-of-Area Operations

The intention of the NATO signatories on the question of territorial responsibility is addressed in Article 6 of the North Atlantic Treaty signed on April 4, 1949, in Washington, D.C.:

> For the purpose of Article 5, an armed attack on one or more of the Parties is deemed to include an armed attack
> —on the territory of the Parties in Europe or North America, on the territory of Turkey or on the islands under the jurisdiction of any of the Parties in the North Atlantic area north of the Tropic of Cancer;
> —on the forces, vessels, or aircraft of any of the Parties, when in or over these territories or any area in Europe in which occupation forces of any of the Parties were stationed on the date when the Treaty entered into force or the Mediterranean Sea or the North Atlantic area north of the Tropic of Cancer.[15]

Despite these limitations, there have been concerted efforts to harmonize out-of-area allied foreign policies from the outset. These efforts have confronted the allies with the fact that the Atlantic Alliance does not and cannot isolate itself from the rest of the world. The United States, as well as other allies such as Great Britain with far-flung interests and France with its active foreign markets, have concerns, often threats, to their security outside the Atlantic area. Those concerns have traditionally been defined to be outside the purview of NATO and the responsibility of the individual NATO member but not without periodic debate of the issue.

Even less clearly defined has been the situation in which an alliance member becomes embroiled in a conflict or dispute outside the defined territory of NATO that requires forces or equipment from the NATO area, even if only airport and landing privileges, with potential implications to NATO defense. Historically, NATO has turned a blind eye despite a depletion of stockpiles, reduced readiness, and even shortfall in forces when members have had to shift resources to other areas. Two striking examples over the past fifteen years have been the British during the Falklands crisis and the United States during the Vietnam conflict.

Initially it was the United States that encouraged strict adherence to the regional basis of the alliance. Coordination of foreign policies took the form of general alliance policy, with any actual cooperation occurring on a bilateral basis outside the alliance. Theodore Draper remarked correctly that the United States was "in effect . . . perfectly content with an Alliance that formally left it with a free hand outside Europe without allied meddling, as if the day would never come when the United States might need allied support outside Europe."[16]

There has been a change in U.S. attitude since the late 1970s, which prompted it to reconsider this stance with regard to the Middle East. Several factors precipitated the change. First, there has been a movement in the United States to force Europe to carry a greater share of the defense budget. As the direct European monetary contribution has not increased, there has been more pressure for European assistance on out-of-area issues. Second, the Europeans are obviously now more economically, militarily, and politically capable of assistance than in the postwar era. Third, expanding economic, political, and military global interdependence has pressured the United States to become involved outside its traditional spheres, and the United States has sought European expertise and support for its activities. Finally, the evolving European Community (EC) has made Europe a natural partner in situations outside the immediate Atlantic area.

Two related issues have predominated in U.S. efforts to engage the Europeans. First and foremost, the 1973 Middle East war impressed the West with the vulnerability of Europe to a cutoff of energy resources and considerably raised the stakes for a peace in the region. Second, a rash of terrorist acts emanating from the Middle East occurred in Europe and made stability in the region even more vital. Although the 1979 hostage crisis in Iran prompted U.S. pressure initially for European involvement, the taking of West European hostages lately in Lebanon and involvement of innocent European civilians in terrorist hijackings has made it increasingly more difficult not to involve NATO. From the U.S. perspective, would not a concerted alliance response to the problems in the Middle East be more effective than individual action?

The U.S. decision to bomb Libya following the destruction in Berlin of the La Belle discotheque by terrorists was accompanied by a request to the Europeans for assistance—if not directly, then in terms of refueling privileges. Only Great Britain accommodated in a limited way. The general European reaction was and has continued to be to look at military response to terrorist actions against individual nations with skepticism. It did not help the U.S. case that the Syrian connection, rather than Libyan, later appeared more convincing in the La Belle investigation. Subsequent attempts to coordinate an Atlantic Alliance policy on terrorism have been difficult and limited to the detection, exchange of information, and possible capture of terrorists. The continued EC debate and pronouncements on Libya following the 1986 raid were not supportive of U.S. efforts. Even the British have warned not to expect them to be as forthcoming in the future.

As perplexing as formulating an approach to terrorism has been the issue of safeguarding Middle Eastern oil and increasing the stability of the region. The United States undertook to reflag Kuwaiti tankers in 1987 with these twin objectives in mind. Again, coordinated alliance assistance proved elusive in the NATO context. The European response had a number of roots; the Germans have a constitutional prohibition[17] that impedes activity in areas of conflict, and the British and French bristle at activities that might appear to condone an extension of the NATO mandate. For these reasons, the Europeans have in the past assumed the more cautious posture of noninvolvement with the argument that out-of-area military action could prove more destabilizing than stabilizing.

The Persian Gulf situation, however, may have prompted a significant turning point in the history of European coordinated action. The fact that the West Europeans harbored reservations over an out-of-area NATO response did not mean that there was no perception of a threat to various European interests in the gulf region. In fact, the French have had a long history and presence in the gulf, as have the British. Prompted by these interests, the WEU convened debate of the issue. The resulting recommendation to European members of the WEU to consider involvement in the gulf was the first time the organization had taken such a course. Although the decision to participate in defending free transit of international waters either with the fleet presence (as France, Britain and Italy), minesweepers (as Belgium and the Netherlands), or assumption of additional tasks in the North Atlantic and Mediterranean (as West Germany) was unilateral, it is clear that the WEU played an important part in the necessary consensus-building process for the gulf action. The WEU reinforced its support of European cooperation with the United States in a communiqué following the bombing of a U.S. ship by an Iranian mine in April 1988. It reaffirmed the principle of free navigation in the Persian Gulf and called for "an immediate end to all mining and other hostile activities" there.[18]

It is also interesting to note that there is a high degree of operational coordination in the gulf among the NATO allies, despite the continued official posture of unilateral action. Before the April mine incident, the European force stood at approximately thirty-two ships, with the French operating their fifteen somewhat more independently.[19]

There is little doubt that the out-of-area issue continues to hold the potential for disagreement among alliance members in the future, particularly with regard to the Middle East. The region is an area of as much, if not more, interest to the Europeans than the United States. Not only may the Europeans be expected to resist redefinition of the NATO area, but the United States can be assured that the European approaches will diverge in the Middle East as well as elsewhere. Reluctance to give assistance by the allies—whether to provide military support or remand a terrorist to stand trial in the United States (as in the case of Muhammed Hamadei in West Germany)—will continue to cause friction.

Ideally a coordinated development of objective criteria rather than the present case-by-case approach would be desirable for the Atlantic Alliance. Preferably the criteria should be as specific as possible with reference to appropriate territorial bounds and issues areas. Simply a reiteration of the 1967 Harmel Report on the problem in this case has already proved insufficient.[20]

More specific criteria could avoid future misunderstandings and limit the degree of subjective decisions influenced by popular opinion or the political climate of the moment in individual countries. Unfortunately, the potential for agreement on such criteria even at the heads-of-state level is small.

For the United States the most constructive development has been the emergence of the WEU and, to a lesser extent, the EC, as consensus-building organizations. Although it remained for each country to forge its own internal support, allied assistance was forthcoming in the gulf. Similar support might be possible in other areas as well, if and when the circumstances and situation dictate.

Trade and Economic Relations

The friction between the United States and Western Europe in the area of trade and economic relations has mounted in the past few years. It affects not only West-West relations but West-East as well. The reasons are manifold and diverse. Perhaps the largest contributing factor has been the recovery and growth of Western Europe since World War II to the status of economic rival to the United States and competitor in world markets.

Western Europe experienced notable political and economic development over forty years, with implications for West-West economic and trade relations. In the case of West Germany, the recovery can only be termed astounding. In economic terms, the total GNP of Western Europe now surpasses that of the United States. With declining agricultural populations and increasing manufacturing (including high-technology) and service sectors, the Europeans compete for the world markets with the United States. In an effort to maintain the disappearing agricultural sector, the EC heavily subsidizes farmers, straining relations with the United States. In the manufacturing sectors the innovative area of high technology has already clashed with both the United States and Japan. Often without the advantages of economy of scale as in the United States or cheap, lean labor pools as in Japan, the West Europeans have found themselves on the losing side of the competition.

While making a valiant effort, the EC suffers from the plethora of cultures, traditions, loyalties, and ingrained differences as well as hatreds among the economic partners of Europe. On the road to the closer integration envisioned in the Treaty of Rome (1957), the West European allies have experienced the high points of success but also the lows of failure. Each country is intent on using the EC to promote its own economic interests, and the result is frequently counterproductive to the long-term objectives of the EC. Fearful of losing national industries, the Europeans are often reluctant to cooperate in order to compensate for the inherent disadvantages involved in merging disparate cultures. For U.S.–West European relations, the resulting subsidies and trade barriers on both sides of the Atlantic have exacerbated relations, with political and economic repercussions and also military implications in the area of joint NATO defense.

But despite its setbacks, the EC has become a global trader with which to reckon. In political terms, the economic development has led to the growing stature of individual European countries and the EC itself. Just on the basis of sheer numbers—economic indicators—the EC cannot be ignored. Its West-West trade is substantial and impressive, and its East-West trade is clearly increasing. The Lome Convention ensures a north-south dimension as well. The sum total of all of these relations has been to increase the political voice and economic weight of the West European nations. The plans to achieve full economic integration by 1992 will increase and reinforce the growing global influence of the EC.

The former U.S. economic and political predominance has been replaced by a relationship of equals, sometimes competitive equals, and this competition often strains relations as national interests clash. Only constant attention to even relatively minor issues often averts clashes over differences. A number of attempts to regulate and bypass potential problem issues have made significant advances. One of these—the regular economic summits of Western leaders—underscores the political as well as economic importance of minimizing areas of potential difference.

The final product of the summits is more often political than economic. On a daily basis, economic sections within the embassies of the countries on both sides of the Atlantic have greatly increased. Bilateral as well as multilateral informal discussions and formal negotiations occur throughout the year. But no amount of negotiation may be expected to eliminate the inevitable differences over West-West trade.[21] There are clear indications that the trend will be to increase trade barriers and thus increase the potential for friction.

A recurring and persistent issue in West-West economic relations has been the question of defense spending. Since the ambitious force plans of the 1952 Lisbon Plan, the Atlantic Alliance has struggled to maintain adequate troop strength. It has faltered as allied democratic governments have not had the means or the political will to increase defense spending sufficiently to meet the desired force levels. Particularly since the late 1960s with the impressive economic gains made by the individual West European countries, the subject of defense spending has caused friction between the the United States and Western Europe. It was at that time that the Senate Majority leader, Mike Mansfield, tried to goad the Europeans into greater participation in their defense with the threats of troop withdrawals.

In response to U.S. concerns and at a time of relative economic prosperity, alliance members agreed in 1977 to a 3 percent national increase in defense spending and an ambitious Long-Term Defense Program.[22] The agreement has since become a source of embarrassment as most nations failed to fulfill the commitment.[23] The United States, particularly the Congress, has continued to apply pressure in the form of amendments and resolutions, the most serious being the recent Nunn amendment.

While most previous criticism of the Europeans had focused on the commitment to the 3 percent increase, the 1984 Nunn-Roth amendment was an attempt to address also the substantive deficiencies of NATO forces. The amendment articulated three specific concerns that had to be corrected within a three-year time frame as a separate avenue for the allies: increase air and ground munitions, increase emergency facilities and semihardened aircraft shelters, and improve the conventional defense capacity.[24] The alternative, as outlined in the amendment, would be troop withdrawals up to 90,000. A compromise was struck, and the deficiencies were corrected, but neither the United States nor Western Europe appreciated this type of pressure. Given the projections for defense spending, a better means of resolving such differences in the future will be necessary.

The friction among Western nations over trade and defense spending is exacerbated by the issue of appropriate West-East relations. The question of East-West trade is certain to aggravate allied relations in the future. While the United States exports primarily agricultural products to the East, particularly the Soviet Union, the West European trade with the East is broader. All trends point to an increase in European trade with the East over the next several years. The reform era initiated by General Secretary Gorbachev portends intensified efforts by the Eastern bloc to import the necessary technology to assist the tremendous task of modernizing Soviet and East European industry and, when this task is accomplished, to enter world markets as a serious competitor.

Although the latter does not pose an imminent problem, the former efforts to attain Western technology have already strained U.S.–European relations and can be expected to continue to cause further rifts. The controversy over the construction of a Soviet natural gasline to Europe in 1982 had ramifications, for example, for a wide range of U.S.–West European issues.[25] The Europeans consider the U.S. sanctions on European subsidiaries of U.S. firms or purchases of U.S. technology to be intrusive and beyond the proper bounds of U.S. dictates. From the U.S. perspective, the specter of the Soviet Union's using technology thus acquired against the United States in future weapons programs has been unacceptable. The incongruencies of the U.S. fear of Soviet use of Western technology for military as well as economic development and West European energy requirements and the European desire to expand its markets could not avoid clashing.

It is not that serious attempts to reconcile the incongruencies have not been tried. The Paris-based Coordinating Committee (COCOM) has had success in negotiating common Western definitions of acceptable trade practices with the East. But with or without COCOM, the potential for problems persists, if not as a result of the clash of differing national interests government-to-government, then in the attempt to regulate private industry where the free market reigns. Problems are inevitable and, in part, unavoidable. The most recent case of the sale of sophisticated technology by private Norwegian and Japanese firms that the United States charges has contributed to the impressive qualitative improvement in Soviet submarine capabilities is only one example. The sales by those firms to the Soviets have been denounced by their respective governments, which are now grappling with the question of formal charges against the firms. Although not sanctioned by the governments, those private sales have had repercussions for U.S. bilateral relations with the countries involved.

Whether West-West or East-West trade, the issues now confronting the Atlantic Alliance may be expected to continue. The increasing interdependence of global markets will pressure national governments into even more attentive scrutiny and protection of their national interests.

Structure of U.S.-European Defense

A final challenge to the United States will be the role of Western Europe in NATO. Elizabeth Pond asked in a recent article, "Europe: a U.S. pillar or rival in NATO?"[26] Although the United States has always encouraged a louder European voice in NATO affairs in principle, the practice has often been different. Unilateral decisions by the United States have not been unusual in the past. While this has become far less true in operational matters over the past decade, on issues with direct implications for the defense of Europe, glaring exceptions remain. The most striking example was certainly the March 23, 1983, announcement by President Reagan of the SDI. The Europeans, neither consulted nor informed on an issue with direct implications for them, were dismayed.

In operational terms, there is close coordination and consultation within NATO on a daily basis. Issues of high political salience are passed on to the defense or foreign ministers or even heads of state meetings. While there continue to be unilateral decisions taken by the United States, there is no guarantee that those decisions will enjoy support in NATO as in the past. As the alliance confronts major decisions over the next few years in the areas of strategy and arms control, modification and/or change will be vital if the allies are to play the role they have come to expect.

Recently an Italian defense analyst addressed the INF decision. Italy, he wrote, had had "only the most limited possibility" to contribute to the initial 1979 decision. Furthermore, although "a sort of pattern seems to have emerged, in that while Italy's role can be decisive in supporting Allied policy," he concluded that the country "still lacks the ability to influence the Allied decision-making process." His prognosis—"filling this gap is the challenge Italian foreign policy faces for the years to come"—is discouraging.[27]

The proposals on how to achieve greater European participation are numerous. They range from former U.S. secretary of state Henry Kissinger's proposal to appoint a European Supreme Allied Commander Europe (SACEUR) to a proposal creating a European seat at the superpower arms control negotiations to more European committee heads within NATO. Often overlooked in the debates over the practicality of these proposals (aside from some realistic objections) is the contradiction in objectives they usually raise. The United States pays lip-service to increased European involvement but would like to ensure continued latitude to make national decisions. The Europeans complain about U.S. dominance in the alliance but are reluctant to assume the risks of decisions themselves and, especially, undertake any new arrangements that would reduce the U.S. commitment. For this reason, the changes within NATO can be expected to remain incremental while making adjustments at the fringes and in the policymaking process.

What then is the likelihood of a separate European voice outside the alliance? Since 1957 U.S. official policy has always encouraged European integration within the EC. It was thought that eventually integration would shift the burden of defense to Europe and gradually reduce the U.S. role on the Continent. Additionally, since the French withdrawal from NATO, many NATO officials have seen European efforts as a way of ensuring closer French coordination and cooperation with NATO operations.[28]

The success of achieving European security policy has been mixed. Since the early 1970s, there has been limited foreign policy coordination among members, and European Political Cooperation (EPC) now addresses at least general security issues. In fact, some issues debated in the NATO councils have been coordinated earlier in the EPC.[29] But more specific arrangements for defense cooperation have not been successful; the Genscher-Colombo proposal to the EC in 1981 met with failure, for instance.[30]

Another scenario in recent years has been outside either NATO or the EC. The creation of the Independent European Programme Group (IEPG) to improve cooperative defense procurement among the Europeans is one example. Projects such as the new European fighter program are encouraging although certainly not without problems. The attempts to expand the purview of the WEU have been only marginally successful but important, as noted in the case of the Persian Gulf.[31]

For those nervous about European integration, the potential dangers are many. Closer coordination outside the NATO structure could disrupt the alliance decision-making process and push the United States into a singular position. What happens if the Europeans finally are able to reach a consensus on issues contrary to U.S. stated policy? Will the United States maintain its leadership role? Would a true equal-among-equals position be acceptable to the United States in the face of its nuclear guarantee for Europe and large number of conventional forces? It is unlikely, particularly given the already long-standing misgivings of some members of the U.S. Congress.

If that integration occurred outside NATO in a European Defense Community or a rejuvenated WEU, it is likely to meet U.S. resistance. The amount of such resistance would depend in part on the effect of the external organization on NATO. Again, as a means of bringing France into the defense structure, it might be an acceptable option.[32] On the other hand, a situation in which Germany had access to nuclear weapons remains disturbing to a significant number of Europeans, and the issue would need to be resolved. There is no question that an avenue(s) must be found for greater European input, both to satisfy U.S. pressure on the Europeans to do more and to respond to European pressure for more input. To be successful, any effort could come only through European initiative but with close coordination with the United States.

Conclusion

The safest predictions for the future are built on the lessons of the past. In the case of NATO, there is little danger in predicting its continuance into the future.[33] Despite the doomsayers, it will continue to muddle through and survive as well as can be expected from an alliance of sixteen democratic nations with some complementary and some conflicting national interests. It is also safe to predict, however, that the task in the future will be more difficult as the predominance of the United States declines and the influence of Western Europe increases. It will also become more complex if the perception of a potential Soviet military aggression is replaced by major reforms to the Soviet system.

The issue of survival that played such an important role in the past for many of the West European nations has faded. The Soviet threat no longer dominates the headlines; for the younger generations, particularly those who may mature at a time of reform and possible rejuvenation of the Soviet system, that threat may become hard to imagine. Furthermore, the political backseat taken by Western Europe to the United States has become an anachronism. The role West Germany played on the issue of the Pershing Ia in the final stages of the U.S.-Soviet discussions over an intermediate-range nuclear arms control agreement has been unprecedented. Finally, the economic devastation of Western Europe at the time NATO was designed has been replaced by a vitality and strength similar to that of the United States. It is no longer a question of economic survival; most West Europeans are now occupied with the task of improving an already astonishing standard of living. Their domestic advances will complicate the difficult task of financing defense. In terms of military confrontation, a recent study by Ambassador Jonathan Dean argues that Europe has reached a watershed and now faces "gradual decline or attrition of the confrontation under the combined impact of arms control, political measures, and budgetary shortages."[34]

This chapter has examined only a sample of issues expected to challenge U.S. policymakers in the future. At the core of U.S.–West European relations will be the question of the continued U.S. commitment to allied defense. The perception of U.S. commitment is important for more than its purely deterrent value against Soviet attack. It is vital to ensure the coupling of European defense to the United States. As World War II fades from memory, Europeans are now asking whether the U.S. sense of its defense commitment and the importance of Europe will fade. Will the myriad arms control agreements simply provide the excuse to retreat? Should the Europeans fear, as de Gaulle often warned, a U.S.-Soviet condominium as arms control negotiations intensify, or is a U.S. turn to the Pacific and Japan possible, even probable?

The issues of strategy and arms control, out-of-area involvements, and trade relations will influence the ongoing debates over NATO structure and organization. There is no question that change is inevitable if the organization is to survive. A balance between the needs of the United States and Europe will need to be struck, either within the existing structure or through the construction of a spearate European capability. The need for mutual respect will never be greater.

Notes

1. Catherine McArdle Kelleher, *Germany and the Politics of Nuclear Weapons* (New York: Columbia University Press, 1975).
2. For complete figures, see *The Military Balance, 1986–1987* (London: International Institute for Strategic Studies, 1986), pp. 200–208.
3. Calls for troop withdrawals and a separate and equal European balance have also come from outside the Congress. For example, see Melvin Krauss, *How NATO Weakens the West* (New York: Simon and Schuster, 1986), and Christopher Layne, "Atlanticism without NATO," *Foreign Policy*, no. 67 (Summer 1987): 22–45.
4. Henry Kissinger, "NATO—The Next Thirty Years," Speech at Palais d'Egmont, Brussels, September 1, 1979.
5. For an in-depth discussion of the French position, see David S. Yost, "France's Deterrent Posture and Security in Europe," pts. 1, 2 Adelphi Papers nos. 194 and 195 (London: International Institute for Strategic Studies, 1984–1985).
6. NATO, "Communique of the Special Meeting of NATO Foreign and Defense Ministers" (Brussels, December 12, 1979).
7. McGeorge Bundy et al., "Nuclear Weapons and the Atlantic Alliance," *Foreign Affairs*, no. 60 (Spring 1982): 753–768; John D. Steinbruner and Leon V. Sigal (eds.), *Alliance Security: NATO and the No-First-Use Question* (Washington, D.C.: Brookings Institution, 1983).
8. Karl Kaiser et al., "Nuclear Weapons: A German Response to No First Use," *Foreign Affairs*, no. 60 (Summer 1982): 1157–1170.
9. For a discussion of the British and French nuclear forces, see George M. Seignious II and Jonathan P. Yates, "Europe's Nuclear Superpowers," *Foreign Policy*, no. 55 (Summer 1984): 40–53.

10. Is it time for West Germany to renounce national unity as discussed in Peter Bender, "The Superpower Squeeze," *Foreign Policy*, no. 65 (Winter 1986–1987): 98–113?

11. For a thorough discussion of the dilemmas, see Stanley Sloan (ed.), *NATO in the 1990s*, (in press).

12. Elizabeth Pond, "The Security Debate in West Germany," *Survival* (July–August 1986): 335.

13. In addition to difficulty over meeting even the 1977 3 percent increase commitment, former SACEUR General Bernard Rogers has argued that at least a 4 percent increase will be necessary. See European Security Study, *Strengthening Conventional Deterrence in Europe: Proposals for the 1980s* (New York: Macmillan, 1983); Andrew J. Pierre (ed.), *The Conventional Defense of Europe: New Technologies and New Strategies* (New York: Council on Foreign Relations, 1986).

14. Johan Jorgen Holst, now defense minister of Norway, warned at the 1985 IISS annual conference held in West Berlin that "in discussing doctrine, it is common to assume greater coherence and consistency than prevails in the real world of basic contradiction and tension between competing requirements and considerations." "Denial and Punishment: Straddling the Horns of NATO's Dilemma," Adelphi Paper no. 206 (London: International Institute of Strategic Studies, Spring 1986), p. 77.

15. "The North Atlantic Treaty," in *NATO Handbook* (Brussels: NATO, March 1982), p. 14.

16. Theodore Draper, "The Western Misalliance," *Washington Quarterly* (Winter 1981): 29.

17. For a review of West German prohibitions, see Joachim Krause, "Die Ruestungsexport-Politik der Bundesrepublik Deutschland," *Europa Archiv*, June 25, 1981, and Joachim Krause and Gale A. Mattox, "West German Arms Sales to the Third World," *Atlantic Quarterly* 2, no. 2 (Summer 1984): 171–182.

18. Julian Baum and William Echikson, "Europe: Pulling Its Weight in the Gulf?" *Christian Science Monitor*, May 2, 1988, p. 4.

19. Ibid., p. 3. The European contribution to the gulf force in May 1988 consisted of Belgium (one minesweeper, one support ship), Great Britain (one frigate, two destroyers, three minesweepers, three support ships), France (one aircraft carrier, four frigates, two destroyers, three minesweepers, three support ships), Italy (three frigates, two minesweepers, one support ship), and the Netherlands (two minesweepers).

20. Marc Bentinck discusses the use of objective criteria. He would, however, base those criteria for the present on the 1967 Harmel Report. "NATO's Out-of-Area Problem," Adelphi Paper no. 211 (London: International Institute of Strategic Studies, Autumn 1986).

21. These are by no means new problems. See Gregory F. Treverton, "Economics and Security in the Atlantic Alliance," *Survival* (November–December 1984): 269–279.

22. The text of the 1976 communiqué and a discussion of it can be found in David Greenwood, "NATO's Three Per Cent Solution," *Survival* 23 (November–December 1981): 252–260. For a copy of the Long-Term Defense Program, see NATO Information Service, *North Atlantic Treaty Organization: Facts and Figures* (Brussels: NATO, 1981), pp. 149–150.

23. Figures for NATO defense expenditures and percentage of GNP (but not percentage increases) may be found in "Documentation," *NATO Review,* no. 1 (February 1987): 32–33.

24. For an in-depth discussion of the Nunn-Roth amendment and the subsequent compromise, see Stanley Sloan, "The Political Dynamics of Defense Burden Sharing in NATO," in *Evolving European Defense Policies,* ed. Catherine Kelleher and Gale Mattox (Lexington, Mass.: Lexington Books, 1987), pp. 79–98. Also Phil Williams, "The Nunn Amendment, Burden-Sharing and U.S. Troops in Europe," *Survival* 27 (January–February 1985): 2–10.

25. For a discussion of the Soviet gas line, see Robert Lieber, "Energy Policy and National Security: Invisible Hand or Guiding Hand?" in *Eagle Defiant,* ed. Kenneth Oye, Robert Lieber, Donald Rothchild (Boston: Little, Brown, 1983), pp. 176–179.

26. Elizabeth Pond, "Europe: A U.S. Pillar or Rival in NATO?" *Christian Science Monitor,* July 29, 1987, pp. 18–19.

27. Marco de Andreis, "The Nuclear Debate in Italy," *Survival* (May–June 1986): 195–207.

28. Pond, "Europe," p. 18.

29. The development of the EPC is discussed in Baard Bredrup Knudsen, "Europe versus America: Foreign Policy in the 1980s," Atlantic Papers, no. 56 (Paris, 1984).

30. In particular, this proposal met opposition in 1982 and 1983 from Greece, Ireland, and Denmark. See John Roper, "European Defense Cooperation," in *Evolving European Defense Policies,* pp. 37–57.

31. For a review of some of these other efforts, see Samuel F. Wells, Jr., "The United States and European Defence Co-operation," *Survival* (July–August 1985): 158–168.

32. It is interesting that Anton DePorte sees the "French problem" as one of the challenges to the "security dispositions" of the Western alliance. A.W. DePorte. *Europe between the Superpowers: The Enduring Balance* (New Haven, Yale University Press, 1983), pp. 188–243.

33. Alliance formation is addressed in detail in Stephen M. Walt, "Alliance Formation and the Balance of World Power," *International Security* 9 (spring 1985): 3–43.

34. Jonathan Dean, *Watershed in Europe: Dismantling the East-West Military Confrontation* (Lexington, Mass: Lexington Books, 1987), p. xiv.

8
Soviet-American Naval Balance and Maritime Strategies

John Allen Williams

T he retirement of Admiral of the Fleet Sergei Gorshkov in December 1985 marked the end of an era. In almost thirty years of service as commander-in-chief of the Soviet Navy, Gorshkov oversaw its growth from a relatively impotent force that could be humiliated by the U.S. Navy in the October 1962 Cuban missile crisis to a first-class navy with global reach and power.

Having lost the unchallenged control of the seas, the United States has belatedly rediscovered the importance of naval supremacy. This is particularly important for an island nation that is both a global power and the leader of a maritime coalition, NATO. The United States is linked to its allies and trading partners by extensive sea-lanes of communication (SLOCs) that form a worldwide network for commercial and military transportation. Freedom of the seas in peacetime and the defense of the sea-lanes in wartime are indispensable to U.S. security. The possibility that the SLOCs could be interrupted—or that the seas could be used to launch an attack on the United States—is a grave problem.

Unfortunately for the U.S. Navy, part of this period of Soviet buildup saw the United States preoccupied with the Vietnam War, when defense expenditures went for an unsuccessful war effort rather than for ships and aircraft. In the bitter aftermath of the war, popular opinion was unwilling to make the necessary investments in defense. As a result of these trends, and a conscious decision by Chief of Naval Operations Elmo Zumwalt to retire over-age ships, by 1979 the U.S. Navy had just half the number of ships it had only ten years previously.

This trend was reversed in 1979, however, when President Carter began supporting increased military expenditures more in keeping with the needs of a global power. This direction was emphasized by the new Reagan administration, which dramatically increased the levels of funding for all the military services and set about augmenting U.S. military capabilities at all levels, from unconventional warfare, through conventional conflicts, to strategic deterrence and antimissile defense.[1] Although the objects of expenditures of the Reagan administration did not differ radically from those of President Carter, the resources made available were significantly greater.

Measuring the current naval balance between the Soviet Union and the United States requires more than just counting ships and aircraft. These items of hardware are necessary, but to be effective, they must perform useful missions in support of a coherent strategy. All of these factors work together in ways that are conditioned by geography and history.

The Naval Balance

The naval balance between the superpowers is the result of serious national commitments of resources. Great navies are very expensive and can be afforded only by great powers. Indeed, a large and powerful navy is arguably more the mark of a great nation than is the possession of nuclear arms.[2] Ships are very expensive in the aggregate—even more expensive than nuclear weapons. Because of this, only a few nations can afford significant navies. In this category one would include the navies of several of the NATO allies, plus Japan and the Soviet Union. Of these, only the U.S. Navy is truly global, although the Soviet Navy is catching up rapidly.

Generalizations

Several generalizations may be useful to consider when thinking about the naval balance and the probability of success in particular naval missions.

1. *Navies are most powerful near home.* This was true for the Greeks at Salamis in 480 B.C., for the Japanese at Tsushima in 1905, for the British Navy throughout history in the English Channel, for the U.S. Navy in the Caribbean since the Monroe Doctrine, and for the Soviet Navy near its bastions today. It would also have been true for the Italian Navy at Taranto in 1940 and the U.S. Navy at Pearl Harbor in 1941 if they had been properly prepared. Even states that are not major naval powers can be quite formidable near their bases. Despite their great advantage in overall military power, a British victory in the Falklands/Malvinas war in 1982 was not assured, and the Argentines may have come very close to sinking a British aircraft carrier.

2. *Naval forces are flexible.* This means, among other things, that they can be used in innovative ways as the circumstances require. In 1982, for example, the British took two aircraft carriers whose primary mission had been ASW in the North Atlantic for use as strike platforms in support of amphibious landings to regain disputed islands in the South Atlantic. In that same conflict, they turned the container ship *Atlantic Conveyor* (later sunk) into an air-capable vessel for ferrying helicopters and vertical takeoff and landing Harrier aircraft to the war zone.[3]

3. *Ships last a long time when they are not being used in combat.* Naval vessels have very long periods of active service—up to fifty years for the large

aircraft carriers—and this factor must be borne in mind during their construction. It is impossible to predict what naval needs and opportunities will be available in the distant future, so growth potential must be built in. Entirely new weapons systems could be mounted on the same platform. For example, the navy is recommissioning its four Iowa-class battleships from World War II and outfitting them with new Tomahawk cruise missiles. These can deliver conventional or nuclear warheads and take advantage of the tremendous size and survivability of these old battlewagons. For a more modern example, the DD-963 Spruance destroyers were poorly armed when built (an eight-inch gun was developed but never installed),[4] but the hull had the capability for further growth and is used for the CG-47 Ticonderoga guided missile cruisers also.

4. *Naval operations must support the land war.* The Soviets have an advantage in wars along their Eurasian periphery in that their army can walk almost anywhere it needs to go, supported by interior lines of communication. This means that maintaining the sea-lanes is not as important to them as it is to the United States. Even the most heroic and successful naval battles will be for naught if they do not affect what is occurring on land. There are many naval missions that meet this requirement, but it must be borne in mind at all times.

5. *Nuclear weapons may not be used.* It is ironic that a threat that cannot rationally be carried out is one of the foundations of peace, but the possibility of nuclear escalation is very useful for deterrence of large-scale conventional war. Nevertheless, a national strategy that relies on such escalation actually to fight a war is an invitation to calamity. Other options must be available. Fortunately, mobile and flexible naval forces can make up somewhat for the diminishing credibility of nuclear weapons for conventional deterrence. Naval forces can also ensure the resupply of Europe so that a U.S. president is not forced to escalate in anticipation of running out of supplies for forces there, help defend maritime states threatened with attack from the land, and tie down enemy forces with attacks in other theaters.

6. *Forces must be usable to be useful.* This means that naval forces must be appropriate for their intended mission, sufficient in number, and maintained in a high state of readiness. Most important, they must be floating. The implications of this for the need to take only prudent risks are apparent.

U.S. Naval Forces

The Reagan administration entered office determined to reverse what it saw as a dangerous weakening of U.S. military power since the Vietnam War. An important component of administration policy was the 600-ship navy goal set by former secretary of the navy John Lehman—himself an aviator in the naval reserve. These ships were to include fifteen deployable aircraft carrier battle groups (plus one carrier in overhaul), a hundred attack submarines (SSNs), four battleship surface action groups,[5] plus amphibious assault shipping sufficient to lift the assault elements of one U.S. Marine amphibious force (MAF, about 52,300 troops total) and one Marine amphibious brigade (MAB, about 15,700 troops total).[6]

In order to pay for these forces, the administration increased the navy budget by 43 percent between fiscal years 1980 and 1985, measured in constant dollars.[7] This "naval recovery program," as it was called by its supporters, emphasized naval construction and will reach the goal of 600 battle group–capable ships (that is, oceangoing combatants) in 1989, assuming that certain older ships are not retired before then.

The problem will be manning and operating the ships once they are in hand. The Congressional Budget Office estimates that an increase of 3 to 5 percent per year will be needed in the navy budget until 1994 in order to do this—a possibility that seems increasingly remote as budget austerity increases.[8] Although not agreeing that such funding is unobtainable, Secretary Lehman accepted the 3 percent figure as accurate.[9]

Table 8–1 shows the change in deployable battle forces between FY 1980 and FY 1987, and table 8–2 shows the progress being made toward the eventual force-level goals of the Reagan administration.

Soviet Naval Forces

The Soviet Navy is primarily a submarine navy now and will be so for the next decade,[10] but it is diversifying rapidly. Two types of submarines should

Table 8–1
Change in Naval Forces

Category	FY 1980	FY 1987
Aircraft carriers (deployable)	13	14
Battleships	0	3
Cruisers	26	35
Destroyers	81	69
Frigates	71	115
Ballistic missile submarines	40	39
Nuclear attack submarines (SSNs)	74	99
Diesel attack submarines	5	4
Strategic support ships	8	6
Patrol combatants	3	6
Amphibious ships	66	62
Mine warfare ships	3	5
Underway replenishment ships	48	57
Support forces ships	41	53
Total	479	567

Source: Caspar W. Weinberger, *Report to the Congress of the Secretary of Defense, Fiscal Year 1987* (Washington, D.C.: Government Printing Office, 1986), p. 179.

Table 8–2
Reagan Administration Navy Force-Level Goals and Level
of Achievement

Ship Type	Goal	FY 1987
Deployable aircraft carriers	15	14
Reactivated battleships	4	3
Principal surface combatants	238	219
Ballistic missile submarines (SSBNs)		
and other strategic ships	20–30[a]	39
Nuclear-powered attack submarines	100	99
Mine countermeasures ships	14	5
Amphibious ships (MAF plus MAB lift)	75	62
Patrol combatants	6	6
Underway replenishment ships	65	57
Support ships and other auxiliaries	60–65	59[b]
Total	597–622	563[c]

Source: Ibid.

[a]Not determined; depends in part on arms reduction agreements.
[b]Includes strategic support ships.
[c]Plus four diesel-powered attack submarines.

be distinguished. First are the attack submarines, which would be used to destroy enemy submarines or surface ships and sometime have cruise missiles for attacks against shore targets. There is even some suggestion that antiair missiles are also on some vessels. These submarines are called SSs or, if nuclear powered, SSNs. The Soviets have over 300 of these, divided—as is their entire navy—into four fleets: the Northern, Baltic, Black Sea, and Pacific.[11] Some of these submarines are reputed to be the fastest and deepest diving in the world.

Second are the ballistic missile–firing submarines, called SSBNs if nuclear powered. The Soviets have seventy-seven of these, and the newest of them have missiles of sufficient range to hit targets in the United States without the submarines ever leaving port. Approximately half of the submarines in the Soviet Navy are nuclear powered, and the percentage increases every year. Because the best way to detect submarines is by the noise they generate, the Soviets have made a great effort to cushion the sound. The United States is ahead of them in this area, but the gap is narrowing.

The Soviets have not ignored their surface forces, however. Of most interest in this connection is the launching of a nuclear-powered aircraft carrier, which will increase the range the Soviet Navy can travel and still have air protection. Currently, when the fleet is out of the range of land-based Soviet naval aviation (consisting of some 680 fighters, bombers, and electronic warfare and reconnaissance aircraft, plus 690 antisubmarine warfare aircraft, tankers, transports, and so forth), it is highly vulnerable to air attack. The Soviets are clearly moving toward the U.S. preference for organic air cover provided by carrier-based aircraft. For now, they are limited to three (soon to be four)

Table 8–3
Soviet Navy Distribution by Fleet

Force Element	Northern	Baltic	Black Sea	Pacific
Surface combatants	382	382	300	443
Submarines	182	45	35	120
Naval aviation	435	265	435	495
Naval infantry	1 brigade	1 brigade	1 brigade	1 division

Source: John F. Lehman, Jr., *Report to the Congress of the Secretary of the Navy, Fiscal Year 1987* (Washington, D.C.: Government Printing Office, 1986), p. 31.
Note: Slight differences with figures in text due to categories and data of information.

Kiev-class carriers that can handle only helicopters and vertical/short takeoff and landing (V/STOL) aircraft.

Although the Soviet Navy has a large number of ships, many of them are coastal and riverine warfare vessels and, very important, mine warfare ships. So although the Soviet Navy is larger than the U.S. Navy, many of the vessels are not seagoing craft useful for extended operations or capable of defending themselves for long against a determined attack by U.S. carrier aircraft. There are, of course, a few noteworthy exceptions to this generalization, including the Kirov- and Slava-class cruisers and Udaloy- and Sovremenny-class destroyers. These are all highly capable—and very expensive—naval vessels.

Table 8–3 shows the peacetime distribution of Soviet naval assets among the four fleets. Of particular note is the growing strength of the Pacific Ocean Fleet, now arguably the most powerful of the four.

Naval Strategy and Missions

Preliminary Considerations

Before looking at the specifics of U.S. and Soviet maritime strategies and the missions required to carry them out, several considerations need to be examined. First, strategy is not made in a vacuum. It must try to determine the prospective opponent's strategy and how best to counter it. It is also affected by the level of resources available to buy the forces necessary to carry it out. Strategy can be more ambitious or less so depending on this factor.[12]

Second, any maritime strategy will be powerfully affected by geography. The United States is an island nation whose primary allies and trading partners are separated by thousands of miles of water. U.S. military strategy must consider how the sea-lanes are to be defended, how the army will be resupplied in the event of a war (in Europe or elsewhere), how to bring pressure to bear on adversaries, how to assist in the land war, and even, if necessary, how to defend the maritime approaches to the United States. Control of the seas is not a luxury for the United States; it is necessary for national military survival.

The Soviets face different geographical constraints. The most important of these from a naval perspective is that their navy cannot reach the open ocean without passing through areas controlled by the United States or U.S. allies. The Northern Fleet, when it is not iced in, must deploy past northern Norway to reach the Atlantic sea-lanes. The Baltic Fleet reaches the North Sea, and eventually the Atlantic Ocean, through narrow straits between Denmark and both Sweden and Norway. The Black Sea Fleet must transit the narrow Turkish straits and navigate the Aegean Sea before reaching the Mediterranean—itself a closed sea. The Pacific Fleet deploys through straits controlled by Japan. Fortunately for the Soviets, they do not need to use the seas to survive, although a considerable amount of traffic moves between the Black Sea and the Pacific ports by way of the 12,000-mile southern sea route through the Suez Canal and the Indian Ocean.[13]

Third, historical factors help to determine a nation's strategy. Even without manipulation by political leaders, Soviet memories of World War II are very strong. They are determined not to be caught unawares again and view any possible threat to their security as a mortal danger. Since the primary threat has historically been from invasion by other continental powers, the main emphasis of Soviet military planners has been on their army. Indeed, it is estimated that the Soviet Navy's share of the (considerable) resources devoted to defense has been only 20 percent or less.[14] Unlike the United States, whose navy has a proud tradition of success for over 200 years, neither the Soviet Navy nor the Russian Navy before it has had a major impact on wartime operations. Admiral Gorshkov had to embellish the history of his navy in his writings to compensate for this fact.[15] The Soviet Union is predominantly a land power; the Soviet Navy, despite its great improvements, is still the stepchild of their military services.

U.S. Strategy

The U.S. Navy has evolved a set of guidelines for employing the fleet in the event of war with the Soviet Union. These are called by supporters and critics alike the "Maritime Strategy" (capitalized to indicate the particular strategy favored by the U.S. Navy). The major assumptions and components of this strategy were laid out in a remarkable supplement to the *U.S. Naval Institute Proceedings* in January 1986 in articles by the chief of naval operations, the commandant of the Marine Corps, and the secretary of the navy. It also included an excellent bibliography of writings related to the Maritime Strategy, collected by one of its early developers.[16]

The Maritime Strategy has been a topic of great controversy, not surprising given the costs of the navy buildup and the fundamental importance of strategy in relating national goals to actions. The Maritime Strategy is, in addition, the basis of planning, training, and procurement in the U.S. Navy. This is not the place for a full review of its strengths and weaknesses as a strategy,[17] but its major features, now unclassified through congressional testimony and articles in professional journals, can be discussed.

The Maritime Strategy assumes that any war with the Soviet Union would be global. This is, in part, a self-fulfilling prophecy, since one of the tenets of the strategy is early offensive action against Soviet forces, possibly including some in the Soviet Union itself. It also assumes that such a war could remain on the conventional level, without the use of nuclear weapons. Given the great destructive power of such weapons and the possibility of the destruction of both societies, it is wise to have the ability to fight conventionally. This is a sensible precaution since a failure to develop viable conventional options could have the effect of forcing the United States to choose between nuclear escalation and surrender.

Three characteristics of the Maritime Strategy should be understood. First, it is a forward strategy, consistent with U.S. military policy generally. The United States has the advantage of mounting its defense far from its own shores, assisted by many relatively wealthy allies. The bulk of the U.S. Army is deployed in West Germany and Korea, and it is doubtful whether there even exists a detailed plan for the land defense of the continental United States. There is no need for one. (The Soviets have no such luxury.) This makes the United States a maritime power, with its land forces in Europe and Asia connected by the seas.

Second, it is an offensive strategy. In the event of war, the U.S. Navy does not plan to fall back to defensive positions (for example, the "GIN gap" between Greenland, Iceland, and Norway). On the contrary, submarines and, at some point, surface ships will move forward to defend northern Norway and the Aegean, sink as many Soviet ships as possible (including SSBNs, to change the nuclear correlation of forces and, the navy argues, both make such escalation less attractive to the Soviets and provide war termination leverage), and, perhaps, attack Soviet forces in their homeland. (A particularly tempting target would be Soviet naval aviation bases, to reduce the threat to surface ships operating in exposed forward positions.) The navy is convinced that the best way to defend the sea-lanes is to reinforce the Soviet defensive tendency to operate out of protected bastions near their territory. Forward operations, especially by U.S. SSNs, would be directed against Soviet submarines of all types and surface ships and could include cruise missile attacks on military targets in the Soviet Union itself. U.S. surface ships and land-based ASW aircraft would participate in these operations as feasible, and amphibious Marine Corps forces would be available for landings in northern Norway, the Aegean, or elsewhere.[18]

Third, it is a joint and combined strategy, relying on the other U.S. military services and on the contributions of U.S. allies. The U.S. Air Force has a particularly important role in maritime surveillance, minelaying, and possibly battle group air defense. Most allied navies have limited capabilities but are fully capable of close-in defense of harbors, antimine operations, and defense of choke points. More powerful navies, such as those of Great Britain, France (still a member of NATO, it must be remembered), and Japan, can perform broader roles in sea-lane defense and ASW.

No one can predict in detail what the U.S. Navy would actually do if war with the Soviet Union broke out, but the Maritime Strategy provides a common understanding of the types of operations required. Although the planning and execution of specific wartime operations is the responsibility of the heads of the unified commands who actually command the operating forces, the Maritime Strategy is the baseline on which specific plans will be developed. For example, the U.S. Navy may or may not strike Soviet naval aviation bases in the Crimea, but it will not fall back to a close-in defense of the sea-lanes. It can be assumed that more specific war plans will reflect the forward and offensive orientation of the Maritime Strategy.

Soviet Strategy

Soviet strategy is defensively oriented although presumably in support of an offensive strategic posture in Western Europe. With a navy that has limited open-ocean sustainability or air protection when away from land-based air defense, the Soviets have made a virtue out of necessity and planned for defensive operations near home waters.[19]

The most important mission of the Soviet Navy is to maintain a second-strike strategic reserve of ballistic missile–firing submarines (SSBNs) and, if possible, locate and destroy those of the United States. U.S. analysts believe that the Soviets would withhold the missiles of their SSBNs during the initial stages of a nuclear war, reserving them for use during the course of the war and as military reserves to affect its outcome.[20] Maintenance of this reserve depends not only on the SSBNs themselves but on the SSNs, aircraft, and surface ships that defend them. Unlike U.S. SSBNs, which are ultraquiet and rely on stealth to operate undetected in the open oceans, the Soviets apparently intend to keep their submarine force in protected bastions in the Arctic Sea, the Sea of Okhotsk, the Sea of Japan, and the Northwest Pacific Ocean.[21] They may also intend to operate under the Arctic ice.[22]

Also important to the Soviets is the defense of the seaward approaches to their homeland. U.S. Navy plans to move forces forward under the Maritime Strategy are taken quite seriously, and carrier battle groups should expect to be fired upon if they come close enough to threaten such an attack. Whether the Soviets would be sufficiently alarmed to launch a preemptive nuclear attack against possibly nuclear-armed carriers cannot be determined in advance.

Another wartime mission, presumably of lower priority, is to cut the sea-lanes connecting the United States with its allies, thereby halting the resupply of Europe. Given the importance of the earlier defensive missions, it is unlikely that the Soviets would devote major assets to this early in a war. Still, one must consider what would happen if this assumption turned out to be incorrect or if they changed their tactics as the importance of the SLOCs became more apparent. The U.S. Navy will attempt to reinforce the Soviets' defensive inclinations by presenting a threat to their bastion forces and to their homeland as soon as possible.

The Soviets would also like to protect their own SLOCs, both their southern sea route and the routes necessary to resupply their allies. Given the extreme difficulty of this during a war with the United States, client states can expect little material assistance from the Soviet Union.

Finally, the Soviet Navy is increasing its ability to perform for power projection missions, using naval infantry (similar in mission to the U.S. Marine Corps but much smaller) and amphibious landing ships. The Baltic and Black Sea fleets in particular have exercised this capability and could be expected to help defend land forces from seaward attack.[23]

Before discussing some uncertainties that could render the previous judgments invalid, it is necessary to meet the objection that discussions of conventional war are marginally meaningful in a nuclear age since such a war would inevitably escalate into a nuclear exchange, at least on the maritime battlefields and the European continent. There is some possibility that this would happen, to be sure. In fact, the uncertainty thus engendered is one of the bases of deterrence. But there is also the possibility that a war would not go nuclear, and it would seem to be in everyone's interest to prevent such an occurrence if possible. The best way to do that is to avoid any kind of war so that the escalatory pressures will not occur. But if a war were to begin, it is well to have conventional options.

There is a great deal of evidence that Soviet leaders are planning for the possibility of a long conventional war. Based on an extensive review of Soviet military literature, analyst James McConnell concludes they now feel there could be a "protracted, general conventional war with the West," one that would not necessarily escalate to nuclear exchanges.[24] He concludes that "the Soviet Union seems to be moving toward a full-fledged conventional option, with its nuclear capabilities basically intended to forestall U.S. escalation."[25] This does not mean that the United States itself is immune from nuclear attack, however. If the United States were to strike targets of theater significance in the Soviet Union with nuclear-tipped Pershing II or cruise missiles, the Soviets might make an analogous response on similar targets in the United States.[26] Thus, if these plans are implemented, even a "limited" nuclear war that involved nuclear attacks on the Soviet Union could result in similar attacks on the United States. The Soviets would determine what they considered analogous, but it does not stretch the imagination to regard such naval facilities as Norfolk, San Diego, and the SSBN bases as candidates for such retaliation.

Uncertainties

Several possibilities could invalidate the foregoing analysis. It is not possible to predict with confidence what will happen in these areas, but it seems useful to review a few of them to see what their effect might be on the Soviet-American naval balance.

Arms Control

The recently signed agreement eliminating intermediate-range nuclear forces from Europe (the INF Treaty) shows that basic changes in nuclear armament levels are possible. Several possibilities would alter fundamentally the naval missions and force structures of the superpowers; two of these warrant discussion here.

The first is to reduce the numbers of land-based ICBMs. This would have the greatest impact on the Soviet Union, since their strategic triad (or "tetrad," if cruise missiles are included) is heavily weighted toward ICBMs. Any agreement drastically limiting the number of ICBMs will make the sea-based deterrent force of each power more important and place an even higher premium on its survivability. U.S. Navy plans for strategic ASW, if successful, would have an even greater impact on the nuclear correlation for forces in such a case. Soviet sensitivities to these operations would also increase, as might the level of their response to them. The disparity between the relative vulnerability of Soviet SSBNs and the comparative invulnerability of deployed U.S. SSBNs makes it unlikely that drastic ICBM reductions will occur without concomitant limits on U.S. Navy operations in the Soviet SSBN bastions.

The second is to eliminate nuclear weapons. The possibility of such an agreement is remote, but severe reductions in nuclear weapons levels would have a significant impact on naval operations. On the surface, eliminating nuclear weapons is an attractive option, but the implications for conventional deterrence and war fighting need to be considered carefully.

From the perspective of deterrence, the uncertainties inherent in nuclear escalation (controlled or uncontrolled) give pause to both Soviet and U.S. leaders in their dealings with one another. U.S. naval operations in support of the Maritime Strategy offer war-widening options that could also have a deterrent effect, but without the risk of nuclear annihilation, as they increase Soviet uncertainties about the possible outcome of aggression in Western Europe. Even their calculation of the correlation of forces is upset since they cannot preconfigure the conflict to remain in the area of their greatest strength, Central Europe.

An elimination of nuclear weapons, or only of ballistic missiles, effectively decouples the U.S. homeland from the defense of Europe (an argument made by opponents of the INF treaty). If this makes Soviet aggression more likely or more likely to succeed, the United States will be thankful for a strong navy that can defend the Western Hemisphere and the Pacific basin and that offers the hope of an eventual relief of Europe.

Technological Breakthroughs

Any number of technologies could mature and have a powerful effect on the way the U.S. and Soviet navies operate. Three of these are relevant to this discussion.

Antisubmarine warfare is the first. As head of the navy's Nuclear Propulsion Directorate, Admiral Kinnaird McKee testified that U.S. submarines are not detectable at operating depths by nonacoustic means and foresees no breakthroughs on the horizon that would make the seas transparent.[27] The impact of a dramatic ASW breakthrough would be great, particularly for the U.S. Navy, which regards its SSBN force as invulnerable. A great improvement in U.S. ASW capabilities would also worry the Soviets and make them less willing to reduce the size of their ICBM force.

On the other hand, the Soviets have made great progress in quieting their submarines, perhaps using information gained from the Walker spy ring. If this trend continues, they could consider the kind of open-ocean SSBN patrols that the U.S. Navy routinely performs. In this case, the Soviets would not need to tie up the bulk of their general-purpose naval forces attempting to keep the U.S. Navy out of their SSBN bastions.[28] This would free forces and funds for other operations, such as sea-lane interdiction and amphibious power projection.

The second area concerns space systems. Whether the SDI becomes a reality in some form, it is clear that space-based surveillance, communications, navigation, and perhaps weapons systems will play an increasingly important role in naval warfare. In fact, the U.S. Navy claims to be the greatest user of space systems in the U.S. military.[29] Great changes in the capabilities and survivability of these systems are possible and would have a strong impact on the operations of the affected navy. For example, naval analyst James Westwood speculates that a successful SDI program could force the Soviets to abandon the SSBN bastions in order to complicate the targeting problem for the U.S. antimissile systems, and perhaps also could increase their reliance on cruise missiles.[30]

The third area is directed energy. Discussions of laser and particle beam weapons have a kind of Buck Rogers quality to them, partly because their state of development is so highly classified that authoritative open discussions of them are infrequent.[31] One can speculate, however, on the effect of a weapons system whose "projectiles" travel at the speed of light. For example, the U.S. Navy is concerned about defending carrier battle groups from massed raids by

Soviet naval aviation, perhaps arriving simultaneously with submarine- and surface-ship–launched cruise missiles. A directed energy weapon, mated to the advanced radar system of the CG-47 Ticonderoga cruisers and DDG-51 Arleigh Burke destroyers, would go a long way toward solving the antiair warfare problem, making the deployment of U.S. Navy surface ship deployments into high-threat areas much safer and mission success more likely. The implications for the U.S. ability to defend the northern and southern flanks of NATO are apparent.

Political Changes

In both the U.S. and Soviet political systems, civilian control of the military is well established. Changes in the priorities of political leaders (either by conversion, as seemed to be the case with President Carter, or by replacement) are likely to be reflected in military plans eventually.[32] Geopolitical realities do not change, but the way in which they are interpreted certainly does. There is little doubt that the military spending policies of a President Mondale would have been different from those of President Reagan. Although there is a good deal of consensus among political elites in both countries on the proper role of military force, many changes in operations could occur quite quickly. In the case of the United States, a president could oppose the navy's plans for offensive sea control and attacks on Soviet SSBNs and relegate the force once again to controlling the sea-lanes by defensive perimeters. The Soviet Navy's bastion defense could be discarded in favor of the kind of open ocean operations that have been the mainstay of U.S. Navy operations for so long. (For this strategy to be successful continuing improvements will be needed in their navy's ability to implement it.)

International political changes could also affect naval operations. An arms control agreement on nuclear weapons could have a major effect. The defection of a maritime state from one or another of the great coalitions could also have an impact. Because NATO use of facilities in the Azores and Iceland is vital for the resupply of Europe, changes in Portuguese or Icelandic politics could affect the U.S. Navy severely. The most pressing problem at the moment in this regard for the U.S. Navy is the possible spread of New Zealand's refusal to permit ship visits unless the United States certifies that they are not nuclear armed, which the U.S. Navy routinely refuses to confirm or deny. Similarly, the Soviets would like to expand their maritime influence, as they have done in Vietnam with their use of U.S.-built facilities in Cam Ranh Bay and would like to do by means of agreements with other states.[33]

Fog of War

Soviet pretensions of a scientific understanding of warfare notwithstanding, no one can predict what will happen once war breaks out. (This is an important basis of deterrence, since the Soviets are quite aware of the uncertainty of such risky undertakings.) At least three factors should be considered.

Competing strategies is the first factor. Strategy is not a game of solitaire[34] and can be evaluated only with respect to the strategy of an opponent. Since the only true test of competing strategies is found in war, it may be too late to make adjustments once a conflict has begun. The Maritime Strategy of the U.S. Navy, for example, cannot be tested short of war but must be evaluated based on reasonable interpretations of what the competing Soviet strategy would be. If the Soviets do not behave as the United States expects, the results of the strategic competition could also be unexpected. Perhaps they will not remain in defensive positions in their bastions or attempt to keep a war at the conventional level as long as possible. They have a significant capability to surge from their home waters and wreak havoc along the sea-lanes, at least for a time, and perhaps they will do so. Every professional military officer knows the necessity of preparing for what an opponent can do, not just what he is expected to do.

The second factor is escalation. One cannot say with confidence that the Soviets would or would not use nuclear weapons against an advancing carrier battle group or, for that matter, that the United States would or would not use them in some fashion to prevent a military collapse on the Central Front of NATO. The linkages between nuclear weapons use on land and at sea also need to be considered. Because of its serious implications, the problem of escalation deserves all the thought that can be devoted to it.

The last factor is effectiveness. Sometimes military forces perform with great effectiveness and sometimes not. So long as they had the materiel with which to fight, for example, the German Army fought tenaciously even at the end of the war when the outcome was clear. Equipment subjected to the stresses of a nuclear battlefield could fail due to electromagnetic pulse, which could also affect communications and surveillance capabilities. Personnel may or may not be able to fight well due to any number of factors, such as their level of motivation and training and leadership. Again, this factor cannot be confidently predicted.

Conclusion

An analysis of the comparative strengths of the Soviet and U.S. navies must include the balance of forces each side could bring to bear in a conflict, whether against each other or against another state. The U.S. Navy has begun to rebound from a period of retrenchment during and after the Vietnam War and has made progress toward the goal of 600 ships set by Secretary Lehman at the beginning of the Reagan administration. Whether the particular force structure based around fifteen deployable aircraft carrier battle groups will be achieved is not certain and will depend on decisions to replace the aging *Coral Sea* and *Midway.* Even less certain is the ability of the U.S. Navy to maintain a level of 600 ships during a time of fiscal retrenchment, given the generally agreed need for a 3 percent increase in navy appropriations each year for the next eight years or so to achieve this.

The Soviet Navy has grown significantly in size and power but is not immune to some of the same considerations that are affecting the U.S. Navy. Even in a command economy, economic choices must be made, and not all resources can go to the military.[35] Increasing the sophistication of naval vessels is as necessary for the Soviet Union as for the United States, and this exacts high costs in technological development, personnel recruitment, and training, and procurement. (The Soviets call their titanium-hulled Alfa submarine—of which there are only two—the "golden fish" because of its great cost.)[36] If each vessel is more expensive and more complicated to build, fewer can be built. Nevertheless, there is a clear trend in the Soviet Navy toward more capable ships that can operate farther from land bases, and it will eventually have its organic air umbrella deployed upon aircraft carriers.

But knowing the naval balance is not sufficient. What will tell in a war is how forces are used and with what effectiveness. For this, one must turn to the strategies and missions of the respective navies. The U.S. Navy's Maritime Strategy calls for early forward movement against Soviet maritime forces in their bastions and permits—but does not require—attacks on Soviet SSBNs and even on the Soviet homeland itself. The primary goal is deterrence, through convincing the Soviets that they will face a prolonged conventional war of global dimensions and that they will not be able to restrict operations to points of strength along their Eurasian border. Should war nonetheless break out, the U.S. Navy intends to use its SSNs and carrier battle groups to defend the NATO flanks in north Norway and the Aegean and to confine as much of the Soviet Navy as possible in their bastions.

The Soviets apparently intend a defensive strategy for their navy, at least at the outset of a war. Soviet SSBNs are expected to surge from their home ports but remain in their bastions protected by general-purpose naval forces. Although plans are developing for nuclear-powered aircraft carriers, it will be many years before the Soviet Navy can hope to match the U.S. Navy in its ability to sustain underway operations at great distances from land bases for long periods of time. Nevertheless, great uncertainties hang over any possible conflict and contribute to deterrence in that no aggressor can be confident of success. One of the greatest uncertainties is the wisdom and political will of national leaders as they make the ultimate decisions that determine peace or war. With the stakes involved, we may all hope they decide wisely.

Notes

1. See John Allen Williams, "Defense Policy: The Carter-Reagan Record," *Washington Quarterly* 6, no. 4 (Autumn 1983): 77–92.

2. I thank Robert S. Wood for this observation.

3. The U.S. Navy did pioneering work on this technique, called "Arapahoe" in the U.S. and "STUFT" (for "ships taken up from trade") in Britain. The main U.S. Navy support for this program is in the naval reserve, which would perform the mission.

4. Frank Elliott, "Navy Drafts Plans for Successor to Battleships," *Defense Week,* October 14, 1986, p. 1.

5. John F. Lehman, Jr., "The 600-Ship Navy," Supplement to the *U.S. Naval Institute Proceedings* (January 1986): 35.

6. P.X. Kelley, in U.S. House of Representatives, Commiteee on Armed Services, *Seapower Subcommittee Hearings on the 600-Ship Navy and the Maritime Strategy,* June 24, September 5, 6, 10, 1985, p. 54.

7. Congressional Budget Office, *Future Budget Requirements for the 600 Ship Navy* (Washington, D.C.: Government Printing Office, September 1985), p. 69.

8. Ibid., p. 47.

9. John F. Lehman, Jr., "Posture Statement by the Secretary of the Navy," in Department of the Navy, *Report to the Congress, Fiscal Year 1987* (Washington, D.C.: Navy Internal Relations Activity, 1986), pp. 4–27.

10. Caspar W. Weinberger, *Annual Report to the Congress, FY 1987* (Washington, D.C.: Government Printing Office, February 5, 1986), p. 67.

11. Figures in the text on Soviet naval force levels are from Donald C. Daniel and Gael Donelan Tarleton, "The Soviet Navy in 1985," *U.S. Naval Institute Proceedings* 112, no. 5 (May 1986): 98.

12. For an earlier snapshot of these issues, see John Allen Williams, "The U.S. and Soviet Navies: Missions and Forces," *Armed Forces and Society* 10, no. 4 (Summer 1984): 507–528.

13. James T. Westwood, "The Soviet Navy: What Will Its Meticulous Planning Lead to Tomorrow?" *The Almanac of Seapower, 1986,* Arlington, Va., Naval League, 1986, p. 31.

14. Ibid., p. 28.

15. Peter Tsouras, "Soviet Naval Tradition," in Bruce W. Watson and Susan M. Watson (eds.), *The Soviet Navy: Strengths and Liabilities* (Boulder, Colo.: Westview Press, 1986), pp. 3–25.

16. James D. Watkins, "The Maritime Strategy," P.X. Kelley, "The Amphibious Warfare Strategy," John F. Lehman, Jr., "The 600-Ship Navy," and Peter M. Swartz, "Contemporary U.S. Naval Strategy: A Bibliography," in *U.S. Naval Institute Proceedings* supplement (January 1986).

17. See John J. Mearsheimer, "A Strategic Misstep: The Maritime Strategy and Deterrence in Europe," and Linton F. Brooks, "Naval Power and National Security: The Case for the Maritime Strategy," *International Security* 11, no. 2 (Fall 1986): 3–88.

18. Equipment and thirty days of supplies for a marine amphibious brigade are being prepositioned in Norway. See William H. Schopfel, "The MAB in Norway," *U.S. Naval Institute Proceedings* 112, no. 11 (November 1986): 33–39.

19. See Watkins, "Maritime Strategy," p. 7, and U.S. Department of Defense, *Soviet Military Power, 1986* (Washington, D.C.: Government Printing Office, 1986), pp. 87–89.

20. James M. McConnell, "The Irrelevance Today of Sokolovskiy's Book, *Military Strategy,*" *Defense Analysis* 1, no. 4 (1985): 248.

21. Daniel and Tarleton, "Soviet Navy," p. 104.

22. Richard T. Ackley, "No Bastions for the Bear: Round 2," *U.S. Naval Institute Proceedings* 111, no. 4 (April 1985): 42.

23. Department of Defense, *Soviet Military Power, 1986,* p. 89.

24. McConnell, "Irrelevance Today," p. 247.

25. James M. McConnell, "Shifts in Soviet Views on the Proper Focus of Military Development," *World Politics* 37, no. 3 (April 1985): 317.

26. McConnell, "The Irrelevance Today," p. 247; "Shifts in Soviet Views," p. 337.

27. Committee on Armed Services, *Seapower Subcommittee Hearings,* pp. 147–168.

28. Ackley, "No Bastions," p. 45.

29. Admiral James D. Watkins in ibid., p. 62.

30. Westwood, "Soviet Navy," passim. This article is also a useful antidote for the feeling that the U.S. Navy planning process is cumbersome.

31. There are some discussions in connection with the SDI. See David J. Lynch, "Tests Planned for Particle Beam," *Defense Week,* October 20, 1986, p. 5.

32. Even presidents do not always get their way, as President Kennedy saw during the Cuban missile crisis when he discovered that missiles he had ordered removed from Turkey were still there.

33. Walter Andrews, "Admiral Points to Soviet Fish Pact," *Washington Times,* September 11, 1986, p. 4-D.

34. I thank Roger Barnett for reminding me of this point.

35. Of course, a much higher percentage of gross national product is spent on defense in the Soviet Union than in the United States.

36. Committee on Armed Services, *Seapower Subcommittee Hearings,* p. 162.

9

The Soviets in the Third World: American Military Dilemmas

Dennis M. Drew

Although American national security policy continues to focus on the defense of long-standing interests in Europe and Northeast Asia (Japan and South Korea), it is ever more evident that the United States also has vital interests and attendant defense problems in the so-called Third World of Africa, Asia and Latin America. While North America, Europe, and Japan contain the bulk of the non-Communist world's industrial capacity and wealth, Third World areas contain the major sources of critical raw materials, and many sit astride or near so-called choke points on international trade routes. For some of the same reasons, it is evident that the Soviet Union also has important interests in the Third World that are in direct political and economic competition with the United States.

Despite these competing superpower interests, the fundamental causes of unrest in these areas have little to do with political ideology or superpower relations. The causes are endemic to the Third World; ignorance, grinding poverty, hunger, corruption, helplessness, and hopelessness. From the American viewpoint, the Soviets take advantage of these local difficulties to foment unrest and revolution in the hope of extending their influence and reducing the influence of the United States in the zero-sum game of power politics. The Soviets and indigenous Communist cadres provide revolutionary movements with discipline, leadership, money, and arms.

Local conditions provide the grist for the Soviet revolutionary mill, but the United States has and continues to cast the Soviet challenge in the Third World strictly in East-West terms. This tendency is so strong in American policy that at times it has been self-deceiving. The conflict in Vietnam illustrated the point. Described as a struggle vital to the containment of Soviet influence and the spread of communism, the struggle was, in reality, a civil war fought by several Vietnamese factions for control of the larger Vietnamese nation. It was a struggle for political power that no doubt would have occurred had the United States, the Soviet Union, and the People's Republic of China played no role whatsoever. Even the 1954 Geneva Accords visualized a struggle for power in Vietnam, albeit a peaceful struggle at the ballot box. The fact that the United States backed one side in the struggle while the Soviets and Chinese backed the other was almost irrelevant to the struggle, although it was critical to the conduct of the war and perhaps to its outcome.

Nature of the Military Threat

The Soviet penchant for sponsoring unrest and revolution in vital Third World areas clearly presents a serious challenge to the United States. However, Soviet sponsorship does not mean that the military challenge to the United States is a Soviet military challenge. In reality the military threat to American interests in most Third World areas is not and will not be a Soviet threat. U.S. or U.S.-supported forces will not, in all likelihood, face massive Soviet forces.

Barring significant and unlikely geopolitical upheavals, the Soviets will continue to face severe difficulties when they attempt to project their conventional military power beyond those areas contiguous to their borders. Unlike the United States with its island-like geography, the Soviet Union will remain largely isolated from the major oceans, its expeditionary forces forced to deploy through constricting narrows that could be closed quickly by a determined and capable foe. Although the Soviets have built a significant blue-water navy over the past two decades, the limitations imposed by geographic accident remain. Thus the ability of the Soviet Union to deploy and sustain major forces well beyond its borders remains a difficult and risky proposition during hostilities. Air power has done little to ameliorate Soviet power projection problems. Air access to most crucial Third World areas often requires long flights through the airspace of nations that may or may not allow Soviet safe transit. Such lengthy and tenuous lines of communication are expensive to maintain and operate at any time and could pose an unacceptable degree of risk during hostilities.

Beyond the question of direct Soviet participation, it is also likely that the nature of the military threat to American interests in the Third World will vary considerably from the conventional European model. Over the past forty years, most Third World conflicts have been internal power struggles, often taking some form of revolutionary warfare featuring guerrilla-style operations waged against the stronger forces of the so-called legitimate government. The insurgent nature of these wars, regardless of the side favoring American interests, creates major military dilemmas for the United States. The United States and its military establishment have had difficulty coping with wars that differ markedly from the conventional European model.

Dilemmas for the American Military

The American military could become involved in insurgent warfare in the Third World in support of either the insurgents, as in Nicaragua and Afghanistan, or the targeted government (counterinsurgency), as in Vietnam and El Salvador. Involvement can come in two basic forms, with almost infinite variations on the basic themes. The first form is to provide assistance, such as training, equipment, and advisers. The second form is direct military intervention, with American forces heavily engaged in combat operations. However, large-scale American combat operations in support of an insurgency would surely dictate the use of conventional tactics and heavy firepower in the hope of eliminating the target government quickly, a circumstance that would eliminate the dilemmas of insurgent warfare.

The qualitative differences between conventional and insurgent warfare lead to three fundamental military dilemmas for the United States: American preparations for war, effective assistance that will reduce the chances of American combat involvement, and the prosecution of counterinsurgent war. Each will be addressed in terms of counterinsurgent operations, although the United States would face many of the same dilemmas when supporting (short of combat) insurgent operations.

The First Dilemma: For What Should the American Military Prepare?

For more than four decades, the American military has prepared itself to engage the Soviet military. In the American view, the Soviets have posed the only serious threat to America's most vital security interests. The American military leadership has structured the problem in terms of offsetting superior Soviet numbers with superior American firepower. Sophisticated technology that produces so-called force multipliers has been the American answer to servicing Soviet targets in a target-rich environment. The target-rich environment has always been assumed to be Western Europe, although in the past decade, at least some thought has been given to countering a possible Soviet thrust toward the oil fields of the Persian Gulf.

The American approach is based on the premise that nations must prepare to fight and win (and thereby deter) the war that they cannot afford to lose. Clearly the United States cannot afford to lose a nuclear war (or, for that matter, to fight a nuclear war) and cannot afford to have Western Europe overrun by Soviet forces in either a conventional or a nuclear struggle. All other risks have paled in comparison to the consequences to these worst cases. As a result, the American military has structured a strong strategic nuclear force and relatively strong conventional forces that are, with few exceptions, trained and equipped to fight a major war against the Soviets and Warsaw Pact forces in Europe. At least partially because of these preparations, nuclear war and a Soviet invasion of Western Europe have become the least likely of the possibilities for future American military involvement.

During the same four decades that it prepared to fight the Soviets, the American military engaged in two major wars, neither of which was in Europe or involved Soviet forces. The most recent of these experiences, Vietnam, was primarily an insurgency, part of an increasing pattern of insurgent conflict throughout the Third World, such as in Malaya, Kenya, Vietnam, Nicaragua, Angola, El Salvador, and Afghanistan. Such conflicts pose the most likely situations for future American military involvement at whatever level and, given the difficulties encountered in Vietnam, pose serious challenges for a military establishment structured to engage Soviet forces in high-intensity warfare.

Insurgencies are not large wars writ small. Although there are quantitative differences, the major differences between conventional warfare and insurgent warfare are qualitative. Insurgent strategists such as Mao Tse-tung, Che Guevara, and Vo Nyugen Giap may differ in detail, but their strategies have much more in common with each other than they do with strategies for conventional warfare.

Insurgencies have the characteristics of civil wars whether or not they fulfill the legal definition of that status. In the Vietnam War, the U.S. government refused to acknowledge that the struggle was essentially a civil war. This position may have been technically and legally correct, but it was also irrelevant to the conduct of the war. The fact was that Vietnamese were fighting Vietnamese. The significance of this reality is found in the fact that civil wars are rarely settled by negotiated compromise. The objectives of each side in such struggles are essentially unlimited; each seeks the total defeat of the other side and total political power. Nothing less will suffice.

The Clausewitzian center of gravity for both sides in an insurgent war is far different from that found in a conventional war. In a conventional war, the military center of gravity is located within the enemy armed force (although strategic bombing theorists argue that the center of gravity is the industrial web that supports deployed armed forces). In an insurgency, however, the center of gravity that the insurgents attempt to attack is the loyalty of the target state's population. Insurgents seek ultimately to disaffect the target population from the target government and thus to destroy the government's support and legitimacy. On the other hand, the embattled government seeks to retain the support of its population and destroy any support within that population for the insurgent cause, support without which an insurgency cannot survive. For both sides the military center of gravity in an insurgent war is the same: the population of the target nation. Therefore military operations are only a small, although vital, part of an insurgency. The hearts and minds of the population tend not to be won, in any lasting manner, through military operations alone. Most insurgent strategies call for a sophisticated mix of political, psychological, economic, and military warfare, each ingredient aimed at winning the allegiance or at least the neutrality of the target population while destroying the credibility and power of the target government. Conversely, the embattled government must somehow counter every aspect of the insurgent strategy. Thus for the target government, military operations are also only a small part of a counterinsurgency.

To counter the generally superior military resources possessed by the government in power, insurgents use guerrilla warfare tactics to prosecute the military portion of an insurgency. Guerrilla tactics present unique problems for the target government and provide unique advantages to the insurgent. First, guerrilla warfare cannot be deterred by strong military force. The guerrilla is always outmanned and outgunned, which is why the guerrilla is a guerrilla. Second, guerrilla tactics can offset the government's superior firepower. Guerrilla tactics emphasize clever target selection, surprise, hit-and-run operations, small unit actions, quick dispersion, and individual mobility—tactics that make it extremely difficult to bring superior firepower to bear. Third, guerrillas either live off the land or from supplies procured from a friendly or cowed population, and they obtain many of their military supplies through raids on isolated government garrisons. These tactics reduce the insurgent's need for a sophisticated logistical system, particularly since the will-o'the-wisp guerrilla forces can control the pace of the action by refusing battle with government troops. Again, the advantage of superior firepower, particularly artillery and air firepower, is diminished. As the United States learned in Vietnam, it is no simple matter to use conventionally trained and equipped troops and conventional strategy and tactics to combat an insurgent force.

Thus the dilemma gains focus. Should the United States continue to concentrate its preparations for the worst-case war, or should its military expend more of its resources to prepare for the more likely guerrilla-style insurgent conflicts? At present, precious few resources are devoted to preparing for the latter possibility.

Finding the correct balance is no simple matter. On the one hand, it is reasonably clear that nuclear or conventional war with the Soviets is unlikely at least in part because of the preparations made by the American military. In the rapidly changing high-technology world of superpower confrontations, there is genuine fear that any significant diversion of American effort from preparation for the worst case might make it a far more likely case than it is now.

On the other hand, without increased emphasis and capabilities, the United States may not be able to respond effectively to insurgent threats in important Third World areas. The fundamentally different nature of insurgent warfare can be countered only with strategies, tactics, force structures, training, and equipment far different from those used by conventional forces and particularly from those forces prepared to fight in Western Europe. More profoundly, counterinsurgent warfare demands the cooperation and integration of military and nonmilitary efforts to a degree that the United States has found difficult to achieve in the past. All of these factors affect the second basic dilemma, which concerns the provision of effective assistance so that American combat involvement will not be required.

The Second Dilemma: Providing Effective Assistance

Although Third World insurgent conflicts may be the most likely to require American military involvement, the United States would prefer that the military involvement not include combat operations. The first priority is clearly to provide the kind of assistance that will rectify the situation without spilling American blood. This task, however, presents many difficulties, most of them directly related to the kind of wars the American military is prepared to prosecute.

The first and perhaps most important problem is providing assistance early enough so the situation can be salvaged without direct intervention. The problem has at least two aspects. First, many Third World areas have suffered from a form of benign neglect that is raised to the American collective consciousness only when ongoing problems reach critical proportions. So much time, effort, and money is spent preparing for the worst-case scenario in Europe that festering situations in other areas either go unnoticed or cannot compete for the required attention. Difficulties in parts of Latin America provide the best example. Latin America, and, especially, Central America, is relatively close to home, is largely in a state of political flux, exhibits the endemic problems upon which revolutions feed, and is host to many insurgent movements. Despite this situation, the resources devoted to bolstering Latin allies and to improving American military capabilities in the area are miniscule when compared to American efforts to combat the Soviets in NATO.

The second aspect affecting the timeliness of American assistance concerns what many have called the Vietnam syndrome. Whenever assistance, particularly military aid and advisers, is proposed to combat an insurgent movement, the cry goes up that the proposal is the first step down the slippery slope to American combat involvement "just as it happened in Vietnam." The problem is that if the area in question is indeed vital to American interests, the failure to provide effective assistance in time will almost certainly lead either to American combat involvement or a serious blow to American interests (or both). The nub of the problem again seems to be the definition of vital interests and the preparations required to defend those interests.

In addition to the timeliness of assistance, Americans face serious difficulty regarding leverage with those target governments it is attempting to assist. Insurgencies feed on dissatisfaction with government policies and practices. Sweeping political and economic reforms are often required if the fundamental causes of the insurgency are to be eliminated and the popular basis for the insurgency destroyed. Unfortunately, the more vital the area is to American interests, the less leverage the United States has in forcing the target government to make required reforms. This is so because if those in the target government believe that vital American interests are indeed at stake, threats to reduce or cease support unless reforms are made will ring hollow. The dilemma is that in order to build support for providing aid in the first place, the American leadership is often forced to extol the importance of the area and government in question. During the Vietnam experience, for example, government spokesmen continually expressed how vital South Vietnam was to American interests, often in wildly exaggerated terms. One would have thought that after the fall of Saigon, a North Vietnamese aircraft carrier would sail into San Diego harbor and demand the surrender of the United States. The more the government attempted to mobilize public opinion, the more convinced the South Vietnamese became that the United States would not abandon them, whether or not reforms were implemented. The situation was exacerbated when American troops were committed to combat, and American blood was spilled in large quantities. It is more than coincidence that many of the major reforms needed in South Vietnam were implemented only after the United States began withdrawing its troops in 1969.

A third problem concerns how military assistance is rendered. Often many of the operational problems faced by those governments the United States supports center on a military establishment that is poorly equipped and trained, badly led, clumsily structured, and ill disciplined. Often the first job of the American military is to provide advisers, training, and equipment to rectify these problems. However, the U.S. military is structured to carry out high-intensity, mechanized, and technologically complex operations against Soviet forces. American doctrine, strategy, training and equipment are centered on the Soviets and on conducting a particular style of combat operations. It is difficult for American advisers to break out of this mold, and it is difficult for the United States to provide equipment that may be more suitable for counterinsurgency warfare.

There is a significant danger of mirror imaging the forces of those we support with the American model, though the situation and circumstances are very different and often inappropriate for the American model. The forces of poor Third World countries combating insurgents on a daily basis cannot afford the elaborate command structure and "tooth to tail" ratio typical of the American force structure.

Proper equipment, however, may be a more serious problem than the structure of the supported forces. The identification and procurement of the kinds of equipment that are most appropriate for counterinsurgent operations is a difficult problem. Figuratively, the most effective weapon to use against a guerrilla is probably a knife, the least effective a heavy bomber. Many modern high-technology weapons may not be suitable for the kind of military struggle in progress, but these are the kinds of weapons in which the American military specializes and that are readily on hand and available.

Beyond the issue of combat suitability, most Third World nations do not have the infrastructure needed to support high-technology weaponry. Worse, sophisticated weaponry is often so expensive that the supported forces cannot afford to purchase the equipment and the United States cannot afford to give it away. Providing more appropriate equipment, however, is no simple matter for at least three reasons. First, virtually the entire American research, development, and procurement structure is devoted to high-technology weaponry appropriate for use against the Soviets. Second, older equipment is hard to find, and maintenance is often a nightmare because of the lack of spare parts. Third, some Third World nations insist on flashy high-technology equipment as a status symbol, regardless of its utility in the struggle they face.

This discussion has certainly not provided a complete catalog of the dilemmas faced by the United States in providing effective assistance to governments in the Third World that are combating insurgencies. However, it does illustrate how complex the problems are and how difficult they are to solve. It therefore remains reasonably likely that the United States will be faced with the prospect of committing forces to combat despite efforts to avoid the situation. This likelihood leads to the third major American military dilemma.

The Third Dilemma: How to Prosecute a Counterinsurgency

Should the United States become actively involved in prosecuting a counterinsurgent war in the Third World, the American government and its military arm will face several vexing problems, among them the rationalization of objectives and strategy, managing time and public opinion, influencing the policies of the target government, and control of the counterinsurgent effort.

Both the insurgents and the government they target engage in an unlimited struggle for unlimited objectives. The prize is total political power; compromise solutions are only stepping-stones to the real objective. The only limiting factors in these struggles are the means available to both sides, means that are generally very limited in Third World areas. Regardless of the means available, the destruction of the enemy is the end sought.

Such unlimited objectives on the part of the principals in the struggle do not necessarily mean that an intervening power such as the United States will also have such draconian ends in mind. In the Vietnam War, for example, while the Vietcong and North Vietnamese sought to destroy the government of South Vietnam and a succession of South Vietnamese governments struggled to exclude the Communists from power in the South, the United States sought to inflict only enough pain on its adversaries to convince them to abandon the struggle. At nearly every turn, the United States sought negotiations and compromise solutions.

Because the United States dominated the relationship with South Vietnam, limited objectives and consequent restraints on actions prevailed. South Vietnam was largely restrained from "going North" and in the end was forced to accept a compromise settlement in 1973 that everyone realized would provide only a short respite in a struggle that was far from over. The North Vietnamese, on the other hand, never waivered in their purpose and ultimately prevailed. One must question whether compromise solutions are possible in such situations. Can an intervening power wage a limited war and still inflict enough pain to change the objectives and commitment of those who are waging a civil war for unlimited objectives? Can limited pressure change the objectives of a society that is fully mobilized for war and steeled to the hardships of a protracted struggle?

In Vietnam, the limited and halting American prosecution of the war was intended at once to inflict pain on the enemy and to project an image of reasonableness that could lead to compromise. The signal that was received by the North Vietnamese, however, was one of a timid giant that would rather not fight, had an overriding fear of escalation, and failed to understand the commitment of the enemy and its objectives. Combined with reports of a growing antiwar movement within the United States, it quickly became clear to the North Vietnamese that time was on their side.

On the other hand, if in the future the United States were to adopt less limited objectives and means and thus threatened the survival of a Soviet-sponsored adversary, the struggle could quickly escalate far beyond a localized insurgent conflict. Although direct Soviet combat involvement may not be likely, the Soviets could bring pressure to bear in other areas or, in the extreme case, rattle their nuclear sabre.

Time is clearly on the side of the insurgents, particularly if the United States is involved. Guerrilla insurgencies are lengthy affairs. For example, the Malaya emergency lasted for a full decade, and the Vietnam struggle (with a constantly changing cast of antagonists) lasted for more than thirty years. Even the Soviets, who can hardly be accused of waging a very limited war, found the rebels in Afghanistan impossible to subdue during years of intense effort. Time is a particular problem for a democratic government in which public opinion is the ultimate arbiter of policy. It is even more of a problem for the United States. Americans are an impatient lot who seek quick solutions to their problems. If the United States is to intervene in future insurgencies, it must find a method to conclude its operations quickly or to mobilize public support and maintain it for the duration of the conflict.

Finally, there is the problem of controlling the multifaceted effort required to combat an insurgency. This problem surfaces at two levels. At the higher level is the question of who controls the overall effort. The target or host government will naturally believe it should control the effort; after all, it is their nation that is in jeopardy. It is also clear that when it intervenes in the Third World, the United States is the dominant partner in a military and monetary sense. It is difficult for any Third World nation to withstand even the most benevolent onslaught of hard-driving Americans with their wealth, technical sophistication, and military power. In the Vietnam struggle, the question was never settled, and the Americans and South Vietnamese formed a very uneasy alliance.

On a second level is the question of how to control and coordinate the various American instruments of power needed to combat an insurgency. Who should integrate and resolve the inevitable disputes between the military and those involved in political and economic programs essential to the destruction of the insurgency? Successful counterinsurgencies require highly integrated operations that often cut across traditional lines of civilian and military command and control. This situation is complicated by the coalition nature of the struggle.

The importance of effective control can hardly be overstressed. Although the political objective of a counterinsurgency may be relatively straightforward, the objectives of each instrument of power and how they fit together to achieve the overall objective form a very complex whole. Worse, if the separate strategies are not closely coordinated, they can be counterproductive. It does little good to build schools and dig wells in a village during the day and bomb and shell that same village at night due to suspected enemy activity. Land reform has a limited positive impact if the beneficiaries become refugees because of gratuitous military actions.

Looking to the Future

It is reasonably clear that superpower competition in the Third World will continue. It is also clear that the Soviets will continue with their general modus operandi, which has met with some admirable successes in the past. As a result, the United States will continue to face difficult policy problems and choices in the Third World. Some of the most difficult choices involve military policy.

Without sufficient preparation, the United States could suffer another Vietnam-style debacle in some other far-off land. Without the proper preparation, the military dilemmas that have been discussed could impose serious limitations on overall American foreign policy. Unfortunately the preparations that could solve the military dilemmas require considerable time, arduous work, and difficult choices. The most difficult problem is the most obvious: deciding the kind of war for which the United States should prepare. Making this decision requires hard choices concerning alternative weights of effort and consequent force structures, training, and, most important, education. Traditionally the United States has structured and trained its forces in a manner largely incompatible with counterinsurgent operations. Additionally, little effort has been expended to educate the American military and its officer corps about the military and nonmilitary doctrines and strategies required to counter an insurgency. If the U.S. military invests in such an educational effort, it will have taken a giant step toward resolving the two more technical dilemmas that have been addressed: providing timely and effective noncombat assistance and prosecuting a counterinsurgent war. Such educational efforts take a great deal of time to reach fruition, and time is fleeting.

10
Move and Countermove: U.S. and Soviet Policy Interactions in the Third World

Daniel S. Papp

T hroughout the post–World War II era, the United States and the Soviet Union have been locked in a struggle for political influence, economic and ideological advantage, and military security. Europe has been the geographical focus of that struggle, but both the United States and the Soviet Union have devoted increasingly large shares of their attentions and resources to other areas.

One of the most notable aspects of this globalization of U.S.-Soviet competition has been the increasingly prominent role that the Third World plays in the U.S.-Soviet struggle for influence, advantage, and security.[1] Both countries have established a political presence in almost every country in the Third World that they can; both trade with and provide economic and military assistance to many Third World states; and both have structured at least parts of their military establishments to facilitate their abilities to intervene in Third World areas.

Perhaps the most startling measure of the role that the Third World plays in U.S.-Soviet relations is that since 1960, the United States and the Soviet Union have only twice moved close to military confrontation. In both cases the arena of confrontation was the Third World. The first instance was during the Cuban missile crisis in 1962. (Cuba at that time had not yet officially joined the socialist world.) The second occasion was in the Middle East in 1973 when the Soviet Union placed its airborne forces on alert and warned that it might take "appropriate steps unilaterally" to end the October 1973 Arab-Israeli War.[2] The United States in response placed its military forces on global alert.

Nor may it be overlooked that at least as far as the United States was concerned, Soviet actions in the Third World during the middle and late 1970s, specifically in Angola, Ethiopia, and Afghanistan, played a major role in undermining and eventually destroying détente. The Third World clearly is an arena of critical importance in U.S.-Soviet relations.

The Third World: Why Washington and Moscow Feel It Is Important

The United States and the Soviet Union consider the Third World important for at least five reasons.[3] First, both see it as an arena of political competition. Second, it is an area of economic importance to both Washington and Moscow, although in absolute economic terms it is of much greater importance to Washington. Third, although the Third World is incredibly diverse, the superpowers both consider it a region of considerable military and strategic value. Fourth, both recognize that the Third World is an arena of real and potential instability. And finally, both sides to a great extent see the Third World as an area of illegitimate and exploitive interest and involvement by the other side. These five considerations are frequently intertwined, but they nevertheless require separate examination.

An Arena of Political Competition

Washington and Moscow compete politically in the Third World on at least three different planes. First, both seek to attract as many countries in the Third World as possible to their own particular political-economic course. When successful, this effort acquires for each respective superpower additional international prestige, possible military and economic advantage, and on some occasions additional political support for its own positions in international organizations and other multinational forums.

The second plane of U.S.-Soviet political competition is to use "pro-American" states and "pro-Soviet" states to illustrate the superiority of the respective Western-style or Soviet-style forms of political-economic organization. For example, during the late 1960s and early 1970s, the United States on occasion hailed Kenya as a showcase of the advantages of capitalism. More recently, the United States has pointed frequently to the newly industrialized countries of Southeast Asia as proof of the advantages of free market economies.[4] Significantly, spokesmen for the Reagan administration have also frequently argued that one of the major reasons that most Third World countries remain economically underdeveloped is that they adopt centralized economic systems.[5]

The Soviet Union points to pro-Soviet states, particularly states of "socialist orientation," as shining examples of countries where new societies based on equity, socialist democracy, and fairness to all are being developed. These states include Afghanistan, Angola, Benin, the Congo, Ethiopia, Madagascar, Mozambique, Syria, and Tanzania. Given the low levels of economic development in these states, the Soviet Union cannot and does not point to standards of living as proof of the superiority of its preferred system; rather, it argues that decades of past colonial exploitation and continued neocolonialism complicate development efforts, but the groundwork is being laid for future advances.[6]

The third plane of political competition in the Third World may be described as "credentializing"; both superpowers recognize that their credentials as superpowers are legitimized not only by their massive nuclear arsenals but also by their abilities to influence and even determine the course of events in regions far distant from their homelands. Frequently this means the Third World. This credentializing aspect of U.S.-Soviet political competition in the Third World is one of several reasons why the United States provides Stinger surface-to-air missiles for the *mujahadin* in Afghanistan, and why the Soviet Union sends Mi-24 Hind helicopters to the Sandinistas in Nicaragua.

An Area of Economic Importance

Economic concerns also loom large in explaining U.S. and Soviet interests in the Third World. Here it should be stressed at the outset that U.S. (and Western) economic interests in the Third World dwarf Soviet interests there. Even so, the Kremlin's economic interests in these countries can be neither dismissed nor discounted.

As far as the United States is concerned, the Third World is an important source for natural resources. It is also an important trading partner and location for investment. In some cases, American levels of resource imports, trade participation, and overseas investment are truly startling. For example, between 1980 and 1983, the United States imported 35 percent of its bauxite from Jamaica and another 34 percent from Guinea. It obtained 35 percent of its cobalt from Zaire and 29 percent of its manganese from Gabon. During the same period it imported 63 percent of its tin from four Third World countries (Thailand, 23 percent; Malaysia, 17 percent; Indonesia, 12 percent; and Bolivia, 11 percent).[7] Equally important, about 5 percent of the total U.S. oil supply came from Persian Gulf states alone in 1986.[8]

From the U.S. perspective, it is also necessary to consider Western European and Japanese reliance on Third World resources. For example, in 1981 Western European states imported 86 percent of their bauxite, 99 percent of their copper, all of their cobalt, 99 percent of their manganese, and 92 percent of their tin. Most of these imports were from Third World countries. Percentages for Japan are in many cases even higher.[9] Nor should it be overlooked that Japan and most Western European states are heavily dependent for oil imports on OPEC, which consists entirely of Third World states.

Lest the importance of resource imports from the Third World to the United States and Western Europe be overstated, it must quickly be pointed out that in some cases substitution of one material for another in production processes is possible, and in other cases alternate sources of resources, including domestic production, are possible. But these solutions to resource dependence would bring higher costs and, in some cases, lower performance. Indeed, in other cases neither substitution nor alternate sources is possible.

U.S. trade with Third World states also is surprisingly sizable. In 1985 U.S. trade with Third World states totaled $191 billion; this was 33 percent of the total U.S. trade turnover. Equally impressive, on a collective basis the Association of Southeast Asian Nations (ASEAN) was the United States' fifth largest trading partner in 1985.[10] Similarly, U.S. firms have over $50 billion invested in Third World states, and the combined debts of Third World states to U.S. and Western banking and lending institutions in 1986 topped $900 billion. Brazil alone owed $107 billion, and Mexico was close behind with a $99 billion debt.[11]

Obviously the Third World is important to the United States in absolute economic terms, but Soviet economic interests in the Third World cannot be overlooked either. The Kremlin imports large quantities of food from Argentina, oil from Libya, phosphate from Morocco, and bauxite from Jamaica and Guinea. One recent study of Soviet relations with Third World states concluded that as much as 80 percent of the Kremlin's imports from the Third World in 1980 may have been raw materials.[12] Soviet trade with Third World states totaled over $26 billion in 1984; this was 13.2 percent of the Soviet Union's total trade turnover.[13] Significantly, between 1975 and 1984 the Soviet Union enjoyed a positive trade balance with Third World states in every year.[14] And while Soviet investment in the Third World is negligible and Third World debt to the Soviet Union is small by Western standards (about 3 percent of the Third World's total external debt), the Kremlin nevertheless found it necessary (or politically expedient) between 1981 and 1985 to grant grace periods to twenty countries that had difficulties in repaying their debts.[15]

Both the United States and the Soviet Union have significant economic interests in the Third World. Those of the United States are much more significant, but the hard fact is that both sides are interested in the Third World for economic reasons as well as other concerns.

A Region of Military and Strategic Value

U.S. and Soviet military and strategic interests in the Third World can best be examined on four separate planes. Both have interests in certain areas of the Third World for reasons of state security; both have SLOCs that run through the Third World; both use bases and have port and airfield rights in several Third World countries to help project their military forces into regions remote from their homelands; and both see the Third World as part of broader geostrategic calculations.

First, in the plane of state security, the United States shares a border with one Third World state (Mexico) and finds many Third World states in and on the Caribbean basin within 1,500 miles of its borders. President Reagan has on numerous occasions pointed to the security implications of Central America and the Caribbean.[16]

The Soviet Union shares borders with two Third World states (Iran and Afghanistan), and four other Third World states (Syria, Iraq, India, and Pakistan) have territories within 250 miles. Sixteen additional Third World states are within 1,500 miles of the Soviet Union. Soviet sources frequently allude to the Kremlin's concern about security implications derived from proximity to these states.[17]

Second, the United States, a seafaring nation, is heavily dependent on ocean-borne trade. It understandably feels that it is in its vital interests to maintain the security of SLOCs around the world. Naval choke points such as the Panama Canal, the Suez Canal, the Strait of Gibraltar, the Strait of Hormuz, and the Strait of Malacca are particular American concerns in the Third World.

It is often overlooked that the Soviet Union has become a major seafaring nation. The Soviet merchant fleet numbers about 1,900 oceangoing ships,[18] and Soviet vessels are the largest single national users of the Suez Canal, at least as of 1980.[19] The Kremlin also attaches great importance to the southern sea route to transport supplies and equipment from the European Soviet Union to the Far East.[20] Perhaps the most surprising aspect of Soviet seafaring presence is that in 1980, 544 Soviet vessels transited the Panama Canal.[21]

Third, both the United States and the Soviet Union use bases and have port and airfield rights in a number of Third World states to help them project military forces. These military forces could be used for offensive or defensive purposes and could be deployed directly against the interests of the other superpower.

For the United States, bases in the Philippines and at Diego Garcia in the Indian Ocean are particularly noteworthy, as are use agreements signed with a variety of nations in Latin America, the Caribbean, and the Middle East. The Soviet Union has access to ports and airfields in Angola, Ethiopia, South Yemen, Libya, Syria, and elsewhere. This listing does not include Soviet bases in Cuba and Vietnam, both of which are technically socialist, not Third World states, and U.S. use agreements with Australia, Japan, and even Western European states that are economically developed. Nevertheless, U.S. and Soviet military forces based in these states can be and sometimes are used for Third World contingencies. One recent example occurred in the April 1986 U.S. raid on Libya, which employed U.S. planes based in Great Britain.

Finally, both the United States and the Soviet Union see the Third World as playing a major role in their geostrategic plans. The United States has long sought to influence Third World states to become part of the American containment strategy[22] and during the 1950s successfully concluded a number of treaties with Third World states—the Southeast Asian and Central Treaty Organizations in particular—in an effort to contain the Soviet Union (and China as well). This strategy was resurrected during the 1980s when Reagan dispatched former secretary of state Alexander Haig to the Middle East in an ill-fated effort to establish a strategic consensus against the Soviet Union among Egypt, Saudi Arabia, Jordan, and Israel.

Meanwhile, the Soviets seek a variety of geostrategic objectives in the Third World, including quite possibly efforts to contain China, to encircle the Arabian peninsula, to deny resources to the West, to jeopardize Western SLOCs, and even to force the United States to pay greater attention to its own "soft underbelly" in Central America and the Caribbean, thereby distracting American attention from other areas of the world.[23]

An Arena of Instability

U.S. and Soviet attention is also drawn to the Third World by the real and potential political instability that pervades it. Both sides see this instability as threat and opportunity. It is a threat since both Washington and Moscow recognize that many of their own friends and allies in the Third World face domestic and international challenges that they might not be able to surmount; Washington and Moscow therefore are cognizant that their own positions and influence are subject to reduction. At the same time, they see Third World instability as an opportunity to undermine the other's position in the Third World.

Until relatively recently, the United States and the Soviet Union persisted in viewing Third World events as essentially a zero-sum game; when one lost influence, the other gained influence, and vice-versa. To a great extent, both retain that attitude today. Nevertheless, during the late 1970s and 1980s as a fundamentalist Islamic government that was both anti-American and anti-Soviet took root in Iran, officials in the United States and the Soviet Union increasingly recognized that Third World events were sometimes more than a zero-sum game. This realization had a dampening effect on both sides' assessments of their abilities to exploit Third World opportunities and simultaneously complicated each side's assessment of threats to its own interests in the Third World.

Despite Washington's and Moscow's greater awareness of the complexity of Third World instability, both remain concerned that the other tries to take advantage of its own weaknesses in the Third World. Indeed, both frequently do move to exploit the other side's vulnerabilities in the Third World. The Soviets often sow disinformation in the Third World in an effort to undermine U.S. prestige and influence;[24] they also on occasion provide arms to insurgencies attempting to overthrow established governments.[25] And for its part, the United States under the Reagan Doctrine has taken steps to aid and support insurgencies fighting against pro-Soviet regimes in Afghanistan, Angola, Cambodia, Ethiopia, and Nicaragua.[26] U.S. willingness to support these insurgencies varies in both scope and scale on a case-by-case basis, but in all instances U.S.-supplied equipment is used against Soviet-supplied government forces.

Thus, despite Washington's and Moscow's recognition that Third World events are more complex than a zero-sum game, both frequently continue to act in ways consistent with this interpretation. As far as their leaders are concerned, then, public protests to the contrary, both sides continue to fear threats to their interests posed by Third World instability and seek to take advantage of the opportunities to undermine the other side's positions that that instability presents.

An Area of Illegitimate Involvement by the Other Side

The final reason that the United States and the Soviet Union assert that the Third World is important is that both consider the other side's involvement there to be illegitimate; both therefore claim themselves duty-bound to protect not only their own interests in the Third World but also the Third World itself. While the skeptic may find such claims cynical assertions on the parts of the superpowers to enable them to pursue their own ends under the cover of moralism, it is difficult to deny that Washington and Moscow reject the legitimacy of the other's presence in the Third World.

As far as most American administrations have been concerned, the Soviet Union has no significant interests of its own in the Third World. Soviet presence there was (and is) considered proof of Soviet expansionist intentions; the Kremlin's attempts to expand its influence in Third World states were viewed in similar lights. During the Nixon and Ford administrations, secretary of state Henry Kissinger argued that Soviet involvement in Angola broke the rules of détente, and the Carter administration reached essentially the same conclusion about the Kremlin's activities in Ethiopia. Under the Reagan administration, secretary of state Alexander Haig told the Soviets to stay out of Latin American affairs. And throughout these administrations, it was U.S. policy to try to minimize the Soviet role in the Middle East and to exclude the Soviet Union from a Middle Eastern peace settlement.[27] Indeed it was in part a continuation of U.S. efforts to minimize the Kremlin's role in the Middle East that led to American willingness in 1987 to reflag Kuwaiti tankers in the Persian Gulf and place them under American protection.

The Soviets have been equally insistent that the United States has few, if any, legitimate purposes in the Third World and seeks only to exploit these states. To the Soviets, the West in general and the United States in particular use multinational corporations, banking and the debt burden, exploitive economic and military assistance, "unfounded" charges of a "Soviet threat," military intimidation and blackmail, warfare and exacerbation of international tensions, and indigenous "class allies" to maintain their neocolonial dominance over Third World states.[28] Mikhail Gorbachev charged that during a ten-year period stretching through the 1970s and into the 1980s, U.S. corporations removed profits from Third World states four times as great as their total investments there. Gorbachev also asserted that the United States annually takes in over $200 billion from Third World states.[29] Other Soviet officials and analysts agree with Gorbachev, as evidenced by one recent Soviet comparison of U.S. and Soviet policies toward the Third World:

> We thus see two dramatically opposed approaches to the destiny of the Third World. Imperialism is still banking on power politics and neocolonialist plunder, while the world of socialism proposes using all opportunities for cooperation with the newly-free states on a fair basis.[30]

As far as the United States and the Soviet Union are concerned, the other has few or no truly legitimate reasons to be involved in Third World affairs. Conversely each side views its own presence there as legitimate and even necessary to prevent additional expansion and exploitation by the other side.

How We Got to Where We Are: A Brief Overview

It is indeed fortunate, given the mix of interests and attitudes, that more frequent and more serious U.S.-Soviet confrontations in the Third World have not occurred as both sides sparred and fenced for position there. In part, the reason is that both sides are aware of the dangers of such a confrontation. But there is a second, probably more important, reason as well. Until recently, U.S. and Soviet policies toward the Third World have been out of phase with each other. When the United States displayed proclivity to intervene in Third World affairs, the Soviet Union did not, and when the Soviet Union adopted interventionist policies in Third World affairs, the United States was self-constrained.

During the 1980s, however, U.S. and Soviet policies toward the Third World have been more in phase than ever before. Never before have both simultaneously had the capabilities, the interests, and in certain cases the will to intervene directly in Third World affairs. This simultaneity has increased the likelihood of U.S.-Soviet misunderstanding, confrontation, and confict in the Third World.

Even so, before we can truly understand the current status of U.S.-Soviet interaction in the Third World, we must examine how that interaction has evolved. We cannot escape the baggage of history, for current perceptions and policies are based at least in part on past experiences.

For most of the post–World War II era, the United States has seen its policies toward the Third World as being based on a mixture of opposition to expanding communism, support for economic development, and promotion of Third World independence and stability. Meanwhile, the United States saw the Kremlin as engaging first in Marxist-driven expansion but has on occasion moved to a position of seeing Soviet policies toward the Third World as motivated by a combination of Marxist ideology and traditional Russian imperialism.[31] At the same time, the Soviet Union considered its own Third World policies to be based on opposition to imperialist expansion, strengthening of Soviet security, and support for the "historical process" of liberation. Simultaneously, the Kremlin believed the United States pursued policies of economic imperialism and suppression of national liberation.

These viewpoints ebbed and flowed through several distinct periods of U.S. and Soviet policy interaction in the Third World. The first period, from the late 1940s through the mid-1960s, was one of clear predominance of American presence and influence in Third World affairs but also witnessed the beginning of expanded Soviet presence and influence there. The second period, from the mid-1960s to the mid-1970s, was a period of transition. In several Third World states, Soviet presence and influence during this period rivaled and even surpassed that of the United States. The third period extended from 1975 to 1980 and was a time of role reversal; its most notable feature was the Soviet Union's willingness to use military force to assert its positions in Third World affairs. Since 1981 the superpowers have engaged in sparring and fencing, with neither side appearing too committed to expanding its own presence and influence but neither willing to concede presence and influence to the other. Indeed, despite mutual recognition that Third World events are not in every case zero-sum situations, Washington and Moscow both deny the other side has significant legitimate interests in the Third World and frequently attempt to undermine the other's positions there. This in turn increases the possibility of U.S.-Soviet confrontation and conflict as their policies interact in the Third World.

Period 1: U.S. Predominance, 1945–1964

Throughout most of this period, U.S. policies toward the Third World were driven by the twin challenges of preventing Communist expansion and buttressing Western influence. The United States also supported decolonization and economic development, but these considerations were rarely placed near the top of the policy agenda. The United States used a variety of policy tools to achieve its objectives, including economic and military assistance, establishment of a system of military alliances that extended into the Third World, and occasional intervention.

Meanwhile, the Soviet Union gradually abandoned Josef Stalin's position that the Third World was not a significant independent actor in world affairs. In a formal sense, Stalin's outlooks were finally rejected at the Twentieth Congress of the Communist party of the Soviet Union in 1956 when Nikita Khrushchev observed that a vast "zone of peace" was emerging in Africa and Asia, allied to neither East nor West. At the policy level, the Soviet Union had in 1955 already begun to supply selected non-Communist Third World states with economic and military aid. Much of this economic assistance was directed toward large-scale projects such as the Aswan Dam in Egypt; the stadium and government complex in Accra, Ghana; and the Bhilai Steel Plant in India. Its military aid remained surprisingly limited throughout the period; nevertheless, it was evident that the Soviet Union intended to become more active in Third World affairs. Indeed, by the time he was ousted as party leader in 1964, Khrushchev had visited Afghanistan, Burma, Egypt, India, and Indonesia.

The Soviet Union had clearly become a player in the Third World, but the United States still enjoyed immense predominance of presence and influence in Third World affairs. The United States nevertheless recognized that the Soviet Union intended to expand its presence and influence. As a result, the United States frequently interpreted challenges to its own and other Western positions as indications of Soviet meddling or pro-Soviet tendencies on the part of Third World nationalists. Sometimes these interpretations were right and other times wrong. The key point is that by the mid-1960s, the United States and the Soviet Union had in fact become rivals in many Third World countries.

Period 2: Transition, 1965–1975

U.S.-Soviet policy interactions in the Third World entered a new phase during late 1964 and early 1965 as the United States became increasingly occupied with the Vietnam War and as a new leadership in the Soviet Union became increasingly comfortable with its hold on power. The entire decade from 1965 to 1975 may indeed be characterized as one of transition in policy interactions in the Third World.

On the American side, the impact of the Vietnam War canot be emphasized strongly enough. The decade began with the United States willing to use military force to determine outcomes of Third World situations, as it tried to do in Vietnam and succeeded in doing in the Dominican Republic. The decade ended with the United States pulling out from Vietnam. Whereas at the beginning of the decade the United States was willing to commit men and materiel to stop infiltration in Vietnam and prevent a perceived left-leaning government from coming to power in the Dominican Republic, by 1975 it was unwilling to commit military forces to combat a main force North Vietnamese invasion of an erstwhile U.S. ally, South Vietnam. Things had indeed changed.

Economic changes were also evident. In 1965, the United States spent $3 billion (measured in 1961 dollars) on economic assistance to Third World states—0.5 percent of the U.S. GNP. By 1974, the United States spent only $2 billion on economic aid, again measured in 1961 dollars—0.28 percent of the GNP. American hesitancy to get involved in Third World affairs had clearly moved beyond the military.

Nor should it be overlooked that the combination of the Watergate affair and a congressional–executive branch deadlock over presidential power in particular and U.S. foreign policy in general raised additional barriers to U.S. activism in Third World affairs. In almost every respect, the United States was reappraising its role in the Third World.

The Soviet Union also used the period from 1965 to 1975 to reassess its position in the Third World but reached significantly different conclusions. Throughout the decade, it attempted to increase its presence and extend its influence in the Third World, but outside of Egypt, it enjoyed few long-lasting successes. Indeed, in several countries the Kremlin received serious setbacks as Soviet friends and clients were removed from power. The Indonesian military removed Sukarno in 1965, Ben Bella was sacked in Algeria in 1965, Nkrumah lost power in Ghana in 1966, and Keita was removed in Mali in 1968.

These were serious setbacks, but the Kremlin's contacts in the Third World nevertheless persisted and even expanded in number. By the mid-1970s, about forty Third World countries received Soviet economic assistance and as many as twenty-eight Third World states received Soviet military assistance. In absolute terms, Soviet economic and military assistance to Third World states also expanded considerably during this time. Between 1955 and 1965, the Kremlin extended over $2 billion of economic assistance and $4.5 billion of military assistance to Third World states; these figures climbed, respectively, to $9 billion and $9.2 billion for the following decade.[32] And on many issues at international forums, including the United Nations, the Soviet Union's positions and the positions of many Third World countries increasingly coincided.

Throughout 1965–1975, the Soviet Union slowly but steadily also improved its ability to project military force. While the impetus for Soviet emphasis on improving force projection capabilities may be tied directly to the humiliation during the Cuban missile crisis over its inability to counter U.S. naval superiority in the Caribbean, ongoing Soviet force projection improvements gave it at least a rudimentary ability for the first time to intervene in areas far distant from the homeland.

Significantly, Soviet officials during the early 1970s began to comment regularly on the external functions of the Soviet military. Soviet naval commander Admiral Sergei Gorshkov wrote a series of articles in *Morskiy Sbornik* in 1972 and 1973 that redefined Soviet naval objectives to include supporting Soviet and pro-Soviet forces throughout the world and that envisioned continued growth of Soviet naval presence in the Third World.[33] The following year Soviet Minister of Defense Andrei Grechko observed that

> the historic function of the Soviet Armed Forces is not restricted merely to their defending our Motherland and the other socialist countries. In its foreign policy activity the Soviet state actively and purposely opposes the export of counterrevolution and the policy of oppression, supports the national liberation struggle, and resolutely resists imperialist aggression in whatever distant region of our planet it may appear. . . . The development of the external functions of the socialist armies is a natural process. . . . It will continue.[34]

Not surprisingly, then, with U.S. activities in the Third World constrained by a combination of reaction to the Vietnam War, the Watergate affair, and congressional–executive branch deadlock over presidential power and foreign policy and with the Soviet Union expanding its contacts in the Third World, building for the first time force projection capabilities that gave it the capacity to intervene far from Soviet territory, and expressing the intention to use them, the stage was set for yet another new period in U.S.-Soviet policy interaction in the Third World. All that was lacking was the opportunity.

Period 3: Role Reversal, 1975–1980

That opportunity came in 1975 as the Portuguese colonial empire in Africa finally fell.[35] In Angola, three indigenous national liberation movements had been fighting not only the Portuguese but also each other for some time.[36] The Popular Movement for the Liberation of Angola (MPLA) had received Soviet support since at least the 1960s. With the attainment of Angolan independence, the Kremlin rapidly and radically increased its support for the MPLA, most notably by transporting as many as 20,000 heavily armed Cuban troops to Angola and providing the MPLA's forces with more arms and munitions. By 1976, the pro-Soviet MPLA was in power in Angola, and the Soviet Union had a new friend and client in the Third World.[37]

Subsequent years saw three more specific instances of large-scale Soviet military involvement in Third World states. Beginning in 1977, the Soviet Union aided and abetted Cuban intervention in Ethiopia. In 1978, Soviet provision of supplies and equipment made Vietnam's invasion of Cambodia possible. And the following year, the Soviet Union itself invaded and occupied Afghanistan.

Clearly the Soviet Union had adopted a new policy of military activism in Third World affairs. Four times in six years, it had used its military might to help determine the course of events in the Third World. If North Vietnam's invasion of South Vietnam in 1975 is included, which itself was undertaken with large-scale Soviet support,[38] the Kremlin five times in six years had helped determine Third World events by its military might. Never before had that occurred. Other indications of a new Soviet forward strategy in the Third World were also evident. The Kremlin extended $9.9 billion in economic aid to Third World states between 1976 and 1980,[39] and Soviet arms deliveries to Third World states totaled $33 billion for the same period.[40] The Kremlin also concluded six treaties of friendship and cooperation with Third World states between 1976 and 1980 (and a seventh as well with Vietnam); previously, it had concluded four treaties with Third World states during 1971 and 1972.

Meanwhile, the United States did not respond in several situations that in earlier years would likely have evoked a response. When South Vietnam fell in 1975, the United States did nothing. When the Soviets intervened in Angola and Ethiopia via Cuban proxies, the United States again did not respond. And when formerly close American allies in Iran and Nicaragua were first challenged and then overthrown in 1979, the United States did not come to their assistance.

This is not the place to argue the wisdom or folly of American inaction or to assess and analyze the factors that led to these decisions. Rather, the significance lies in the fact that five times in six years the United States did not respond in situations that in earlier years would probably have evoked its responses.

For all practical purposes, the United States and the Soviet Union had reversed roles in the Third World, at least as far as their willingness to intervene was concerned. Before 1975, it had been the United States that was willing to apply its military forces to Third World affairs in large enough quantities to influence and even determine situations; U.S. interventions in Lebanon, Vietnam, and the Dominican Republic were specific cases in point. In contrast, the Soviet Union had not intervened militarily. After 1975, the situations were reversed.

It was also apparent that role reversal could not last. Despite its unwillingness to become involved militarily in Third World affairs during the last half of the 1970s, the United States retained too many interests in these areas to remain passive for long. As the 1970s drew to a close, the questions were how long the United States would remain passive, what interests the United States would defend once it began to reassert itself in the Third World, and how U.S. and Soviet policies would interact when both superpowers asserted themselves in Third World affairs. To many, it appeared that the 1980s would be a decade of potentially dangerous U.S.-Soviet confrontation and conflict in the Third World.

Period 4: Sparring and Fencing, 1980–Present

Perhaps surprisingly, the feared confrontation and conflict have not yet come—at least in part because U.S. and Soviet attitudes and policies toward the Third World have become more refined.

The United States, galvanized by the capture of American hostages at the U.S. embassy in Tehran in November 1979 and the Soviet invasion of Afghanistan the following month, began to adopt more active policies toward Third World affairs in early 1980. This trend was accelerated as Ronald Reagan, himself more disposed toward activist and interventionist policies, assumed office in 1981. The Soviet Union meanwhile adopted less activist policies and tried to consolidate its positions in the Third World. Several factors influenced the Kremlin's new conservatism; resource limitations, questions about benefits, a succession crisis, and greater U.S. assertiveness were the most prominent.

On the American side, Jimmy Carter gave notice that the United States was abandoning the passivity of the previous five years during his 1980 State of the Union message. Stung by events in Iran and Afghanistan, Carter declared that the United States considered the Arabian peninsula and Persian Gulf vital to Western security and warned that the United States would militarily defend its interests there.[41] Carter's warnings, quickly dubbed the Carter Doctrine, were given teeth as the Rapid Deployment Joint Task Force, soon to be converted into the Central Command, was strengthened.[42] Additionally, the United States sought and gained access to ports and airfields in Egypt, Kenya, Somalia, Oman, and elsewhere. U.S. military equipment was also prepositioned at Diego Garcia in the Indian Ocean.

U.S. activism in the Third World became more evident after Carter left office and Reagan assumed power in January 1981. In 1981, the United States and Libya confronted each other in the Mediterranean; the United States shot down two Libyan fighters. U.S. military forces landed in Lebanon in 1983 and invaded Grenada later the same year. In 1986 U.S. planes attacked Libya on two separate occasions, once because of Libyan actions against U.S. ships operating in the Mediterranean and a second time because of Libyan support for terrorists. The United States also applied subtle behind-the-scenes pressures that helped lead to changes of governments in the Philippines and Haiti in 1986. Additionally and importantly, the so-called Reagan Doctrine also gave notice that the United States would provide military assistance to national liberation movements fighting radical pro-Soviet regimes in several Third World countries; the United States thus gave military assistance to UNITA in Angola, the *mujahadin* in Afghanistan, the contras in Nicaragua, and the non-Communist resistance under Norodom Sihanouk in Cambodia, all under the auspices of the Reagan Doctrine.

Meanwhile, the Kremlin pursued a more moderate policy course in the Third World during the 1980s. It did not abandon any of its previous commitments, but neither did it take on any new ones. It must be admitted that Nicaragua and Grenada may or may not be considered exceptions. Thus, although Soviet ties with Nicaragua and Grenada strengthened considerably during the 1980s, a strong case can be made that the groundwork for both the Soviet-Nicaraguan and the Soviet-Grenadan alignments was laid during the preceding period. For example, five Soviet generals visited Managua within a few weeks of the Sandinista's July 1979 victory,[43] and the Sandinistas and CPSU signed a party-to-party agreement in March 1980. Nevertheless the Soviet Union did not provide Nicaragua with significant quantities of economic assistance until 1982.[44] Similarly, in Grenada, small contingents of Cuban construction crews working under Soviet and East German engineers began constructing a new maritime facility in late 1979, and in October 1980 the Soviet Union and Grenada signed an agreement in which the former promised Grenada 4.4 million rubles in military and civilian equipment to be delivered during 1980 and 1981. The Soviets also agreed to train Grenadan servicemen to use and maintain the equipment.[45]

The Soviets appear to be trying to consolidate previously attained positions rather than taking on new commitments. This phenomenon is taking place in Angola, Afghanistan, South Yemen, Ethiopia, and elsewhere; Nicaragua and Grenada may be interpreted in this light as well. The Soviets are also helping no fewer than six pro-Soviet governments—in Afghanistan, Angola, Cambodia (via Vietnam), Ethiopia, Mozambique, and Nicaragua—fight smoldering civil wars. Outside the formally defined Third World, the Kremlin is propping up the Cuban and Vietnamese economies with massive infusions of aid—as much as $5 billion and $3 billion to each, respectively, on an annual basis.

Given the state of the Soviet economy, it would be understandable if Soviet authorities questioned the wisdom of diverting greater quantities of scarce funds to the Third World. Many authorities may also be questioning the rewards the Soviet Union receives for the attentions it pays its Third World friends and allies. The Soviets, like the Americans, have found their Third World friends and allies to be less than fully reliable.

Additionally, Soviet attentions may have been diverted from Third World affairs by the ongoing succession drama. Leonid Brezhnev died in November 1982, and it was not until March 1985 that a leader came to power who appeared to have a chance for an extended period as general secretary. It would be understandable if Kremlin politics during the extended succession uncertainty attracted greater attention from local notables than did Third World affairs.

Equally troubling from the Soviet perspective was the course that U.S. policies might take if the Kremlin sought to strengthen its positions in the Third World. With the United States demonstrably over the Vietnam "hangover" and with a president in power ready and willing to employ military force in Third World contingencies, Soviet leaders may simply have concluded that the benefits to be gained from further adventures in the Third World were not worth the risks.

To this point, then, the dangers of U.S.-Soviet confrontation in the Third World that appeared so high in the early 1980s have been avoided. Can they continue to be avoided?

Sparring and Fencing: The Future of U.S.-Soviet Policy Interactions in the Third World

With both the United States and the Soviet Union maintaining their own sets of interests in the Third World and with neither side understanding the scope or accepting the legitimacy of the other's interests there, the possibilities for misunderstanding, confrontation, and even conflict between the two nations remain considerable. While the Soviet Union no longer is pursuing as expansionist a policy in the Third World as it was in the late 1970s and while the United States is no longer as prone to intervene in the Third World as it was in the 1960s, the fact remains that both superpowers have the capability, the interests, and in certain locations the will to intervene militarily in Third World affairs. And this breeds potential for confrontation and conflict.

To their credit, leaders in Washington and Moscow recognize this. Discussions of regional conflicts occupied a prominent (although not primary) place at the Reykjavik summit meeting between Ronald Reagan and Mikhail Gorbachev in October 1986, and both before and since Reykjavik, other U.S. and Soviet officials have met to discuss Afghanistan, Cambodia, Central America, the Middle East, and southern Africa. Additionally, Washington and Moscow have proposed several steps that could lead to amelioration of or solutions to regional conflicts. For example, the Soviets have regularly argued for an international conference on the Middle East, and in early 1987 they began to imply that they were seeking a political end to the conflict in Afghanistan that led to the start of withdrawing forces in 1988. On the American side, President Reagan in his 1985 address to the United Nations General Assembly proposed that the United States and the Soviet Union encourage warring parties in regional conflicts to seek political settlements and that they then enter into bilateral talks to end their own military involvement in regional wars. At the same time, congressional leaders urged the establishment of centers where U.S. and Soviet experts could discuss regional issues, thereby increasing understanding of each side's interests and decreasing the likelihood of confrontation and conflict.

The relative merits of these proposals vary. Some were doubtlessly undertaken more for propaganda appeal than policy impact, and others were clearly stacked to one side's advantage. But some were also the result of sincere desire to minimize the possibility of U.S.-Soviet conflict in the Third World.

Nevertheless, to this point nothing concrete has been accomplished to lessen the likelihood of U.S.-Soviet misunderstanding, confrontation, and conflict in the Third World. Both sides recognize that their own interests in the Third World remain vulnerable and are equally cognizant that the other side's interests are at risk as well. Further, each side sees many of the challenges to its own interests as emanating from policies pursued by the other side; in many cases, this perception is right, but on some occasions it is not. Even so, it is undeniable that Washington and Moscow frequently work to undermine the other's positions in Third World countries. This is undoubtedly an inevitable by-product of superpower rivalry that will continue as long as both sides maintain interests in the Third World—and neither side shows any intent to abandon its Third World interests. But rivalry need not necessarily lead to conflict.

To this point, U.S.-Soviet conflict in the Third World has been avoided more out of good luck than good policy. Before the 1980s, U.S. and Soviet policies in the Third World were out of phase with each other; when the United States pursued activist policies in the Third World, the Soviet Union did not, and when the Soviet Union adopted interventionist policies, the United States did not. Thus, the probability of conflict was reduced.

This is no longer true. The United States is once again acting assertively in Third World affairs. So is the Soviet Union. For the first time, both superpowers have the capability, the interests, and in certain locations the will to intervene militarily in Third World affairs. Both sides understand that the costs of direct confrontation and conflict could be considerable—a recognition evidenced most clearly by their willingness to discuss regional conflicts at the summit, by occasional discussions of regional conflict at working group and other levels, and by the various proposals put forward to ameliorate and solve regional conflict.

By themselves these efforts are not enough. Both sides must now develop the capacity to recognize the legitimacy of at least some of the other side's interests in Third World affairs and to allow that recognition to affect at least some of their own policy responses to the other side's Third World activities.

This is a call for neither U.S. or Soviet surrender in the Third World nor for superpower hegemony over Third World states. Both superpowers have definable interests in Third World affairs, and both must be expected to defend those interests. Nor should it be expected that the United States and the Soviet Union will agree on definitions for their own and each other's interests. Similarly, in no case can it be argued that superpower interests in Third World affairs are as great as or greater than those of Third World states themselves.

For Washington and Moscow, the challenge is clear: to develop clear understandings of their own and each other's interests in the Third World. This understanding need not be complete; indeed, it probably cannot be complete. But without some mutual understanding, chances for confrontation escalate, and with them chances for conflict.

U.S.-Soviet disagreements over Third World affairs will continue. They are inevitable, a part of superpower rivalry brought about by different needs, different outlooks, different ideologies, and different historical experiences. But misunderstanding can and must be reduced. As the United States and the Soviet Union continue to spar and fence for position in the Third World and elsewhere, with their policies nearly in phase, if not in phase, for the first time, we can no longer continue to rely on the good luck that has so far sustained us in avoiding conflict in the Third World.

Notes

1. For the purposes of this chapter, the Third World is here defined as all states that are not "countries of developed socialism" or members of the "capitalist center." This is a definition widely accepted in Soviet analytical literature and accordingly excludes the Soviet Union, Mongolia, North Korea, the Eastern European states, China, Cuba, Vietnam, Laos, and Cambodia from the Third World, as well as the United States, Canada, Western Europe, Japan, Israel, New Zealand, Australia, South Korea, and Taiwan.

2. *Washington Post*, November 28, 1973.

3. The following general listing and discussion of U.S. and Soviet reasons for attaching importance to the Third World should not be construed to imply that either the United States or the Soviet Union views all parts of the Third World as equally important. They do not. For detailed discussions of the different levels of importance

that the United States attaches to different areas in the Third World, see, for example, William J. Olson, *U.S. Strategic Interests in the Gulf Region* (Boulder, Colo.: Westview, 1987); and Harold Molineu, *U.S. Policy toward Latin America: From Regionalism to Globalism* (Boulder, Colo.: Westview, 1986). For detailed discussions of the Soviet Union's perspectives, see Daniel S. Papp, *Soviet Policies toward the Developing World During the 1980s: The Dilemmas of Power and Presence* (Montgomery, Ala.: Air University Press, 1986).

    4. See, for example, Secretary of State George Shultz's address to the Wilson Center, "ASEAN: A Model for Regional Cooperation," May 27, 1987, in U.S. Department of State, *Current Policy Number 965.*

    5. See, for example, the address by Deputy Secretary of State John C. Whitehead to the Meeting of the Organization for Economic Cooperation and Development, "Promoting Economic Growth in the Developing World," April 17, 1986, U.S. Department of State, *Current Policy Number 827*; and the address by U.S. ambassador to the Organization of American States Richard T. McCormack to the Conference of the Great Cities of the Americas, "Obstacles to Investment and Economic Growth in Latin America," June 20, 1986, in U.S. Department of State, *Current Policy Number 862.*

    6. For details, see Daniel S. Papp, *Soviet Perceptions of the Developing World During the 1980s: The Ideological Basis* (Lexington, Mass.: Lexington Books, 1985), esp. chapter 3.

    7. Derived from U.S. Department of State, *Atlas of United States Foreign Relations* (Washington, D.C.: U.S. Department of State, 1985), p. 61.

    8. *Time,* May 25, 1987.

    9. American Metal Market, *Metal Statistics 1985* (New York: Fairchild Publications, 1985), p. 187.

    10. See *1986 Direction of Trade Statistics Yearbook,* p. 401.

    11. Investment data are from the address by Under Secretary of State for Political Affairs Michael H. Armacost to the National Third World Studies Conference, "U.S. Policy toward the Third World," October 17, 1986, in U.S. Department of State, *Current Policy Number 894.* Debt data are from the World Bank, released March 26, 1986.

    12. Papp, *Soviet Policies,* p. 99.

    13. *Vneshnyaya Torgovlya SSR,* no. 3 (March 1985).

    14. Ibid., appropriate years and issues. See also Papp, *Soviet Policies,* p. 100.

    15. Pyotr Koshelev, *Soviet-African Economic and Technical Cooperation in the 1980s: Records and Prospects* (Moscow: Africa Institute, 1986), p. 11.

    16. See, for example, President Ronald Reagan's address to the nation, "Central America and U.S. Security," March 16, 1986, in U.S. Department of State, *Current Policy Number 805.*

    17. See, for example, *Pravda,* November 19, 1982, October 12, 1981, June 20, 1982.

    18. *The Military Balance, 1986–1987* (London: International Institute for Strategic Studies, 1986), p. 40.

    19. Theodore H. Freidgut, "The Middle East in Soviet Global Strategy," *Jerusalem Journal of International Relations,* no. 1 (1980).

    20. See James T. Westwood, "The Soviet Union and the Southern Sea Route," *Naval War College Review* 35, no. 1 (January–February 1982): 54–67. More recently, during a 1986 trip through Southeast Asia, a number of U.S. military attachés and

Southeast Asian scholars and government officials confirmed that Soviet maritime traffic through the Strait of Malacca was considerable, although no number of ship passages was provided.

21. *Panama Canal Company Annual Report, 1980.*

22. See Terry L. Deibel and John Lewis Gaddis (eds.), *Containment: Concept and Policy* (Washington, D.C.: National Defense University Press, 1986), 2: esp. chaps. 18, 19, 22, 23, 24.

23. See Papp, *Soviet Policies,* pp. 36–38.

24. The Soviets call these efforts "active measures." See ibid., p. 74. See also U.S. Department of State, *Soviet Active Measures* (Washington, D.C.: Government Printing Office, September 1983).

25. The Kremlin frequently provided arms to so-called national liberation movements during the colonial era but has been rather circumspect about providing them to insurgents seeking to overthrow established Third World governments. Nevertheless, such arms transfers do occur.

26. For one explication of the Reagan Doctrine, see President Reagan's March 14, 1986, address to Congress, "Freedom, Regional Security, and Global Peace," U.S. Department of State, *Special Report No. 143,* pp. 4–5. For an interesting assessment of anti-Soviet insurgencies, see Mark N. Katz, "Anti-Soviet Insurgencies: Growing Trend or Passing Phase?" *Orbis* (Summer 1986): 365–391.

27. The only exception was for a brief time in 1977 when the Carter administration entertained thoughts of Soviet participation in an international conference on the Middle East.

28. See, for example, Papp, *Soviet Perceptions,* esp. chap. 4.

29. Mikhail Gorbachev, *Selected Speeches and Articles* (Moscow: Progress Publishers, 1987), pp. 359–361.

30. Vitaley U. Vasilkov, "Soviet Foreign Policy and Developing States" (paper delivered to the 28th Annual International Studies Association Meeting, April 15–18, 1987, Washington, D.C.), p. 6.

31. More complex American views also exist. See, for example, Papp, *Soviet Policies,* pp. 29–38, which identifies six objectives of Soviet policies toward the Third World: the reduction of U.S. and Western presence and influence, reduction of Chinese presence and influence, expansion of Soviet presence and influence, enhancement of Soviet security, obtaining economic benefits, and pursuit of geopolitical and strategic advantage.

32. Papp, *Soviet Policies,* pp. 14–20.

33. See Sergei G. Gorshkov, *Red Star Rising at Sea* (Annapolis, Md.: U.S. Naval Institute, 1974), p. 173.

34. Andrei Grechko, quoted in U.S. Department of Defense, *Soviet Military Power* (Washington, D.C.: Government Printing Office, 1982), p. 9.

35. It is possible to argue that this period actually began in 1973 when the Soviet Union threatened to intervene militarily in the Arab-Israeli War and when the Kremlin provided large-scale military assistance in support of North Vietnam's invasion of South Vietnam. However, the Soviet Union did not send its forces into the Middle East, and Soviet support for the 1973 North Vietnamese invasion (and the 1975 invasion as well) could arguably be construed as part of the Kremlin's ongoing support for North Vietnam. In the case of Angola, no doubt exists qualitatively and quantitatively the Kremlin's

activities in support of the Popular Movement for the Liberation of Angola (MPLA) were different from any Soviet activity previously seen.

36. For details, see John Marcum, *The Angolan Revolution* (Cambridge, Mass.: MIT Press, 1975, 1978), vols. 1–2.

37. This does not imply that the MPLA held power unopposed. Civil war continued to rage in Angola over a decade later as anti-MPLA forces, chiefly the Union for the Total Independence of Angola, sought to overthrow the MPLA government.

38. See Daniel S. Papp, *Vietnam: The View from Moscow, Peking, Washington* (Jefferson, N.C.: McFarland, 1981), pp. 153–154.

39. U.S. Department of State, *Soviet and East European Aid to the Third World 1981* (Washington, D.C.: Government Printing Office, 1983).

40. *Congressional Record—Senate,* April 14, 1983, pp. 54610–54612.

41. See *New York Times,* January 22, 1980.

42. For a discussion of U.S. rapid deployment capabilities, see Sherwood S. Cordier, *U.S. Military Power and Rapid Deployment Requirements in the 1980s* (Boulder, Colo.: Westview, 1983).

43. Robert S. Leiken, "Fantasies and Facts: The Soviet Union and Nicaragua," *Current History* (October 1984): 315.

44. *Latin American Regional Reports: Mexico and Central America,* June 4, 1982.

45. The October 1980 agreement may be found in document 000190, captured by U.S. forces in Grenada and released to the public on November 4, 1983.

Index

About the Contributors

Stephen J. Cimbala is professor of political science at Pennsylvania State University. An extensive contributor to the field of security studies, his most recent works include *Extended Deterrence* (1987) and the editing of *The Technology, Strategy and Politics of SDI* (1987).

Dennis M. Drew, a colonel in the U.S. Air Force, is director of the Airpower Research Institute at the Air University Center for Aerospace Doctrine, Research and Education. The author of numerous articles and chapters, his most recent books include the coauthorship of *Making Strategy* (1987) and *The Eagle's Talons* (1988).

Robert C. Gray is associate professor of government at Franklin and Marshall College. A former Council on Foreign Relations fellow who served as a policy analyst in the Office of the Secretary of Defense, he has also been a research associate at the International Institute for Strategic Studies in London. He is currently conducting research on the arms control implications of land-mobile missiles.

Gary L. Guertner, professor of international relations at California State University, Fullerton, has served on the staff of the U.S. Arms Control and Disarmament Agency and the faculty of the U.S. Army War College. He recently coauthored *The Last Frontier* (1986).

Gale Mattox is associate professor of political science at the U.S. Naval Academy. An International Affairs Fellow of the Council on Foreign Relations, she has been a Robert Bosch fellow in West Germany and is a member of the International Institute for Strategic Studies in London. Her most recent work includes the co-editing of *Evolving European Defense Policies* (Lexington Books, 1987).

Daniel S. Papp is professor of international relations and director of the division of social science at the Georgia Institute of Technology. A widely published author, his most recent books include *Contemporary International Relations,* 2d edition (1988), *Soviet Policies toward the Developing World during the 1980s,* and co-editing of *International Space Policy* (1987).

David S. Sorenson is associate professor of political science at Denison University and senior research associate at the Mershon Center, Ohio State University. The current chairman of the Section on Military Studies, International Studies Association, he has published articles and book chapters in the areas of military doctrine and technology and defense expenditures and is currently working on a book on NATO logistics.

Paul R. Viotti, a colonel in the U.S. Air Force, is professor of political science at the U.S. Air Force Academy. His most recent books include *The Defense Policies of Nations* (1982), *International Relations Theory* (1987), and the editing of *Conflict and Arms Control* (1986).

John Allen Williams is associate professor of political science at Loyola University of Chicago and vice-chairman and executive director of the Inter-University Seminar on Armed Forces and Society. A former faculty member at the University of Pennsylvania and the U.S. Naval Academy, he has published in the areas of U.S. maritime strategy, U.S. and Soviet naval forces and missions, strategic nuclear policy, and other defense policies.

About the Editor

Donald M. Snow is professor of political science at the University of Alabama. He has also served as secretary of the Navy Senior Research Fellow at the U.S. Naval War College and as a faculty member at the U.S. Air Command and Staff College. His most recent books include *National Security* (1987), *The Necessary Peace* (1987), and coauthorship of *The Eagle's Talons* (1988).